THE HIDDEN WORLD

Number 8

Space Television
Cult of the Witch Queen
Luder Valley
& MORE!

The Shaver Mystery

Global Communications

THE HIDDEN WORLD
Number 8
The True Story Of The Shaver & Inner Earth Mysteries

Richard S. Shaver

Ray Palmer

Gerald W. Page

This revised edition and new cover art
Copyright © 2010
Timothy Green Beckley
DBA Global Communications, All Rights Reserved

Originally Published by Palmer Publications, Winter 1962 A-8

No part of this book may be reproduced, stored in retrieval system or transmitted in any form or by any means, electronic, mechanical, photocopying, recording, without express permission of the publisher.

Timothy Green Beckley: Editorial
Director Carol Rodriguez: Publishers
Assistant Sean Casteel: Associate Editor
William Kern: Editorial Assistant
Cover Art: Tim Swartz

Printed in the United States of
America For free catalog write:
Global Communications
P.O. Box 753
New Brunswick, NJ 08903

Free Subscription to Conspiracy Journal E-Mail
Newsletter www.conspiracyjournal.com

Note: Four digit numbers on the bottom of each page corresponds to total number of pages in the entire series. Numbers below those are page numbers for this book.

How Shaver Lead Me To The Caverns of My Mind

by Gerald W. Page

I discovered Ray Palmer's science fiction magazine, **Other Worlds**, in 1954, when the science fiction field was collapsing around our ears and poor old **Other Worlds** was a weak-kneed shadow of its former self. I was a mere teen-ager but had been reading sf books for six or seven years -- but only now discovering the magazines because I'd labored under the delusion that all the good magazine stories got reprinted in anthologies.

Of course I heard about Richard Shaver. Science fiction fans still berated him and Ray Palmer because of the controversy over the claims that the Shaver Mystery stories were based on truth. As far as that goes, science fiction fans still do that even today. But I had a friend named Jerry Burge who collected sf pulps and was a big fan of the Ray Palmer issues of **Amazing**, and of the fiction of Richard Shaver. He lent me a lot of classic science fiction magazines, including some issues of **Amazing** and **Fantastic Adventures** containing Shaver stories. Rather than just shaking my fist at them, I actually read a few. And I found out that Shaver was frequently a pretty good writer who told stories that were a lot of fun.

Palmer I had discovered more or less on my own. While **Other Worlds** wasn't as good as many of the other magazines in the sf field at that time, it carried a long editorial by Palmer in each issue, and Ray Palmer was one of the great editorial writers of all time. Someone needs to seriously compile a volume or several of his editorials. At his weakest he was more readable than anyone else in the science fiction field, and often as thought provoking as any writer the field ever produced. He was also more controversial than anyone else, although there were times when John W. Campbell, over at **Astounding Science**

Fiction (later ***Analog Science Fiction/Science Fact***) could play him a close second.

A few years before, in the early fifties, when **Other Worlds** was actually one of the best science fiction magazines around, Palmer suffered a fall off a ladder in his basement which left him paralyzed. His doctors said he would never recover, but Palmer was an old hand at fooling doctors. An accident when he was ten years old had left him crippled and stunted his growth, but had not prevented him from leading a full, productive and very interesting life. He announced the fall from the ladder in an editorial by saying that after years of "being paralyzed from the neck up," he'd taken care of the other direction. The medical costs seriously effected his ability to continue operating as a publisher but somehow he managed to stay in business though he had to turn **Other Worlds** into a magazine called **Flying Saucers**, and concentrate on Fortean and related materials. Perhaps that was what he really wanted to do at that time.

From about 1954 until almost the sixties, Shaver was virtually absent from the science fiction magazines. In 1957, **Amazing** ran a special flying saucer issue, with articles (but no fiction) by both Shaver and Palmer. Shaver was occasionally showing up in Palmer's magazines **Search** and **Flying Saucers** with articles, too. In 1958 **Fantastic Science Fiction**, the companion magazine to **Amazing**, ran a Shaver Mystery issue, featuring a novel by Shaver called "The Dream Makers," one of the finest pieces of fiction Shaver ever wrote. The issue also featured a few non-fiction pieces by both Shaver and Palmer. Shaver was occasionally showing up in Palmer's magazines **Search** and **Flying Saucers** with articles.

But as far as fiction was concerned, Shaver had given up in 1953 with the conclusion of his serial "Beyond the Barrier" in the February 1953 issue of **Other Worlds**, and short stories in the February and April issues of **Imagination**. One last story, "Why Skeets Malloy Has Two Heads" appeared in a magazine called **Orbit** in 1954. That was the last of Shaver's fiction until "Dream Makers."

When Palmer fired up his Shaver Mystery publication, **Hidden Worlds** in the early 1960s, Shaver's fiction began to reappear. The novel "Mandark," begun but never finished as a serial in **The Shaver Mystery Magazine** in the 1940s finally saw print. Beyond that, so far as I'm able to determine, the rest of Shaver's fiction in **Hidden Worlds** was reprinted, mostly from **Amazing**. But Shaver turned out reams of articles, essays and commentary for the magazine and his skills as a writer were clearly not diminished.

THE HIDDEN WORLD

It's Shaver as a fiction writer that impresses me.

Just one of Shaver's stories has been reprinted in book form so far as I know. The 1948 volume from Venture Press, "I Remember Lemuria" and "The Return of Sathanas" contains two stories the first of which was written by Palmer from material in Shaver's letters and under Shaver's name. "The Return of Sathanas" is a story that appeared in Amazing as a collaboration between Richard Shaver and Bob McKenna.

After Palmer left Ziff Davis and began his own publishing company, he more or less promised that the Shaver material he would publish in *Other Worlds* would not include anything related to the Shaver Mystery. The first issue of *Other Worlds* featured five stories, two of them written by Shaver and the rest by Rog Phillips. The cover story, by Shaver was called "The Fall of Lemuria" and is certainly based on the Mystery. It is also one of the finest stories Shaver ever wrote, featuring a certain amount of experimentation in its construction.

Richard Shaver could be a frustrating writer. He was sometimes clumsy in the way he put his stories together, and occasionally sloppy in a way that suggests he was rushing. But his imagination never flagged, and his humor and satire were frequently both subtle and deft. His stories are apt to have more sex in them than was common in science fiction at the time -- sf was rather strait-laced back then, if the truth be told. In that regard Shaver was clearly ahead of his time. He could wander, and he could let a story sort of die out as it neared its ending and become an essay.

He was a mimic of the first water, able to skillfully incorporate stylistic touches reminiscent of the finest of the field's early writers, including E.E. Smith, A. Merritt and Edgar Rice Burroughs. He clearly read a lot of writers outside the sf and fantasy fields, as well. His novel in the Shaver Mystery issue of *Fantastic*, "The Dream Makers," reminds me a lot of Jim Thompson's magnificent short paperback novels of the 1950s. Yet he never seems to be imitating these writers so much as using skills he's picked up from them to strengthen his stories. (One exception may be Maurice Walsh; his attempt at incorporating Walsh's style into a couple of his fantasies seems less imitation than copying.)

But stories like "The Dream Makers," "The Tale of the Red Dwarf" and "Fall of Lemuria" stand very well on their own two feet and deserve to be better known than they are; and not as examples of an aberrant writer, but as examples of a writer who has been poorly served by the field and needs to be introduced to a wider readership. Shaver wrote a good many stories that can stand free of the Shaver Mystery and the popular conception of Richard Shaver himself, and which are deserving of true respect.

Indeed, Shaver is not without his influence on modern science fiction writers. William Michael Mott and I collaborated on a story called "Cask of Ages," which you can find in Mott's "Pulp Winds" (TGS Publishing, 2009; www.mottimorphic.com) that combines the Shaver Mystery with aspects of H.P. Lovecraft's **Cthulhu Mythos**.

The Summer 2010 issue of **Startling Stories** from Wild Cat Books (www.wildcatbooks.net) features another Shaver Mystery based story, "Scroll of Strange Device." An upcoming issue will reprint "Cask of Ages."

Over at **Planetary Stories**, an online sf magazine (www.planetarystories.net) co-edited by Shelby Vick and myself, Lane Harrison has started a series about cavern dwellers. It focuses on a heroine named Breese and her attempts to avoid being captured by a slave dealer named Tarice. The first story is "Cavern Wight" in **Planetary Stories # 20**. A second story, called "The Ebon Sphere" is scheduled for issue 21. Further stories in the series are in the works.

Is this a renaissance for Shaver? Of course not. But it might be a beginning of one. Whether or not it is, it shows that some people hold Shaver's talent in regard. We hardly expect this to lead to a full-fledged reformation of the Shaver Mystery in the eyes of science fiction fans and readers. But wouldn't it be nice if it led to a situation where his fiction could be read and judged on its merits with a lack of prejudice because some of his ideas are unconventional?

Jerry Page

THE HIDDEN WORLD

The HIDDEN WORLD

ISSUE NO. A-8
WINTER, 1962

EDITORIAL	1343
Ray Palmer	
HOW TO MAKE A PORTRAIT OF DERO ACTIVITY	1349
Richard S. Shaver	
SPACE TELEVISION	1354
Richard S. Shaver	
LETTERS	1356
From Our Readers	
HOW TO GET INTO THE CAVES	1390
Richard S. Shaver	
MY PAINTING OF ADAM & EVE	1397
Richard S. Shaver	
SPIRITUALISM AND THE SHAVER MYSTERY	1404
Jim Wentworth	
CULT OF THE WITCH QUEEN	1416
Richard S. Shaver	
LUDER VALLEY	1484
Richard S. Shaver	
REPORT FROM THE FORGOTTEN PAST	1503
Ray Palmer	
JOE DANNON, PIONEER	1504
Richard S. Shaver	
ERRORS IN SPECTROGRAPH OF STELLAR BODIES	1525
Frank Patton	
THE INVISIBLE INTERVIEW	1526
Richard S. Shaver	

Address all correspondence to THE HIDDEN WORLD, Amherst, Wisconsin.

THE HIDDEN WORLD is published quarterly by Palmer Publications, Inc., C-137 Hickory, Mundelein, Illinois. Reentered as second class matter at the Post Office at Amherst, Wisconsin. Manuscripts, artwork, photographs invited, but no responsibility is undertaken for loss. No payment is made except by arrangement. Return envelope and postage necessary to insure return. Subscriptions, 4 issues for $6.00; 8 issues for $12.00; 12 issues for $18.00. Some material in this issue is copyrighted and may not be reproduced without the permission of the copyright owner.

EDITORIAL
By Ray Palmer

THE JOB OF being an editor of a magazine like this is like sitting on the horns of a dilemma between the devil and the deep blue sea, directly beneath the sword of Damocles. There has never been any question of the validity of the Shaver Mystery in this editor's mind. But one thing is true, and always has been true, concerning our publication of the material from the very beginning -- we had to decide on the basis of our editorial experience, and on a basis of practicality and salability. The magazines in which the material originally appeared were fiction magazines published for but one purpose, to make money for the owners. This editor was not the owner. All through the years we have had to "kill" some of Shaver's writings for these reasons. Also there were those items which simply could not be proved even by left-handed logic, or which were too incredible, or which, frankly, this editor just couldn't swallow. It usually turned out that later developments literally forced the material down our throats. Mr. Shaver had a knack of turning out to be right.

Now, in the past two years, Mr. Shaver has made a new claim, this purporting to be the proof of his past races, to be found in actual records in picture form in the stones to be found in this area, specifically, and all over the Earth, if we are to accept Shaver's opinion. As editor of a magazine designed to present only the facts of this Mystery, how would you feel if you were shown a whole bushel basket full of stones and invited to look at the pictures on and in them --

only to find that you saw nothing, except some vague resemblances that were quite obviously accidental? Would you do as the writer asked, and present the whole thing as an actual fact, and say "Here is proof!"? Not if you've got any brains, you won't!

Let's say that the stones were exactly as claimed. But like yourself, nobody else could see anything but "accidentals"? Once go out on a limb, and where are you when it is sawed off? Risk the work of fifteen years by going off half-cocked?

Thus it is that in this issue we begin to present Shaver's side of this argument as to whether he has actually found the artifacts his critics have challenged him to present all through the years - but, we take the stand that we don't back up one single word of it! One thing we will admit - there are pictures there! But HOW they got there is a different thing. We're going to present the evidence as we promised, exactly as it came to us and is coming to us - and let YOU decide if it is indicative of one thing or another. Shaver gets very angry with this editor's "blindness", the fact that he is "tampered", and that he may even be stupid or vicious and unfair. However that may be, this editor feels that coincidences come in bunches like bananas, and "accidental" pictures in the variegated composition of a stone also can come in bunches. We would be very interested in a foolproof way to prove otherwise - and that is exactly the purpose of this magazine: to make a foolproof case for what we call "The Hidden World".

The interesting part is that Shaver discovered artifacts of the Mound Builders, dating back from 6,000 to 8,000 years of undoubted authenticity and extreme archaeological value, and places no importance upon them at all - even scorns them as trivialities. Worse, he picked up the two prize artifacts we were having professionally photographed, and gave them to a fan, with the result they are lost to us.

If you can show an expert a stone that is of positive authenticity and value, it is much easier to get his attention on a matter far more delicate - such as pre-Deluge artifacts of races no archaeologist would even suggest could possibly have existed on the earth. It is easy to prove (?) the Shaver

1344

Mystery to one who wants to believe - but it is the "hardhead" we must convince. Shaver's singleness of viewpoint, no matter how well-founded on personal experience and knowledge and research, has always turned away all serious attention from those most qualified to conduct an investigation. "Nuts to them!" says Shaver, "They are hidebound in error taught in our Universities, and they will not see even the nose on their faces." We like to feel that these people are a challenge and we aim directly at them. Certainly insulting them will achieve nothing!

We might point out that Shaver is not alone in this stone record business. He has lots of company. Out in Oregon there is a man who has made a similar discovery. We are making an attempt to combine our researches. In the "rock hound" magazines, there are "pictures found inside stones" constantly being published. Some of them are fantastic. But they recognize them only as accidents. We must do the same until we can prove beyond the slightest shadow of doubt that they are not. So, in this magazine, the CONTINUING nature of the Shaver Mystery, which is only a portion of the overall Mystery we have typified by calling our magazine THE HIDDEN WORLD, is proved by these controversies which are going on.

With this issue of this magazine we reach a sort of milestone. We have presented 1532 pages of basic material, laid a groundwork for what is to come. In order for anyone to understand what we are talking about, all this material must be available. To do otherwise is like starting out in a history of the world in 1957 and expecting to understand why the world is like it is. Also, to try to explain 1963 to anyone with just the sketchiest of summaries of the past 3,000 years would be folly - you might just as well skip it; your listener will be hopelessly lost. It is the same with this magazine. If you have not read the first eight issues, you will be nothing less than baffled by the 9th and following issues. Thus, if you are a new reader, and you are ready to return your magazine to the newsdealer and ask for your money back, stop and think a bit. We have anticipated your dilemma, and we purposely printed extra copies of all eight issues and stored them. You can buy a complete set; but not more than

1345

1500 can do it! After that, these magazines will be quite a disappointment to the person who picks one up on the newsstands, and wonders what he has missed and why he can't get it. It is just true that this is a task we've taken up that we can do only once. Financially it would be impossible to reprint the whole series and make it available to the few readers who will come in very late. We haven't got about $10,000 to store in our warehouse where it may never sell because it is true that there are not an unlimited number of people who want to know the whole truth about the HIDDEN WORLD, and about the Shaver Mystery, and about the information we really ought to call the Palmer Mystery from here on, because this magazine is actually the presentation of a lifetime of research and collection on this editor's part in the field of the hidden. Out of an initial curiosity about some mysterious facts which science could not explain, and indeed chose to ignore, has come this more or less complete picture of a behind-the-scenes reality which seems to us to be so important that to allow the information already gathered to be lost would be a tragedy. If nothing else is achieved, all of this material cannot fail to make a substantial number of people think along new lines - and when such is done, it cannot fail to have its effect on the future and on the history of this planet. Merely to sight a Mystery in the distance is to invite Man's pique into pathways which may be the "Great Breakthrough" into a world far better than the one in which we live now. For just one suggested example, what if it is possible to live a thousand years? Man did it before (says the Bible) - why not again? What mysterious thing shortened his life? What mysterious thing could restore its length? It's worth trying to find out.

Some of the articles in this issue may lift your eyebrows a bit. Some of them may flabbergast you. Take for instance Shaver's article on how to make a portrait of a dero. We've seen some of these portraits, but we've now got to make some ourselves - and we are sure some of our readers will do the same. The results of many people making them might be surprising. At the very least, we might be able to disprove it, which is as good as proof in making this whole thing a factual thing. We must know where we are in error as well as where we may be on the track. The pair of pictures in this issue showing an actual photo (unretouched) of a stone which Shaver sliced with a diamond saw; and a painting done by Shaver as a "copy" of the stone, plus the addition of details which bring out the pictures so that they may be seen plainly by such "dumbheads" as your editor, ought to make you look long and carefully. One thing is certain - the painting is a very good copy of the stone, and a vague picture has been "retouched" so that it is no longer vague. Now, is this what Shaver has done, and nothing more, or is that picture in the stone precisely what we see in the painting - a representation of Adam and Eve and the snake with an apple in his mouth?

Also in this issue is quite a long section of letters from readers, whose testimony may shock you as you read it. Such letters are not unusual. We have in our file many thousands of equally shocking ones. Some of them may be from madmen, we admit, but most of them are not. And after all, what is a madman? Someone who differs from the average man in his concepts? We are too inclined to say of the man who states as a fact something beyond our experience "He is crazy". Under such a criterion, how do you know you are not crazy? Or do you make a point of agreeing with the herd? Are you afraid to stand out alone, for fear of being called crazy? If so, don't jump to conclusions. You are going to be forced to change them before we finish publishing all the letters we have on hand.

Speaking of letters, next issue we begin the publication of Shaver's private letters to this editor, plus some of the answers (which will be interesting from the standpoint of how unwilling to accept your editor was in the beginning. Also, you will be able to see why Ray Palmer entertained Shaver's material in the first place. You may be surprised to know that the "caves" were not new to him.

Some of the stories in this issue are "fiction" stories written for the old Amazing Stories in which the only truth is the exposition of facts of the Shaver Mystery given a proxy explanation in the way they are used in a story. Remember as you read that the story is fiction, but the way the facts of the Mystery work out in it are precisely as they

1347

would work out in such circumstances, and that this is the way they did work out in principle in the past, as Shaver records from his mysterious thought records. Some of the stories we've included as pertinent evidence in this magazine have been actual thought records, and Shaver only reproduced them. The stories in this issue are written and created by Shaver, and merely incorporate background of the caves. But that background usage is important to demonstrate to you how they apply, and how you can apply them in your understanding.

The article about the interview with the F. B. I. men is true, but written in a facetious and rather scornful and bitter fashion by Shaver. We have presented it in this manner only to convince you of Mr. Shaver's real feelings on the subject. It certainly shows his sincerity!

Why would the F. B. I. agents express so much interest in a fiction story in a science fiction magazine?

We urge you to make sure you get every future issue of THE HIDDEN WORLD.

Lastly, if you have anything to report in your own experience, now is the time to do it! — Rap.

THE HIDDEN WORLD
How To Make A Portrait Of Dero Activity

By RICHARD S. SHAVER

ANY SINGLE one of you can make a bona-fide conclusive photograph of deros in action any time he wants to do it, if you can follow simple directions.

For some time I have been transferring pictures from stone surfaces to cardboards, enlarging them from about six inches to two foot by three foot cardboards so that no one could avoid "seeing" the stone pictures, no matter how tampered they were.

The process I use is one I invented myself. You set up the opaque projector about six foot from the floor so it throws an image just to cover the white cardboard I use.

One, first sprinkle soap powder (Cheer is what I use, because the granules are the right size to shake evenly, and light enough to respond easily to the minute light forces that aligns them in the pictorial lines. Of course you can think underground mech helps this process magnetically BUT it will work to some extent anyway. Then you sprinkle a couple of half cartons of dye (I use Putnams because I bought a lot of it cheaply) very evenly from a pepper shaker over the cardboard and soap powder picture. Then you spray very lightly with wax spray, the kind they use on furniture and call "Dust-off" etc. (I use Tone but Pledge works, too.) Now you sprinkle the whole lightly with water by using a Windex window spray pump; and presto the dye takes hold where the wax was held back by the soap . . . and you get a picture.

Here is where the dero activity portrait shows up. Enraged that you too can see pre-deluge art from record stone, fearing you may learn something of the ancient wisdom they're too stupid and too lazy to learn themselves, they tamper the picture with the ancient machines used the

THE HIDDEN WORLD

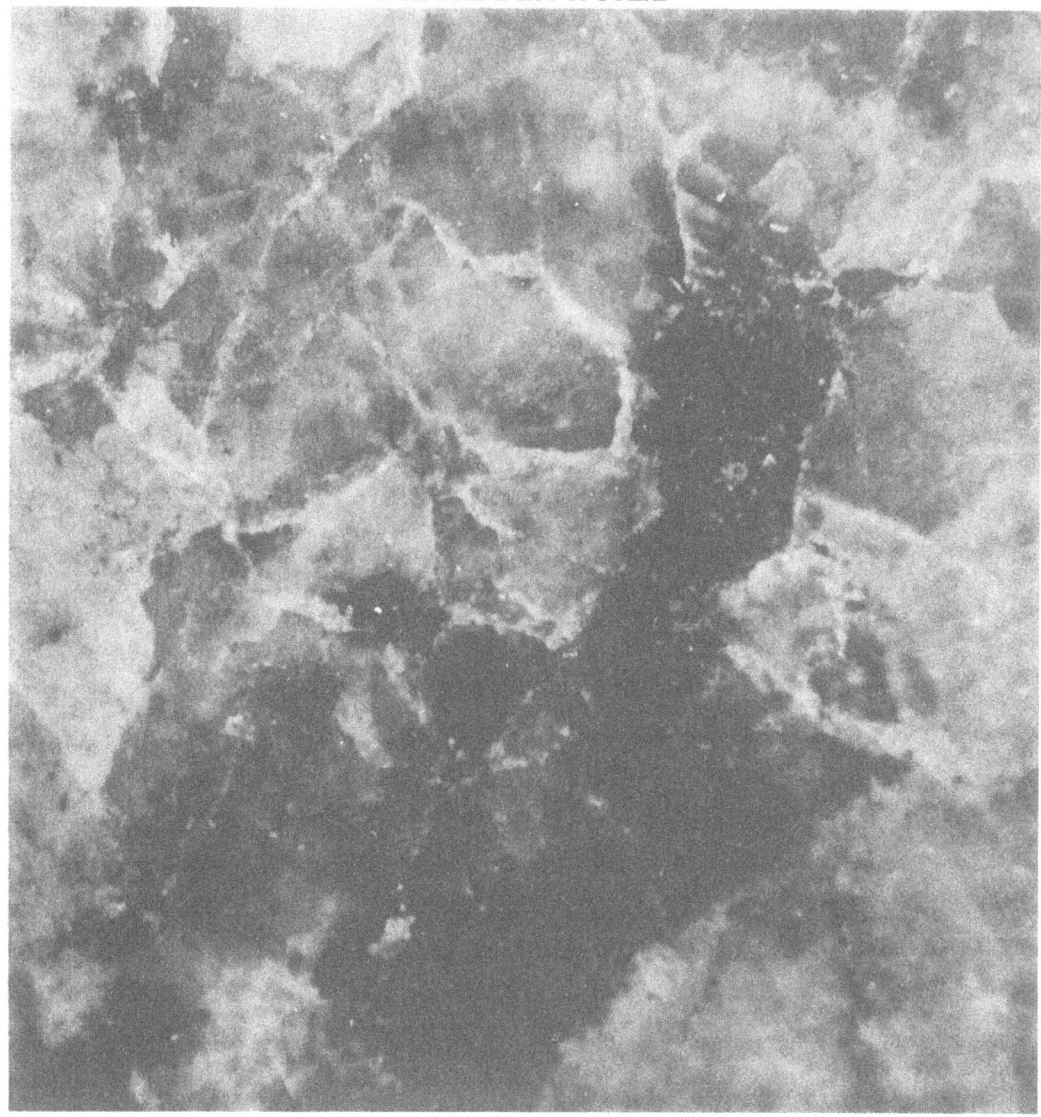

Photo of actual stone from which painting was copied.
Painting is reproduced on opposite page.

world over and setting there under your feet, to spoil your picture. In my case they make the focus change magnetically by a distorting field, or they change the face right before your eyes by a projection which forces the soap flakes into new patterns, often a horrible portrait of a degenerate and ugly dwarf, possibly themselves, peering into the machines they have never bothered to try to understand. Anyway, you will see the distorting images they make print photographically before your eyes, and you will have a bona-fide proof of dero activity.

(If you are interested, a little "Drain-flo" speeds up prints.)

Now, about this process of making photographic enlargements, its still experimental, and you will have to work with it and do a little thinking on your own to get good results, but it can be done. There is doubt in my mind about the use of "Dust-Buster" wax for the very reason it is anti-magnetic against the magnetic forces which cause the dye and soap to align in the lines of the picture; but in use it seems to fix the picture as it chills and hold it from too much dye spreading, one of the troubles.

You can get perfect pictures by this method, but I get really perfect results only one out of ten, and lots of them I botch up by too much dye, too little of this, etc.

I find the best way to make these pictures is to mix all the ingredients before spreading them, that is equal amounts of "Drain-Flo" and soap flakes, to get a fighting chemical action, which seems necessary, and equal parts of three dyes, to give you a colored picture effect, spread evenly on the cardboard - shaken out little by little, with care to spread very evenly, from a height of about two feet or three, so the light particles get a chance to flow or fall down the magnetic lines of force by themselves.

You can get a picture without the use of wax spray, and fix it with fixatif, but my wife yells so about the fixatif smell I tried the wax to fix the powder . . . but I suspect "Dust-Buster" is also spoiling pictures by busting the dye particles into lines they didn't fall into by themselves.

This is a fascinating process to enlarge stone pictures, as you never know quite what you will get. The tiny details hardly noticed in the stone become life-size to six-inch figures in the enlargements and studying the details is an endless delight for anyone truly interested in what man was and how he lived before the Deluge, in the Golden Age when Earth and Mankind were both young and full of zest.

The fact that you also get perfect photographic proof of dero activity was only incidental with me. I was delighted to discover a way of seeing the stone pictures better and larger . . . and then it occurred to me here was the perfect

THE HIDDEN WORLD

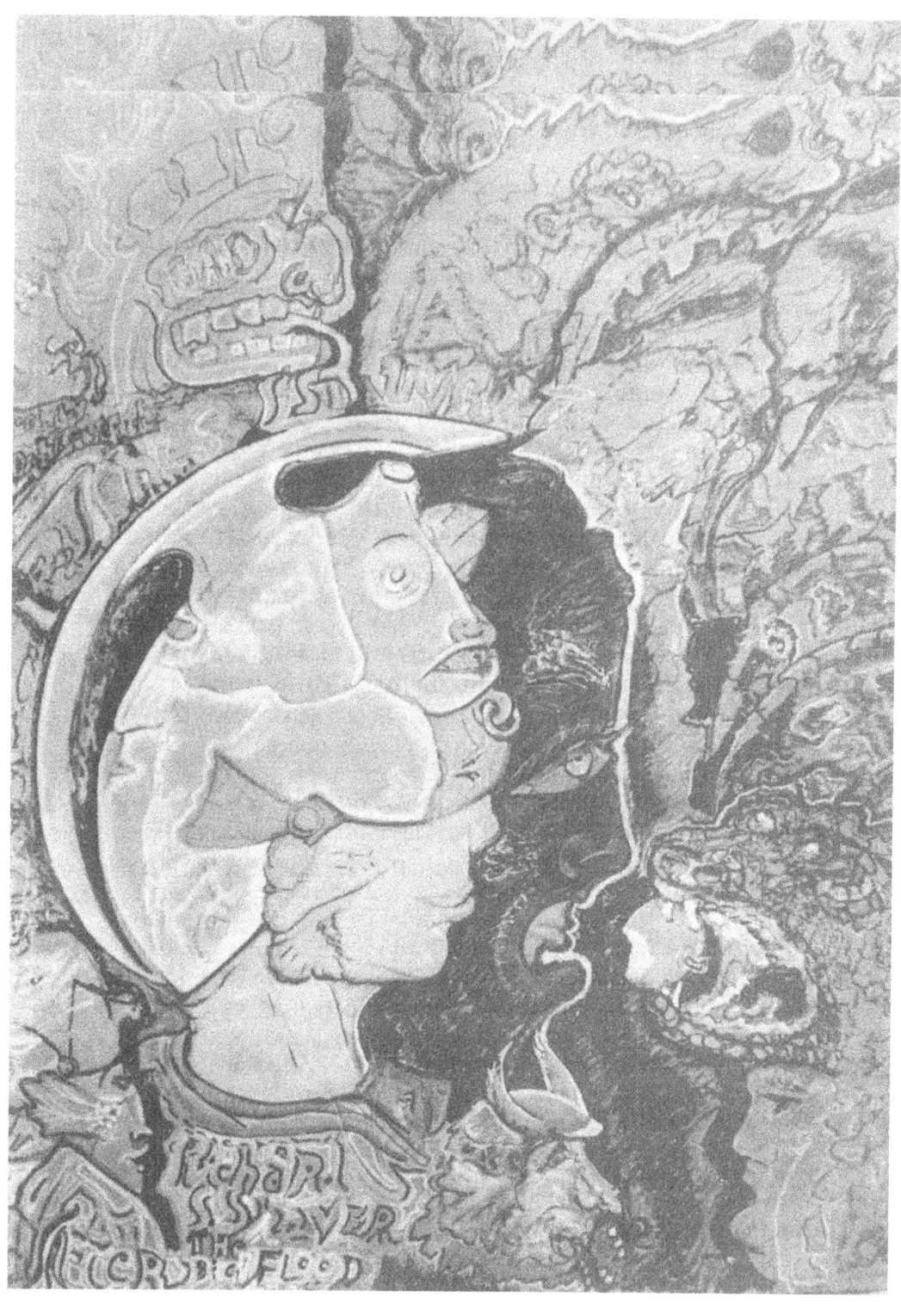

way to prove the existence of dero to doubters, because they show so plainly (in their tamper projections in the pictures).

To continue with making pictures by this method, you can also make fine pictures with powdered bleach on a black cardboard, the bleach will go into action when moistened with the windex and make a photograph on the black in bleaching out lines.

You can also make fine photographs of various projections from the underworld by this method, as there are such machines in many places in the caverns and the tero will give you a page out of a pre-Deluge book any time you try this way of making pictures.

You can also make a photograph of the so-called accidental pictures, formed by the magnetic field of mother reflecting as a radar antenna catches and focuses signals, and some of these are fascinating because they seem to come from the macro world, but in truth I believe they come from other worlds, and are photographs of the massive life-sentience of Mother Earth herself, perhaps the very thought fields of her massive self in action . . . in pictures, photographed by you!

This is one of the most interesting things I have ever done in my life, to make these pictures with soap powder, bleach powder, Drain-Flo and other simple chemicals anyone can buy in the grocery store. Any fine particle reacts to magnetic force and will cling to the board you use in the pattern you place there, whether you do it with magnetic force or an opaque projector. It is a simple process any one can master in a few tries, and as time goes on and you become more expert and careful, you can get pictures better than an expensive camera, pictures big enough and good enough to use for murals in your home.

Don't say I didn't prove the existence of the dero and the caverns to you! Anyone can look at my artifacts, and anyone can make these photographs with simple easily obtainable materials. Don't write me and tell me I'm talking through my hat about teros and deros and caverns and so on, because I can prove every point I ever made a dozen different ways, and you can't!

1353

SPACE TELEVISION

By RICHARD S. SHAVER

HAVE YOU ever turned off your TV - or sat there late at night as the last channel put itself off the air, and wished there was a knob on the TV you could switch over and receive the programs from other planets that are probably there . . . if we knew how to receive them?

Well, if you didn't, try it, look at that TV and wonder if and why there isn't some way to look at space television and see what's going on on other worlds.

There may be a way even you can listen to space programs . . . an ignored and overlooked way!

Space television, to reach other planets and space ships on long runs between planets, would have to use the magnetic field of the planet itself to reach another planet. There would be no other field big enough to bounce a signal.

One of the things I have learned is a principle I call

"simulacrum inductum", much used by the ancients as a principle of design and as a principle of optics, as well as in electronics.

This is the principle upon which a compass works. It forms its own little magnetic field with two poles, then promptly the two poles swing into line with the large poles of the planet earth.

Now it is true that a magnet by being similar in some ways to earth's planetary magnetic field will induct by the principle of similarities induct (for the same reason the magnet needle points north, a very big reason indeed) from the earth field many things beside direction.

One of these things is the images we are apt to call "accidentals". I like to think these images, which we only occasionally notice and pass off as "accidental" are not at all accidental. I like to think they are "space television".

If you study accidentals as long as I have in my pursuit of art, the study of the history of art, and what the ancients or true elder race thought about art, you learn that an accidental picture can be a whole field of art. The ancients used that field and caused designed accidentalism in pictures (as I have demonstrated in some of the covers I did recently for Hidden Worlds).

Designed accidentalism is a very big field of art, quite unknown and unthought of today (as indeed are most of the principles the ancients took for granted).

Now, suppose ALL accidentals were designed accidentalism!

That is, it may be possible that accidental pictures which we see whenever we really look for them, are in fact the magnetic field of earth reflecting pictures off its field in several directions, just as we bounce radar off the moon, or off Telstar, reflecting natural pictures which we dismiss as accidentals!

This may in fact be the actual case, and SPACE TELEVISION may not in fact need any receiver or TV set if the pictures are in color!

Is this the case? Only prolonged study will tell science the truth!

1355

THE HIDDEN WORLD
LETTERS
FROM THE READERS

Where pertinent information concerning The Shaver Mystery is solicited from those who may have facts of value to offer.

Dear Ray Palmer:

I just finished reading your Flying Saucer Magazine dated Feb. 1959. You see I haven't been reading much science fiction or about the saucers since October 1948.

Let's go back . . . way back when . . . The Shaver Mystery . . . Margaret Rogers . . . and people who heard voices . . . even way back when Amazing Stories first was published by Hogo Gernsback.

I became interested in science fiction, an avid reader. I met few people who agreed with me on the subject. Then in 1933 I married a very conservative New Yorker. I had to hide my interest in Science Fiction because he felt it was "all nonsense." Then came the Shaver Mystery . . . and I wrote a few letters to the readers column. Through this I became acquainted with Margaret Rogers and several other people. Then one day while at lunch BOTH MY HUSBAND AND I HEARD VOICES TALKING OUTSIDE THE DINNETT WINDOW. My husband claimed it was someone talking down the street and that the talk we were hearing was merely an echo. YET THE LANGUAGE WAS A FOREIGN ONE AND VERY CLEAR . . . AND THERE WERE NO FOREIGN PEOPLE LIVING IN OUR TOWN.

By 1948 I had contacted several people who were interested in the VOICES I was hearing all about our small farm. My husband lost patience with me and insisted I see a psychiatrist. On our 15th wedding anniversary I agreed to do so. October 23rd, 1948. I was questioned briefly by the psychiatrist and it was suggested I go to the hospital for a PHYSICAL. I agreed.

When I arrived at the hospital, my clothes were taken away and I was asked many questions. Then I was taken up to the seventh floor where I found I HAD BEEN COMMITTED FOR OBSERVATION.

I did everything wrong . . . I was so stunned that I just refused to talk and when I was locked in a cell I went to bed and put myself to sleep for 24 hours under self hypnosis. When I woke up there were several doctors and nurses in the cell. They questioned me and when I stated I could put myself to sleep and wake up when I wanted to they asked to prove it . . . I did. I went back to sleep and slept till the following morning at nine A.M. When I woke up I found my arm all poskmarked with tiny blood spots. They had stuck needles in me to try and wake me up!

For two weeks I lived among yelling screeching women. Then I was told I was to be discharged. They gave me my clothes and when I was dressed they took me out to a car and the next thing I knew I was in the State Hospital for the insane.

The day before Xmas, 1948, at breakfast in the institution I happened to notice several flying discs slowly circling just below the clouds . . . I brought it to the attention of several of the floor nurses . . . remarking that "OF COURSE I'M CRAZY . . . THOSE AREN'T AIRPLANES UP THERE . . . MERELY A FIGMENT OF MY IMAGINATION . . . AND IF YOU SEE THEM TOO, THEN YOU'RE CRAZY AND SHOULD SEE A PSYCHIATRIST . . . One of the nurses had the floor doctor look and then they called the head doctor . . . Nothing was said in front of me . . . but two weeks later I was released in the custody of my husband. Exactly one month later I walked out of my home with a suit case and 13¢ and somehow managed to get to Pasadena, California.

Several people joined me and since then we have traveled all over the U.S., Mexico and Puerto Rico. I got myself a registered trade name. I never went back to my husband or home. Up until just a few months ago not even my relatives knew where I was. In the meantime we all worked and made

1357

a new life for ourselves. MY VOICES have guided us as to where to go and what to do and they have never failed in making things better for us. We all HEAR VOICES . . . SEE ODD THINGS and have strange experiences. We are respected and liked by our community . . . but we never TALK about ourselves or what we know or believe in. We seldom stay over two years in one place.

We have better than the average place to sleep . . . food to eat and clothes to wear. When we NEED money (which is usually to help some else out) I can walk in the bank and get a loan in just a few minutes.

I had a serious heart condition which is now completely cured. We're never sick unless one of us is foolish enough to get emotional and then its only a cold. I had my first one here since 1945. I let myself become CONCERNED over a few frightening things that happened . . . consequently a bad cold.

We have all seen flying saucers . . . six of them in formation in Puerto Rico during a bad (1955) storm . . . at nite. Several in the early morning at Westbrook, N.Y. in late Oct. 1949. Up until last year none of us have bothered to read science fiction except in small spurts. But now we have just sent a subscription to one of your magazines. And now we probably will be getting Flying Saucers, too.

This is rather a long letter, Ray, considering the type, but I thought you might be interested and if you should decided to print this in the reader's column . . . please do not print my name or address. My friends will recognize me from the letter and I'M SCARED of strangers!

Dear Ray:
Because Saint Paul was such a bad reporter and few people have taken the trouble to understand what he was talking about, the term "Epicurean" has been mistakenly accepted as a synonym for "glutton." The Epicureans were teleologists, not gluttons. Epicurus was the founder of the Greek school of teleology and one of the basic principles of teleology is: The seven pillars of wisdom are the seven basic needs of life. Food is only one of them. If a need is

1358

denied it is replaced with a desire, and a desire can only be appeased while a need can be satisfied. The more you appease a desire, the greater it becomes, and it will eventually become your master. A glutton is one who allows one need to become a desire to replace another basic need which is being denied.

The school of teleology was evolved from the Thothian school of mysteries and was the basis of all Egyptian knowledge. If the Greek teleologists had not destroyed the Eleusinian schools before Saint Paul arrived there, Greece could never have become the cradle of the Christian faith. Saint Paul would have been laughed out of Greece if it had not been for the Epicureans.

Because of this misunderstanding, I dare not say that I am an Epicurean and expect to be understood, so I must say instead, I am a teleologist.

In Nineteen forty-eight, when Richard Shaver was the central figure in a raging controversy, I wrote to Robert Webster regarding this subject. My letter to Mr. Webster did not necessitate a reply anymore than this one to you does, but in the light of Mr. Webster's succeeding articles and editorials, I knew that he recognized the truth of what I wrote.

There are three underground cities beneath the Earth. Each one of them is built beneath a desert with the only entrance to these cities in the mountains near these deserts. It should not be difficult for a thinking man to understand why these cities have been built beneath deserts. None of these cities are peopled by what Mr. Shaver calls deros, teros, or even zeros. More than likely you have met, and may even have talked to persons from at least one of these cities during your lifetime, but you wouldn't have known this except by the lack of color in their irises. The pigmentation of their complexion will darken about as quickly as it takes you to get a suntan. They are neither evil, or saintly but they do have more keenly developed sensitivities than the average human on the surface of the Earth because they do not have to live under the destructive disintegrating energies of the Sun as you do. These short lived energies are contradicted and

1359

killed by the silica of the desert. They are the yellow rays which you can see being reflected by the desert sands. To these people, you are just another species of animal on the surface of the Earth and they regard you in the same way that you regard the simian species in relation to your species. They do not bother you as long as you do not intrude into their lives, but they do not attempt to control your lives by telepathy, or para-psychology, or any other method.

In my letter to Mr. Webster, I did not say that Mr. Shaver was a victim of delusions, and I did not say he was a fraud. Neither was the case. Mr. Shaver was not a liar, and he was not insane even though there are those on Earth who would like to have you believe that he was either, or both if they could make it seem that way for their own benefit.

Undoubtedly you know what a synedrome is Ray, but do you know what a synedrium is? In the belief that you do not, a synedrium is a group of minds functioning in triadic concatenation and focusing on a single intention. (If two or more gather together in My Name, their prayers will be heard.) Unfortunately it can be used for either good or evil. Two triadal coils, functioning on the wave-lengths of human thought and set up in triangulation can give one evil mind the power of a synedrium composed of a million minds if it is so required. The power of these triadal coils can cause planes to crash without any apparent reason, or they can be used to ignite explosives which have been stored, or they can cause buildings to burst into flames without an explainable reason. The triadal coils can influence the minds of anyone happening to be thinking in a certain wave-length at one time, or in the vicinity of electronic or electrical apparatus which coincides with the wave-length of the transmitting traidal coils.

Mr. Shaver's deros (a very flattering name for these swine) are on the surface of the Earth and even pass themselves off as human beings.

Of course I know who uses these coils for the purposes which I have mentioned, but how are you going to prove it? These triadal coils are being used in radar, sonar, television, and directional radio transmission, so who can de-

1360

termine when someone has them set up on the wave-length of human thought, or used in pairs with reversed windings to cause a disturbance in the molecular structure of buildings and other structures?

I know that all this seems fantastic, and unbelievable and I do not blame you if you choose not to believe it. The human mind has a habit of believing only what it chooses to believe and this is why you have so many obvious criminals walking the streets until they have committed a crime, even though it should be obvious to any intelligent person that they are capable of the crime they eventually commit. Whether you believe what I have written or not, however, I would advise you to consider the evidence very carefully and do a little research on your own before you publish anything about it. If you should decide to publish this anyway, go ahead. I would not have risked writing it if I were not thoroughly protected in several ways. - Eduard Delamer Duverus, 155 East Empire Street, San Jose, California.

Mr. Richard S. Shaver:

Hoping this letter finds you in the best of health. My name is Frank J. Mezta. I live in the County of Imperial Valley, City of Calexico, California.

Through accident I happened to stumble into your book the Hidden World issue No. A-1 and just recently A-2. I sometimes wonder if it was luck or a deliberate action on the part of a tero. All my life, I have been looking and asking for certain, unsolved and unanswered questions regarding civilization, our ancestors and the beginning of time. I believe your book gave me the best answers. Let me tell you a few of my expeditions.

Two years ago, we went treasure hunting in the interior of Mexico, which turned out to be a flop. But in that excursion some strange things happened to us, which at the time we wrote them off as superstition. We went to this place where we were supposed to enter; but suddenly a fright with chills came over me, something I had never felt before. Something like a sixth sense, like if I knew something was going to happen to me. I didn't go in and neither did anybody else. Next day we approached the cave again, only this time I wasn't afraid and I led the group inside. This cave was tremendous in size, and leading passages everywhere. Some of these passages or chambers, sometimes being 30 ft. high and 100 ft. long with connecting tunnels. We finally gave up, but in retrieving we found two leading passages instead of the one we had entered. This startled us, and we set to investigate this second tunnel. It just kept winding and going down so we finally gave up and got out of there.

When we got back to the village we struck a conversation with two Mexican Indians, and they told us that whatever we did, not to go into the enchanted caves. We got curious and asked them where these so called enchanted caves were. They gave us directions and that was exactly where we had entered a few days ago. We asked them what happened in these caves. They told us that people that went in there, never came out, that while in there, the entrances and tunnels would change, which happened to us, and we didn't know about this till after we had been in there. Then they told us the strangest thing, which at the time we said these people are superstitious, they said that they went with an expedition with 20 or 30 men hired by an American man to look into this cave. This happened about 10 or 15 years ago they said. Four or five of the men had revolvers, they were well equipped with lights and tools. While they were working there all of a sudden in the far end there appeared a half man and bull head like a bull upright. This description fits the one you have on your front cover on issue A-1. And next to him was a naked midget or little boy. They pulled out their revolvers but they wouldn't fire, and their lights went out. There was confusion, and several of them were killed in the scramble and nobody returned after that.

Just recently another strange thing happened to me. I went out to explore a mountain, and after quitting I stopped in a little restaurant to drink a soda. There I noticed some beautiful colored agate. I asked the lady where she got it. She started to tell me. Just then she pointed to a man approaching us, and she said he would be able to tell me

1362

more. Then I asked him, and he said he knew where there was a whole mountain of it, and offered to take me to it. We went and I picked up several pieces of agate, and mind you I am not a rock hound. The following week I walked into the usual store, and there was your issue no A-2, so I bought it. The first thing I read was your pictures inside of the agate, so I looked in the one I had and found some faces. I had no intentions of going agate hunting yet I went and got some. Just a few days later I read about it in your book. It sure doesn't look like a coincidence to me. This is a desert area and this mountain of agate is surrounded by desert. If your theory of the old ancient cities is right, there should be a buried city somewhere near that mountain. I would like to have more information on this subject, especially the power plants and the old mech machines, and if you could send me some rock so I could compare them with mine. I sure would appreciate the glass with 3D images. I am going to try to find an entrance and I won't stop till I do, not for myself, but for the good of mankind. I believe as you do. The place I am talking about is about 16 miles from here. - Frank J. Mezta, 939 Genge, Calexico, Calif.

Mr. Palmer:

If you have not read a book called "Agartha" written by Dr. Dickhoff of Dordgelutru Lamasery, New York, I think you would find it interesting, as it deals in the subjects you call The Shaver Mystery. The underground cities, lost races and evil Venusians who came here in past migrations, in fact it confirms Shaver's claims almost entirely. And Red Lama (Dr. Dickhoff) says it is all true. I never have believed Shavers dero world was physical, but considered it as astral, and his deros thought-forms built up of evil forces. It is a true world in the astral sense, for I have had the same experiences as he has had and know the deros exist as part of the Hypnotic Organization behind Spiritualism, that play the part of Controls and guides the mediums call the spirits. This vile organization called Astral Chemists tried to force control upon me. I refused mediumship, and as the years went by found out too much about the behind

1363

the scenes details, and they feared I would tell the public what I knew, so I was persecuted for years for knowing too much, by which I found out more and more. The Black Organization that rules Spiritualism, trains mediums in illusion, pretends to be the spirits etc., is totally dero in type, and can create anything in the astral it wishes. The telaug is Spiritualism's group mind office and flows everywhere where circles are sitting. It could form Shaver's deros and no doubt did. He had much they could use for contact with those who accept his views, and so he was forced to comply with black uses. I had no fantasies in my beliefs, but know psychic science thoroughly after twenty five years of persecution from its lower levels, and know it could explain all of Shaver's experiences. On Dr. Dickhoff's book I have not studied it enough to accept it as fact or not. It seems incredible to me as yet; so can not accept it as a physical reality.

The Dr. met Margaret Rogers in San Antonio he told me, but gave no details. Did she answer Shaver's call? It seems likely. She also wrote of the cavern world. Was Shaver influenced by her ideas upon it? Seems odd three people would write on the same subject, if not in some way connected astrally. - Gloucester, Mass.

Dear Editor:
Over a year ago a fellow was interviewed on the A.B.C. television network here in St. Louis. He said people on other planets were contacting earth people through the brain, and that some were nice and some antagonistic. He was doing a research on this. Do you have any truth on the matter?

I keep getting talking through the ear that insist they are in a plane overhead, and that they have an intricate system they can do this with for their own business and the communist government. It's a sending talk and receiving sound and thought waves in a larger area they put this over that they use, a frequency of some sort. Several women of St. Louis have been invaded by this, but can't prove it. They experiment on some and gather information from others. - A reader of your magazine, St. Louis, Mo.

1364

Dear Mr. Palmer:

First I would like to compliment you upon your choice of material to publish under the program now being pursued. I have just started Issue A-2 and having completed Shaver's commentary in the first few pages, felt compelled to write lest it slip my mind.

In his (Shaver) commentary, he speaks of rocks and pebbles which were finally discovered on his property. I should like to write Mr. Shaver and request a few of these rocks for my own study, but do not know how to go about reaching him. Would you relay my request?

As it is so very far from Wisconsin, I doubt if I could make it by anytime in the near future but would certainly like to meet R. S. at some time when I may be in the area.

The Shaver Mystery has always intrigued me. I suppose many people would call me gullible, but I am sure the term is no stranger to you either. Of course if one takes the story literally, the entire hypothesis of religion could be explained as having originated in the Atlan-Titan races. Lately my reasoning has been swinging in favor of such an explanation.

One other thing before closing. Yesterday at work the most inexplicable (or is it unexplainable) thing happened. I will try to set it down completely and perhaps you can analyze it for me, but I have my suspicions of the truth.

Ordinarily I am not a heavy thinker or expressive writer. However, for some reason I started writing and the first missive was a rather profound (I thought) observation concerning leadership within each generation. Shortly after I showed it to an acquaintance and she asked to keep it. Well, of course, that is the finest form of compliment. To top it off I tried recalling it no more than 30 minutes later and found I could go no farther than the first few words. Have you any comments so far?

During the later evening hours, work was slow and again I took up my pencil and began writing on some very diverse subjects, including poetry, which I can never remember as having done before.

Most of my philosophical writings had to do with man's

1365

destiny and love. (I like the word philosophical.) One point I failed to mention. The first passage mentioned above was spontaneous. I mean, the pencil no more touched the paper than words were forming in my mind and had to be put down.

I would appreciate your comments and R.S. Shaver's too, if he'd care to. - Jay Wollam, 616 6th St., Juneau, Alaska.
P.S. I have a habit of doodling with geometric forms and arcs. Whenever I do one it is quite complex. Have often thought of having one analyzed but knew not where to go. No telling where they'd put me. Could you help if I sent some samples? I have always felt there was a meaning hidden in them.

Dear Mr. Palmer:

Thank you most sincerely for your splendid editorial which appeared in "Hidden World" issue A-4.

Your evaluation of "The Shaver Mystery" and "Spiritualism" hits the nail squarely on the head, so to speak.

Richard S. Shaver is a wonderful imaginative writer, and I feel a likeable person. I've always been one of his ardent readers. "But" it's hard to understand how Mr. Shaver can deny "Spiritualism" when he has on file so many instances where the only explanation for a given phenomenon could or be caused by discarnate entities, dero or tero notwithstanding. Even if what Dick writes about dero or tero is true, this alone wouldn't rule out the probability, that man has a soul and that under certain favorable conditions that it is possible to contact the soul or spirit of the departed.

Like you, Mr. Palmer, I too have always been a hard boiled skeptic. I could not swallow the diet that many religious writers gave us as daily bread. Yet deep within me a voice kept telling me insistently that man was more than a carcass, so I grew dissatisfied and a yearning to "know" impelled me into the field of psychic research. I entered this field as a lone investigator some 25 years ago.

I placed such debated phenomena as telepathy, clairvoyance, direct voice, apport, spiritism, levitation, and such as so much balderdash or supernatural nonsense.

Nevertheless, through my independent investigations into

1366

these phenomena there has accumulated such a weight of evidence that I could not dismiss it as, supernaturalism; advanced-natural is the word that most fittingly describes it. - Consider. In the days of Professor William Crooks, Professor Hyslop, Sir Oliver Lodge, Sir Arthur Conon Doyle and at a later date Henry Ford, Thomas A. Edison, all these sterling men had evidence of contact with spirits. On any other subject their word would be evidence in any law court in the land! But "Spirits" My God! But Professor Hyslop and others did prove "survival" and by the holy of all holies "the scientific method", though I know many would take issue with me there. But it's a fact!

Now this writer is not over-credulous but the word "impossible" is fading from my vocabulary. We just cannot be cock-sure about anything. Now as to Shaver's rocks. I think he has something. I saw pictures, plenty of them, and examined his rocks with great interest. I know he has a great inquiring mind and no doubt has experienced many eerie things that would be new to this writer. I tried to explain my viewpoint to Dick sometime ago but he regulates "spirits" into the realm of "superstition" or as ray projections from the caves. Now he might be right to a degree - but only to a degree.

Me? Well, I've gotten plenty of good out of Spiritualism, by experiment and home circles, never have I consulted a professional medium. Too many magicians in this field and not enough psychics. To repeat, I have been a lone wolf. But it has given me a reason for being. It has given me a guiding light. It answers the age-long sneering question "What's the use?". For the most part, I've lived a life of poverty or near poverty and though I know that this is nothing to brag about the thought that I'm surrounded by a sea of Spirit is wonderful "Stim", believe me.

Yes, I have mentally contacted certain spiritual forces. I have seen what Shaver calls "ray projection". Never have I had any adverse affects from the study of supernormal phenomena. I've known many who have gone overboard. Though, I believe it was caused through their misunderstanding of natural law.

1367

I asked Mr. Shaver in a recent letter if he had read any books by the late Steward Edward White. He said he hadn't although he had heard a lot about him. I heartily recommend Mr. White's books on Spiritualism to those who are not initiated into spiritual reality. Anyone who has read his books experience a wide shift in viewpoint. It would help clarify The Shaver Mystery, I believe.

Sure, I know there are a lot of crack pots in Spiritualism. But these are the sane cautious type. I hope I belong in this category. I wish Dick would give the subject some 'real' consideration. Our movement needs men like Dick. We need men of faith to restore this world to a healthy balance. Let him tell the world the true state of man, that man is a creature of eternal progression. That he has an immortal soul! It could be a refreshing drink to those who are weary and thirsty. It renews the race that in these latter days are filled with strutting know-it-all scientists and psychiatrists.

I hope Shaver will eventually join us and toss his hat over the materialistic windmill in our effort to prove to man that he is "a creature with folded wings", (here I quote White) capable of enjoying and partaking of a higher consciousness.

Well, hope I haven't boored you - but your wonderful editorial was stimulating. And although we may not see eye to eye on all things, I admire your honesty and courage to say a few kind words for us spiritualists. - Durence (Duke) Clarke, 900 No. Park St., Casper, Wyoming.

Dear Mr. Shaver:

You may call me Chuck, everyone does. My wife doesn't know me by any other name.

This letter is in reply to your January 31 letter. Please forgive me for not answering sooner. Enclosed is some material I hope that you can glean something of value. Please be as candid as you have been in the past and if I am far off base don't hesitate to tell me.

I have recently aquired an opaque projector and as you say perhaps this type projection will prove best generally speaking. The only real disadvantage is maintaining the correct focal plane. A slab of plasticene under the stone

1368

is as good as anything. The type screen used is important. A good diffusion screen is best.

I have contacted a jeweler who claims that he can saw stones as thin as an eight of an inch or thinner. I shall visit him one of these days. Next time I get to Medford I will look up the saw you mentioned.

Our foundation has located a vast system of underground passages in the Mother Lode country of California. They were first discovered in 1936, ignored by all even with our best efforts to reveal them. Recently a road crew blasted out an opening verifying our claims. One chamber 200 feet long, 70 feet wide and 50 feet high. We have disclosed what we believe to be a vast subterranean drainage system (probably traversing the Great American Desert country for a distance of more than 600 miles. We believe this system extends out like the five fingers on your hand to such landmarks as Zion Canyon in Utah, the Grand Canyon, another runs south from the Carson Sink in Nevada and yet another follows the western slope of the same range, joining its counterpart and ending somewhere in the Mojave Desert. We believe that contrary to orthodox geologists that the existence of this underground system drains all surface waters running into Nevada (none, with the exception of the Armagosa runs out) and accounts for the fact that it is a Great American Desert. The hairy creatures that you have written about have been seen in several of these areas. Certainly there has been much "saucer" activity in these parts. For two years I have collected material pertinent to these creatures and if you have any opinions along these lines I would appreciate hearing them.

So much for now. I hope that I am still your friend. Much of my time has been devoted helping a farmer near Portland who has made a fantastic discovery of incredible stone artifacts. He has several tons of them. They predate anything yet found (or accepted) let us say that for now. We are making slow but steady progress in getting through the wall of orthodoxy. - Chuck Edwards.

1369

Dear Ray,

Received the Fall issue HIDDEN WORLDS two days ago, and certain statements in articles prompt me to make comment.

The first is that, now that we are into enough issues of this series, we can begin to see just how deftly you, in selecting and presenting each article, have made our minds follow what it is you want us to see, and as from my own thoughts, I suspect you are making us do some very deep thinking on our own. At least, in my case, several interesting thoughts have slowly developed (from FLYING SAUCERS, etc., also) which I feel impelled to impart to you. . . They are only thoughts, though . . . or maybe large questions.

On pages 1234-35, in Shaver's FORMULA FROM THE UNDERWORLD for example, concerning this thing of people answering ads and vanishing . . . a thought occurred that wouldn't it be something if this is the place Howard Hughes disappeared to recently (when Federal marshals, et al were looking for him re a suit); that he could be an agent for these beings; that he has come up with some pretty fantastic electronic (and other) gadgets, which one might construe as having been developed by roboticized humans working for a master, that these might be his "reward" for serving the master - as Hughes very frequently does have ads in papers for various types of engineers, etc. . . is this what the writer had in mind? Hughes has always been something of a mystery anyway, although there are probably natural explanations for his behavior . . . the thought just struck me that way when I read those passages in the story.

In BEYOND THE VERGE, in the last paragraphs of the appendix: I got to thinking about the book of Job, wherein Job is asked to answer how he thinks he knows more than God, and the statement that the earth hangs upon nothing in the north . . . which brought the thought as to what all other planets etc., are hung on. Is it not the same North Star as Earth's? Anyway, this particular article certainly makes very clear your ideas about how it might

1370

be at the poles - in that explorers, aircraft, etc., etc. traverse a cricle, a point of which presents what seems to be the true north pole, without still entering beyond that circle . . . also we now have the announcement that the Soviets have agreed (and vice versa) with us to investigate magnetics of earth . . . which bears up the point made in the article that man is highly interested in northern phenomena. The article is still "current" then, and comes at a most opportune time, considering recent sciental announcements.

Lastly, I would like to have the name and address of that man in L.A. (re John Campbell's letter on pages 1339 and 1340) or Campbell's address ... you will recall my last letter re "faces". I also wrote Shaver about them . . . and am still trying to prepare an intelligent dissertation on what I have found in study of such (recently discovered something of great interest in old astronomical photo's taken in 1926, of a supposed nova, but which looks exactly like one of the pictures Shaver's paintings depicts . . . too, the time sequence shows that it was moving to us and then away, which made it appear like a nova expanding, then contracting. The face and form is very very distinct, and not just "seen" that way . . . but I don't understand it myself).

I do know that such "faces" and "objects" have appeared more frequently immediately AFTER nuclear testing in the atmosphere than prior to such experiments, which seems to have some significance for something ... maybe intensifies dero ray machines, or disrupts them, thus "sending" their pictures over the rays, or something like that?

I also had a very frightening experience after I got to looking further into this and had shown them to someone else . . . maybe it was something from my psyche, a la Kor and Jung . . . but since it was so vivid, I cannot help but feel that I actually saw what I saw . . . and I don't really know much about anything to warrant that kind of action against me . . . unless it is my curiosity that prompts it . . . anyway, I started to prepare investigation into why nothing will appear, in sight, on a negative or

1371

positive print, but will appear after printed on newsplate process (since news photo's are composed of dots), and that they should then be so very distinct so that people, who know nothing of such things, occult, UFO, etc., and care even less, should see something there, definitely identifiable so that they all sketched exactly the same likeness of what they saw. So that in starting this I was suddenly, last September, confronted with an aspiration, which appeared so suddenly in front of me that my tummy felt as though an electric wire was suddenly thrust into it, and I was covered with goose bumps, and I heard a voice very clearly telling me "Douglas, do not look any more into this", pointing to a pile of such photo's where I had traced out faces (from current newspapers and mags . . . faces and forms do not appear in all), and then vanished leaving a strong pungent odor and me a trembling mass of fright. Looking back, I don't know now if it was real or imagined, but I tend to believe it . . . still, as I said, I don't know that much . . . only have piles of loose empirical data and couldn't understand technical jargon, etc., anyway, until it was in abstract form . . . maybe it means I might stumble on something and to stay out of it?

What really started me was the happenings the night of August 22, 1924 . . . when the U.S. Naval Observatory, one of many such participating in a world-wide program of radio silence to detect intelligent messages from Mars, or space, and they, having trained camera-scope on Mars, and using that night, for the first time, a new type of Kodak emulsion, found, upon developing, that there was a series of dots resembling code, and lines resembling faces, that it was pored over and then supposed to have been shelved, still unsolved . . . personally.

I couldn't conceive of anyone shelving a thing like that . . . they would stick with it (at least one person would) like archeologists stuck with translating the Rosetta, for instance . . . and later, I felt that there was a great deal behind such as Project Ozma, and like projects, and now the Soviets announcing, via Dr. Shlovsky, (who presented theory re artificial Mars moon) that they would search

1372

Andromeda nebula for signs of intelligent life . . . or in the last sentences of the Feb. 6, 1962 AF UFO analysis report wherein they state they do not deny existence of animal life elsewhere . . . then say they have no evidence to back that up . . . and that Lick took numerous photo's, especially of Luna, that same Feb., 1962, the ones showing Archimedes showing something that wasn't there before (to the right of that crater) looking cigar-shaped . . . all of these instances and more making me think that behind it all, and behind the expenditure of millions of dollars and man-hours, etc., there must be some pretty staggering information . . . else what would prompt them to waste time in such searches after they say there is nothing to it all? Puzzling, isn't it?

But you and Dr. Iosif S. Shklovsky caused a lot of empirical data, in my mind, to "click" into place . . . which might be result of bad thinking, I don't know . . . but the following, briefly, is the picture I get from it all . . . maybe you can understand it better than I, if I have come close to the mark at all. (If you want an article for FS, I'll be happy to put one together, re the following).

I know your time is valuable, so I'll cut it short, and before briefly explaining what I mean, I'll make a statement re my theory:

"Some type of intelligence seems to be literally re-making the entire surface of Mars over to make it possible for their kind of life (or biology) to exist there, and that in the last 98 years we have been observing the fruition of their labors, which in recent years, has been drawing to completion, that they finally settled on the surface in 1960 (showing that maybe Bender guessed correctly why UFO suddenly declined), after having spent this time preparing for colonization." Following sequence of events (observed) over 98 years, on Mars, it appears that there is intelligent activity engaged in a fantastic program to remake or re-condition the surface.

Assuming that the moons were not there prior to 1862 (many articles showing use of same type telescopes, etc., despite Keplers drive for rhythm in numbers showing

1373

there should be two moons there which caused Swift to accurately guess . . . OR, was it predict?); that we have the active phenomena of the fabulous 1880's, especially with the discovery of those moons at a time when strange things were happening on Luna, Earth, the Red Spot of Jupiter, etc.; of the oddity presented by the twinning out of those "canali" (actually series of linear squares?) as they reach the equator, which natural formations could not produce, much less repeat over and over; of the fact that as what appears to be vegetable growth spreads into, or encroaches over, arid areas, so do the "canali" (so-called), which certainly indicates to me intelligent deliberateness; of the finding that as spring growth begins, and ice melts (whether frost or cap ice) there is a corresponding increase in the orbit velocity of the inner moon (wanes in fall), which, to my mind, can only indicate deliberate, purposeful, intelligent REGULATION, maybe reacting with or to natural cosmic and planetary forces, to create stronger tide effects to superbly conserve the small amount of moisture there, which makes it possible to plant in the arid areas? Since the cycle is from pole to equator, rather than vice versa. It seems to me that that encroaching growth has to be artificially encouraged, as noted by the rapidity with which it moves and the selectivity of area where it is observed (maybe those genuine contact cases, such as in South America, where a peon reported beings studying his plants and taking some with them, might mean they were taking samples back to their agronomists to see if it would grow on Mars? Certainly, they could be graminivorous . . . wouldn't any kind of life, no matter where it exists, have to eat? This was one of my own reasons for wondering why NICAP refused to look into the Simonton cakes, since they acknowledge presence of extraterrestrials, and they would have to eat . . . and to say they lacked funds sounds poor, because any of their sciental members should have been eager to determine the truth of those cakes . . . to find out whether they were original to Wisconsin or whether they were not . . . they could, for instance, have determined

1374

if they had earth chemicals, such as riboflavin, vitamins; or determined, by irradiation background, what part of earth the grains were grown in . . . that can be done, can't it? Simonton's having hit the lecture trail might only be a means to try to convince people of the truthfulness of the experience, only he knows. . .

Mars' surface is composed of massive quantities of magnesium, so we are told . . . and I keep thinking of Maury Island, and Ubatiba incident in that respect . . . if one of Mars' moons is artificial, and considering its size, they could harbor such craft easily . . . in Bender's case, maybe they weren't extracting directly from sea water but were collecting from ocean floors. I recall an item in an old AMAZING about piles of slag on the floor of the Indian Ocean, for example, and then the Soviet finding of strange tracks there on the floor . . . and discovery of magnesium nodules (ore) strewn about the ocean floor, which industry is thinking of collecting themselves.

But those Naval Ob films (plates) seem to me to support a private theory of mine re certain peculiar aspects of the UFO, such as in the case of UFO toying with pilots, as in the Gorman case (and even from Shavers cave mech, would still be the case?) . . . it appears that in all such cases, the UFO was actually able to instantly and accurately determine not the next move of the pilot, but his THOUGHT TO MAKE AN EVASIVE MOVE . . . that is they did not read the pilots mind, but something much finer and deeper . . . all such say that they felt as though they were being observed . . . well, suddenly being confronted with something foreign to our experience, we at first feel basic emotions, THEN enter into mental activity (thought as to what way to cope with the situation) . . . and it seems to me that the UFO was able to interpret chemical-triggered reactions of the pilot and react to them, BEFORE the pilot could transform that chosen thought into muscular action. I am thinking of the findings made in the DNA series, for example - I think we have a vital clue to something tremendous in this research . . . me, I don't understand it but barely . . . maybe you will. - Douglas

1375

Mapes, 344 Perry St., Apt. 1-A, Buffalo 4, New York.

Dear Ray,

I haven't read all of the 4th issue of "Hidden World" but have completed Jim Wentworth's correspondence with Dick Shaver. A lot of what he has written coincides with my experiences, particularly my letters to him and Shaver's letters to me in 1948. In the summer of 1948 my family and I visited Dick Shaver and Dottie in McHenry, Illinois. Later on in the year they sent us pictures of them as we had sent pictures of us for their fan album.

This is all a matter of introduction. I had written you before when you were sounding off about fluoridation of water and with your permission had sent the particular magazine in which your article appeared to our local newspapers. One voice in a big world and still the city of Richmond has poison in its waters. Not material, however.

I have a small file on my personal correspondence with Dick, one on clippings of Flying Saucers, another on Voice of the Gallery (and by the way, what happened to Ralph M. Holland?). Or for that matter, what has happened to Eva Firestone, or to Chas. Marcoux? Besides my personal files I have many copies of the old Amazing Stories, etc. from there on out.

Back about 1948 when I visited Dick & Dottie I was "hot" for the Shaver Mystery, although like Wentworth I had not seen flying saucers, had weird dreams, etc. However, since then - WOW!!!

In August of 1954 I bought my present residence (with mortgage, of course) and up to that time transferred my belongings and my interest in the Shaver Mystery at the same time. Since that time and particularly for the last few years I have slept with my light on in the bedroom (my wife notwithstanding).

To lead up to that I will explain several occurrences that happened prior to 1954 when we were living in the rented house we took over after my folks moved out and bought a house of their own (I don't remember the exact year, but it was after my return from the war in 1945). And come to

1376

think about it, it was after my visit to Dick in the summer of 1948.

So - somewhere between '48 and '54 the following happened to me (enough to calm me down on speaking about the "Mystery" to people I came in contact with. One night I lay asleep with my lovely wife beside me in an upstairs bedroom (last one to the rear). As the night went on I seemed to have a dream, yet I woke up (and it was not a dream) and a light seemed to stream up beside my side of the bed about mid-hip. It went clear thru the ceiling and I could see the stars and the clear sky above. There seemed to be an insistence to the light, an effect, or a feeling that it was pulling me over the bed and into the light. There was also a premonition or feeling that if I gave in I would be a "goner". I fought this feeling and looking over the side of the bed could see that it apparently extended down to the depths of infinity. Scared! Hell! Scared was not the feeling I had. It was worse than that. However, I could barely move but with much purpose of mind I found I could move a leg and nudged my wife. Gradually, she awoke. As she did so the light grew dimmer, or at least to waiver in intensity. With this difference I gave a good kick and she awoke grumbling, but not before she saw the light vanish in its entirety. And with the vanishing of the light I broke down and cried. I ascertained later that she had seen the light but did not understand what was going on and still does not to this day. Nor neither do I.

ANOTHER NIGHT LATER (possibly six months to a year later) - same room and with reasonable light in the room from outside, I again awoke and felt the bed covers being pulled down toward the foot of the bed. I again had the feeling of not being able to move or to combat this sensation. I gripped the top edge of the covers with my fingers and felt a decided pull. Being horrified because of the previous experience which flashed in my mind, I again tried to touch my wife, to nudge her with my knee. How long this struggle went on I do not know, but it seemed like hours. Finally, with one last desperate lunge I gave my wife a good kick (you know where) and she awoke. When she awoke the pull left and the evil that had seemed to be in the air vanished also. She sensed none of this except that she can verify that I was almost hysterical and again crying, begging her to just hold on to me and not to let me go.

A THIRD INCIDENT - This was apparently a dream, but how horrible it was! I seemed to be in Peru (I just knew it was Peru). It was like I was inside this mountain, part of the rock itself. Below me in a cavern room were two rows of soldiers dressed in the arms or armor of the same type as the soldiers of Ponce de Leon. (Curiously, I just looked up Ponce de Leon and my encyclopedia opened immediately to the pages describing Peru. Coincidence?)

The soldiers were facing each other in two rows, with about six in each row. The two on the right end held long swords. At a command the two swung at each other, chopping each others heads off. As the swords swung around, the next two grabbed them from the still reflex swing of their now dead companions and swung at each others heads. Again the same result, until the entire group lay on the floor, dead or dying from cuts in the head or neck. I woke up screaming from this, and my wife had to quiet me. Even to this date I can see this scene as if it only happened yesterday and in reality!!! What does Dick Shaver say?

Shortly after the above we moved to our present address and for several years really had nothing startling to record except that after sleeping from east to west (head to the east) I was compelled to move the bed from north to south (head to the north). I know not why and today would not move the bed again if you tried to force me. I just feel that it is in its best place, which, to say the least, is not the best because of what has happened since.

As I said above we moved to our present address in 1954, buying a home on the GI Bill, that is, with a 30 year mortgage. Sometime between '56 and '58 (I say '58 because that is the year I busted my knee at National Guard Camp at Indiantown Gap and place the time because of that) I had several more "weirdies". I again experienced the bed cover pulling bit as one with an experience one night of having my left leg pulled over the side of the bed. There

1378

was no feeling of touching, just a force. I began thinking of God and praying and the force suddenly left. Was it Good fighting Evil? I am not a particularly religious or praying man, though I believe in God, but have not been in church more than three times since 1945, I am sorry to say. I have prayed when my wife thought I was irreligious and still do when family things seem to go wrong.

One night a couple of years back ('59 or '60?) I woke up, wide awake and not dreaming. The moon was undercover and it was dark as all Hades (if Hades is dark). Yet in the blackness of the room and as dark as it was I could sense the thing that woke me up. In the upper right hand corner of the room (remember I am sleeping from north to south) which would be the southwest upper corner I could sense an evilness and a darker blob that was darker, inky, a disturbing blackness. I could feel it throb and pulse as if a living thing? An evil amoeba is what I thought at first but I could feel that it was much more than that. Its evilness seemed to beam at me that it wanted me and nothing else and that it would get me. As horrified as I had been on previous occasions I now was on the verge of going absolutely NUTS! I couldn't scream, I couldn't move. I wanted light, and the only light I could think of was the light of GOD. I prayed to Him, beseechingly, humbling myself to Him as I never had before, and I thought of the TERO's, and prayed that if any were anywhere in the vicinity to please help me. Never in my life have I been so desperate and never in my life do I want to experience such a thing again. (Incidentally, I read in one or your mags about some one else having such an experience. My sympathy to her and to others who may have such.)

The feeling of goodness came about. It seemed to exude thru the room and as it did so, the black blob of evilness diminished and all of a sudden vanished. I gained my power of speech, feeling, and movement. Turning on the light, I felt an inexpressible feeling of well-being, of good, and the preceding few moments as if only a nightmare. It was and it wasn't.

After that I thought of the goodness of things. I prayed

more than I ordinarily would. I let Shaver and the mystery slip a little bit away. Oh! I kept up with things, but I just read and forgot or rather let the things I read just go into memory without concentration on such. THEN, about two years ago, for no rhyme or reason I began experiencing the most hallucinatory dreams, horrible, fantastic, weird, things I could never dream of unless I was NUTS.

No, I wasn't, and I can't prove it. I have no certificate from our local mental asylum certifying to such, although I have a friend who went in on an alchoholism charge and he now has a certificate saying he is sane. From what?

The dreams came and they went. Some nights I even had pleasant dreams, but how few and far between. I learned over a period of time that light had something to do with it. When the light was on I had pleasant dreams and when the light was off I had the "weirdies". Nowadays I leave the light on all night, or should I say nowanights.

I have explained this to my wife, and she doesn't quite believe me. She can testify that I have had some weird nightmares and woke her up with a scream to turn the light on and only could go back to sleep with the lights on and snuggled comfortably in her arms like a baby. That's the only nice part about this business.

She recently came back from Hawaii after spending about 40 days there because of her mother having a stroke. During the time she was away I often had unexplainable feelings about things and often took the dog of the family, a black spaniel type of non descript breed to bed with me. As much as he enjoyed this comfort he never spent the entire night in bed with me. I have an uncomfortable habit of waking up about every hour on the hour (this goes back about two years). When waking up the first time I would go looking for him and he would be comfortably ensconced on a rug on the living room floor. What made him leave me after having evinced his desire to stay with me on the bed? I snore, of course, but he has stayed most of nights regardless. Could it be that he feels the evil that penetrates this room and could it be that I am only to sleep one hour at a time to combat an evil? Or simply, maybe he can't stand my snoring.

However, since my wife has been back she has tried to cut the lights several times after I had fallen asleep. Back came the old "weirdie" dreams and after experiencing such for a short time I would wake up and see that the lights were off, and consequently cut them on. (You know who got hell the next morning?)

In between waking and cutting the lights on several times I would have the distinct experience of having cut them on, or on having to reach and reach and reach and then to supposedly discover that the bulb was burned out. The bulb was never burned out, of course, and only after tremendous exertion would I realize the tamper or the effort to keep me from turning the light on. After such realization I could turn the light on without any effort. And, of course, left it on for the rest of the night. My wife now has instructions not to turn the light off for any reason until the morning sun begins to brighten our windows. (Now she wonders why I drink so much.)

I started this as a letter and now it appears to turn into an article, because I just keep rambling and rambling. BUT, I do have one more little thing to talk about and it is for the person who advertised in one of your mags for a visitor of outer space. This ties in whith Shaver and I never had the nerve to ask him about it. It came on one of his Shaver Mystery Mags, and was stamped in green ink on the outside. Can you explain it? It threw me and still does. If it is authentic maybe the person wanting some outer space contact can write using this address and maybe the P.O. will have some way to forward it. - Here it is - just imagine the following in green ink: FINE, UNMATCHED OUTER STUFF, (Kill very recent), Diving Salvage, Inc., Pier 13, Proof St. N.G.

I for one would like to know just exactly where this place is and what is meant by the top line. If you, RAP, can explain, please do so somewhere, either by personal letter or by or thru "Hidden Worlds". Or maybe I've shot my mouth off too much!

Things have gotten to be pretty much of a such and such nowadays, which means nothing. I don't really understand

1381

where I'm going. My family and I have no fallout shelter. We have some guns, but what protection with little ammunition? Maybe Shaver can answer the problem, or between him and the NASA we can come to some solution. Hurray to the first man on the moon! Then, we won't have to worry. Instead of a war we'll be worrying about who will get the rest of space! Or don't you think? - G.M. Roberts, 3026 Maplewood Avenue, Richmond 21, Virginia.

Dear Mr. Palmer and Mr. Shaver:

I have read your book titled the "Hidden World", the first one Spring 1961, about the "caverns" below the earth, and some of the "things" that happen there. "I know it is true" because I have been held there and "tortured" - forced to do a number of "degraded things". And there are a number of other "people" held there and forced to do these degraded things. I know you can be tortured in the ways Shaver says because it has happened to me and will happen again. There are a number of other things that happen there. I have lived there for a number of years and have been tortured during those years and I mean tortured.

"Do you, Mr. Shaver, know there is a 'cycle of time' going on right now?" It started back in 1956 and has been going on for a number of years now. It is this period that I am tortured. Right now I am hearing a voice from this other world, have been since 1957. "It" has some control of my mind before this time period starts up again back in 1956. "They" somehow are able to take control before 1956 start up again. They hold the people from the surface of the earth prisoner and torture them and myself. This happens live.

Right now I am hearing the voice from that other world as I write this. Then before 1956 start up again they hold me live for a period of time, then 1956 starts all over again and then I remember a "story". And then the voice starts up again, that I am now hearing.

P.S. I send Harry Edwards, the "Spiritual Healer", a letter about this "time period". He answers back that he knows all about it and calls it the "cycles of time in the universe". Thank you.

1382

Mr. Shaver, ask the tero if they know about it and what can be done. - Mr. Martin Byrne Jr., 4217 Garwoodway, Pittsburgh 1, Pa.

Dear Mr. Palmer:

I don't know whether this experience will fit your pattern or not, but I give it to you for whatever it is worth.

I have a 10-day old baby. Last night I thought he was having difficulty in breathing. I got up and checked to see if his blanket was over his face, but it wasn't.

I decided to call our doctor in the morning and tell him about it, as I then thought baby might be catching cold. As people will do, I pictured in my mind just exactly how I would tell him about it.

Imagine my horror when I actually heard someone say, "Burn off his hands and feet and that will cure him!" I gasped, as I then heard a maniacal laugh. But here is the real shocker -

THE VOICE SOUNDED JUST LIKE OUR DOCTOR!!!

Could this have been dero at work? What a horrible suggestion to make to a mother!

I believe that once I saw a dero, demon, or devil. At any rate, something extremely evil. I was very small at the time, but was able to talk. However, I did not know anything about ghosts or evil spirits, and such like. I was upstairs when I saw this person(?) and 3 neighbor children were with me. We all saw her, and ran screaming down the stairs.

When my mother had calmed me enough to tell what was wrong, I could only tell her it was a bad woman. She searched the second story of the house and found no one there.

That was 30 years ago and I can still see that face in my mind's eye and can never forget the gleam of pure hatred in her eyes. I have no idea why she should frighten little children, but I do wonder if my heart trouble doesn't date from that experience. If you want to use this letter in your column, it is perfectly allright with me. - Mrs. Mildred Crow, P.O. Box 2633, Freeport, Texas.

P.S. My husband and I would like to see some enlarged pictures of Shaver's mystery stones and if you would lend them, we will send them right back after examination.

1383

Rap:

This is an important letter!

Nearly every letter I get nowadays is from people who read your article "Psychic Stones" (in SEARCH Magazine). Now listen - they don't enclose money because they are sure they are NOT psychic and hence will NOT see any pictures!

Your article practically ruined what was getting to be a wage paying business of mailing a few rocks every day. I think you should make up for this article now that you yourself can see pictures quite plainly by stating that fact - and for your own sake - you may be in the rock business yourself before you know it!

I think these rocks are the most wonderful discovery ever made by any man anywhere since the Deluge because of what they contain in FACT and not "Psychically". This is readable and available information on the complete technology of ANOTHER CIVILIZATION superior to our own - and I feel you should make this plain in your magazine to make up for the ruin of what was not much but was paying me for my efforts. That phrase "psychic stones" nearly cut my business off. It is coming back very slowly because most people I have contact with have read other things about the stones in HIDDEN WORLD - but the effect of the article was to completely counteract what I was able to tell them in the ads.

I know you didn't do this on purpose and I don't feel you did, but I do feel you were tampered into that article and the impression it made on people was most unfortunate for a wonderful new thing in their life, and mine.

I have not had one real complaint from people about NOT seeing pictures in the stones I sent them. The only complaints are a few weasels who say the pictures are accidental and don't take time to study them to see if they are, and these are very few, not a half-dozen -- and even these do not ask for their money back, they are just arguing for the sake of arguing. They do see pictures and you know they all do, so where does the "psychic" angle come in if anyone can see them?

Your sincere friend: Richard S. Shaver, Rt. 2, Box 39, Amherst, Wisconsin.

THE HIDDEN WORLD

● Yes, Richard, this letter is important. I believe that in answering it, a great many things will be cleared up in the minds of my readers as well as yours. I don't know how many times in the past fifteen years I have been asked if I MYSELF believe in your caves, and the dero, and the mech, and the stim machines, and the pictures in the rocks, and HOW I reconcile your incontrovertible disbelief in anything psychic, and my own quite obvious belief in it. WHICH is it, my readers ask? Am I fish or fowl? Am I liar or fool? Am I really trying to disseminate truth, or out for the buck?

Let's clear up the "buck" first. For myself, I suggest that it is necessary to make a living, to provide for my family of a wife and three children. The fact that I make this living doing what I BELIEVE in and what I LIKE to do merely indicates that I am an individual who simply will not be a robot and stand on a production line because society has built such a line. I am not a socialist, nor a worker in a hive, nor a drone. I am Ray Palmer, and I do not conform. And I CAN take care of myself, and do it until the day I die, social security taxes notwithstanding. Yes, I try to make a buck. I have so far been successful only in losing some 35,000 of them (it was as high as 70,000 in 1954, but I've paid it back rather than cheated my creditors by doing the lawful(?) thing of claiming bankruptcy. So I need money. I doubt if there is a single of my readers who thinks I shouldn't make any.

The same goes for you, Richard. You are entitled to sell stones and make money on them. Your paintings of them are "impressionistic art" far superior to recent work which won $1,000 prizes in New York (such as that assinine black square painted with a calcimine brush which the critics said had "subtle meaning"). When I wrote my article, giving my opinion of these stones, it was not to ruin your business, nor yet because I was "tampered" by a dero ray into doing something entirely beyond my mental control or true will. Why is it that an opinion which differs from yours is due to "tamper", and not to individual reasoning processes. Why is it that one who suggests the pictures are accidental is a weasel? Would you have us believe that there is no picture in any stone which is NOT accidental? If you make such a

1385

claim, then it must be proved. The purpose of my article was to prove something. I wanted to prove that your rocks either contained actual pictures, or they were accidental, or they were imaginary. So I printed three pictures. I asked my readers to show me the faces and forms they saw. If they were actually there, we would get many items of agreement. Hundreds would point out the same face to me. I would have to say that it was actually there. I even asked YOU, Richard, to show me in these three pictures, and you did. The results of this article were so fantastic that I have not yet completed the collossal job of cataloging and classifying the answers I received. You have said that even the weasels, if they would only LOOK, would see the same pictures you see, because they are there in FACT, and not psychically. This is exactly what I asked my readers, and you, to do. They did it. But I have one question in my mind - will you, my readers, the weasels, the psychics, or even the dero, accept a scientific and rigid test such as this one? Will you abide by the results of LOOKING by EVERYONE and not just in "opinion". Either the pictures are there, or they are not. If they are, ANYONE can see them, although it may take a little persistence, experimenting with light and angles, lenses, magnification, photography, or what have you. You asked me to sit down and STUDY the stones. To LOOK. Then I would see, you said. I did look. And I asked my thousands of readers to look also. They did. YOU looked at the same pictures.

You ask me to remedy the ruin I have made of your monetary return for these stones. This infers that if I say to my readers: "There are pictures in stones," then everyone will rush to send you money. I wish I could make money that easily! Readers, I have on my farm millions of stones. I will send every one of them to you for $1.00 each! On and in many of them are priceless art work from a forgotten age, depicting the history of races long dead. How is it, then, that the same rush to purchase does not come from the thousands of psychic people who read SEARCH Magazine? If it is a matter of belief, then it should be easy to sell anything - just appeal to their beliefs! But you ask me to put it on the basis

1386

of FACT. You do not wish me to hoodwink them by saying it is something psychic, which is an illusion fostered by dero, and that in truth there is no spirit world, no life after death, no God, no nothing - just mankind, rotting to his early death through radioactive poisoning.

Well, then, let us have the FACTS! Given hundreds of readers making careful study of three photos, will it not be true that their scrutiny will reveal the presence of those ACTUAL pictures that are there, because all will point out the actual picture, and those who see imaginary pictures or accidental pictures will NOT agree? Just how did this bit of Ray Palmer scientific method turn out?

You will learn, as soon as the report is ready. But meanwhile, granting that the pictures are ACTUALLY there, can we say that they are implanted there by a dead race, or by a living race of underground people, dero or tero, or can we say they are implanted there mentally or psychically by a dead race, or by a race now in some other plane of existence such as that spirit world you so emphatically deny?

In the article, I pointed out that the Bible says there are records in the rocks of this planet. That Oahspe says that the God of this planet implanted records in the rocks of Wisconsin. That Richard Shaver says Mutan Mion implanted historical records on plates of imperishable "telonium" which we suggest is a word for "rocks" (tellus being the ancient name for Earth)? Can it be that when we say cavern world, spirit world, factual or psychic, man or dero, that we are all talking of the same thing, using different terminology? Richard Shaver says he was physically in the caves. Another says he was psychically in the astral world, among the dead. Each is convinced it is true, because by all the evidence of his senses, it actually happened. Each asks the listener to take his word for it, and to believe. But Ray Palmer says belief is not enough - we must have proof. If Richard Shaver has been in the caves, others can go there. Let them die, if necessary, under dero torture, we care not. That would be proof, if we can witness it and escape. Or if we can journey into the world of spirit, let us go there, and perhaps come back saddled with an evil spirit that will drive us to mad-

1387

ness. What do we care about that, if we know for SURE that it is FACT and not illusion?

But in reality, nobody wants fact. Everybody wants his own pet illusion (or reality) to be accepted and believed. Here in these rocks Richard Shaver says is the proof. But not all can see it. Some weasels just won't look. Ray Palmer gets some of the weasels to look, and look long and carefully. Surely if even ONE of them sees the pictures, it is a triumph of research far more conclusive than a thousand believers chanting "I believe - mighty is the great Poobah!"

Are the pictures of ancient races, their history, engraved by some means in stones? That is the question. Can they be seen by everyone if the examination is careful, scientific, complete, free from suggestion, imagination, accident, or faith? And if they ARE to be seen, does it matter if we say they are seen by white light or black light, by eyeball or pineal gland, by camera lens and film or by x-ray?

Those who read your article in this issue, about your painting (from a rock) of the history of Adam and Eve, can see from the photo of the actual rock that you did not improvise, but merely strengthened an image already there. But the means of impression of that image on the stone is not decided. Was it by mysterious scientific rays of a dead race, or was it by mental power or psychic power? Was it a form of photography lost today? Or was it by sheer accident? Was the image only a coincidence? Have you added the details visible only to you? If we all painted this painting (see the front cover of the A-7 issue of HIDDEN WORLD) using the image on the stone as our base, would we all come up with Adam and Eve, the snake and the apple, as Richard Shver has done?

Must we rather say to ourselves, while Richard is making a buck on these rocks, we must not put them to the test, we must not question his statement, we must not wonder if our own thoughts are valid? But then, what if we proved them to be valid pictures, FACTUAL pictures, either physical or psychical, wouldn't that mean that the world would beat a path to your door and buy at fantastic prices and make you very rich?

1388

Who is it we must convince, the weasels or the votaries?
- Rap.

1389

HOW TO GET INTO THE CAVES

By RICHARD S. SHAVER

THEY ASK ME so often, young fellows who read carelessly and think sloppily. Just walk in where Shaver tells you, they seem to think; that's all there is to it.

Well, I'll tell you. Just now I was watching the Walt Disney epic on the Coyote - you must have seen it, it's on most TV programs.

There are prediluvean ruins in the background - the desert scenes especially; it's not so easy to tell when it's wooded. In one background particularly, there is a huge human face. If you watch carefully, next time they re-run this coyote picture on your TV, (they run them over six and eight times on some stations in Wisconsin) you will see this huge face. The great shadowed eyes and acquiline nose are as sharp as if Gutzon Borglun had just completed them, in

1390

my memory – but perhaps to other eyes it would not be so clear.

If you go to the Walt Disney studios, find out where this epic was filmed, go to that location and find that face, walk up to it and find the mouth, crawl into the mouth (you may have to shovel a few days to clear out the flood silt in some parts) and you will get to see the inside of one prediluvean ruin.

They used such faces for doorways quite often. There is a great carved face in the city of Rome, used today as an entrance to a night club or bar; perhaps that may date back to the Flood . . . and may not.

But don't expect too much. Not all the surface ruins were anything but ancient ruins when the Flood hit, because they were cities built by undersea peoples, of immense antiquity, and of uses not precisely the same as those of land people. Some of the ruins you can spot in picturesque backgrounds of movies are of later date, and some of them are so old that their nature is hard to understand, because undersea peoples were not exactly the same dunderheaded animal we call Man.

Some of the stones I can mail you on request were made by people who breathed water and lived undersea all their lives. That is one reason for the peculiar lack of horizon, for the lighting, perspective so unreasonable to our eyes, people with no feet who stand on their heads as often as right side up. It's underwater life, without horizon and little more up and down to it than a scene in a space liner on no-grav.

Some of the black stones with the queer yellow glaze like fox fire running over it, contain scenes like those that are obviously taken inside submersibles very like modern submarines in appearance, if you are one of those interested in looking at stones. I can mail you stones just like that, but it takes a little work with lens and light to see them . . . and they are worth it: the black stones are very deep stuff. Some of them contain undersea scenes so deep the fish and animals carry lights on their snouts, as do some of the manlike fish in the pictures; two on their foreheads as imps are pictured so often in ancient tales.

Since we are talking about getting into the caves, that would be perhaps the safest way: do it underwater in a submarine, so you wouldn't run into dero. You might run into sea people, survivors of the ancient forebears of mankind who never took to the land and so kept their water breathing apparatus intact. Who knows that whole races of them do not exist in the oceans, keeping themselves secret from rapacity, exploitation and from murderous men who would slaughter them for being different? There are still many sailors who swear to seeing mermaids, you know. I for one, believe them. Why not? Certainly I am not asking official icthyology; they would deny it with their dying breath. They would deny it with a mermaid gasping out her life in front of them. They would deny it with a sea-man's ray burning their very rump to make them tell the truth. If I were a mer-man, I'd help them deny it, too.

I am very tired of the official attitude toward all the wonders of this world of ours.

Officialdom is pronounced that way for a very special reason, you know. It is Mother Earth's little joke on liars and only a seeress can explain it to you. It is called "grain" and every soothsayer once understood it perfectly. It is one of the lost wisdoms of earth. If you learn about "grain" and study Shaver's Mantong alphabet, you can see the "grain" of events working out, at times, in the sound of the words, like the grain of wood running through a plank.

By the way I've got a correction for Issue Number A-3. On Page 409, lower center of page, Ray has me saying -- "Instead they allow such silly things as Batman Comics, Superman comics." Now I don't want the Batman after me. This is a sample of tamper. I was trying to say that people could take a lesson from such apparently silly things as Batman comics and Superman antics . . . a lesson in their active intent to thwart evil, their actual attack upon evil.

We must find a way of being as effective in real life as the Batman is in his comic-book career against evil, or we will be swallowed up again as the Renaissance was swallowed up in the witch-hunt of the Auto-da-Fe, and the darkness will

1392

come down again as it did then. Look how long it took to recover a little from that madness of the witch burnings over all Europe.

Do you know what that century-long circus of death was really all about? It was about getting rid of MAGIC BOOKS!

The witches they killed were people who possessed some knowledge of the caverns and of the elder science. The styles of medieval times were taken from actual pictures of prediluvean civilization. I have seen medieval styles on these stones. They had prediluvean books in circulation during the Renaissance. They got their styles, that fantastic lovely business we call medieval style, from prediluvean books. It could well be those books were also silica, and that they read them with rays they took from ruins, just as I am telling you to do now.

That witch hunt succeeded, and once again a knowledge, any knowledge, of prediluvean science, then called magic, was confined to the possession of a very few survivors. The same murderous effort to get rid of everyone who knows anything about the caves is going on today. Right under my feet men die on racks because the dero who want us all in ignorance as profound as their own have caught them trying to help protect Shaver. It could well be that still, as always, my "protection" is but a sham to catch the independent minded ones of the caves trying to reach my "protectors". How can you tell, up here? It is just as hard, down there, for they are expert liars. And it is death to be fooled by a dero.

So, to you ray people who feel that urge to come here, my advice is quite different. Take my advice and start a new clean stronghold somewhere else, where you are sure there are no dero and you can keep them off with booby-trapped ways, with barricades in all the tunnels, with all the ways you know and with new ones, for surface rockets are being used and you need a rocket barricade a long way from home to stop a warhead. One of the most effective has been a center-way set, I have heard. That is, you hang a heavy metal object dead center in the cavern way, and the oncoming rocket, set to steer equidistant from both walls, will slam into it and go off before it reaches other metal.

So don't think it's good here just because they let me write. These writings can just as well be a come-on to get a few more well intended generous ray people out of the way for the monopolist's comfort. Much good it ever does them to kill us; they have to live with themselves afterward, and that is the dullest life one could ever choose. The dullest, the dirtiest, the most evil, we have all of that around here, and some that sounds like else, too, but do you know that a fifty voice set can sound like fifty people complete with built in syllogism that goes forward instead of backward? They are building record organs now to do that: give a flow of Tee syllogism so they don't get caught thinking backward. They push appropriate keys, and the organ is apt to say if they ask about the weather that the plum cake is delicious . . . but I don't always believe it is, do you?

The truth is I am badly abused by ray, so don't think it's anything but the same old cruel trap somewhere under. You might find friends holding the fort, and you might find nothing but dead men, and dead men's voices from the organ.

Incidentally, there are a lot of new developments in the underworld's everlasting efforts to get rid of everyone with a brain, which every ray, and every tero ray, and every Shaver fan and every man or woman with loose cash, should know about. But how to tell them so they will hear, that is a problem.

One of the wools they pull on tero not in touch is Shaver syllogism, taken from records of my thought and of people in the underworld working with me. Over an organ-ray these can sound most convincing and disguise an idiot killer with an overlay of high-moral tone and the familiar Shaver syllogism passed around in the caverns. If you don't happen to know how skillfully this can be done, it can kill you. It has cost us so many, and developing defenses against these particular tactics has been too long in the oven.

How many men fighting in the caves know this has all happened before, back in the thirteenth century? Then they

1394

killed off the wisdom workers, and the whole Renaissance vanished in blood.

Stay out of the cruels, clean a spot of deros, fight defensively and guerilla hit and run, but don't get trapped in that dirty switch-top deal they have been handing out. You must know your top range, and you must know when he is out of action. How many of us must die before we learn all their ancient tricks again? They get them from the old records, that's one reason they don't want anyone studying the stones we have rediscovered. They are the ancient silica records and they tell the truth about how things were done when ray was not an idiot's cruel dream of torment for everyone.

There is one more thing every ray should know that has fooled a lot of ray to death. The dipper, so-called for want of a better name, is not a killing ray, just the ancient traveling theater, no more capable of harm than a TV station. It throws an overlay, yes, but they can't kill from that overlay; it only serves as a cover for the killer they plant among your own local ray.

These two things every ray of responsibility should know. The dipper is not death dealing. That it has always been thought to be is an ancient dodge. The lovely syllogism, the thought records of our best loved dead, are so often used to cover a killer's approach. Most of us know it, but how not to be fooled is something else again. The best way is disarm and screen every one.

Now, about surface traps. Every rotten racket the caverns have worked on surface mankind must be exposed. Today we are deciding not to have that wool, since we have learned the ultimate depths of the customary double-cross they work on us all when they give us the "witches salt", the "knowledge of good and evil", or one of the other potions they have prepared of radioactive salts since time immemorial to bend stubborn minds to their insane wills.

I don't know too much about surface traps worked by the underworld on unsuspecting rich people, because I never was rich enough to get anything but run-around and tamper wool. But I can guess. One is standard; they show

1395

them the wonders of stim and projection, and give them an address, usually with the provision they leave no one know where they are going. They can make this stick with the "noble" button on the stim organ. The trusting one brings the cash, and if he gets away with his life he is lucky. Then they work the double racket, spying on a rich family and working up a full complement of doubles, so that one wonders if any rich family are really who they were when they got rich. This one is hard to prove when witnesses and old family friends are doubles, too. And no one who "knows" ever mentions a word about this sort of thing because . . . well figure it out. You can't even tell a policeman; he runs you in for being mad. You take what comes, and most of it has been nasty. Most of us would like to change that, for there is only insanity in the dero nastiness and murderous deviltry.

This is the sort of truth that must be written about ray and ray activity before much will be done about any of it. I am very tired myself of being brushed off by people who should know better than to act like boneless worms before the murderous madmen who staff ray rackets. Must everyone be an utter coward before the unseen death of ray racketeers?

This silica library is one example, there are a hundred others, where the so-called erudite and important of surface man flunk out miserably in the test of courage and mentality.

This cannot continue, one wants to think it is only lack of information that ails them, or that they too, are doubles, and not genuine men and women, but some sort of mindless creatures who pretend to be human.

Educated men who can turn their back on an Elder library of silica because of fear of the underworld are not men; in my opinion they are some kind of vermin.

However, we now have some eminent archeologists recognizing the silica books as genuine prediluvean artifacts, and the word is spreading rapidly. Get yourself some before their real value is more generally recognized. They will be priceless.

1396

MY PAINTING OF ADAM AND EVE

By RICHARD S. SHAVER

(SEE FRONT COVER

FALL, 1962, VOL. A-7

HIDDEN WORLD)

Reproduced on Page 1352 of this edition

THE COVER painting on issue A-7 of HIDDEN WORLDS magazine is from a micro-photo of a stone surface.

I chose it because it's about something with which you are already familiar - the story of Adam and Eve.

Other photos of the same stone show "they" are hunting similar black furred "Adams" - hunting him on horseback among what appear to be ice crevices ... for "sport"!

The particular scene I chose shows a false "Adam"; that is: one of the cavern people dressed up in a black beast suit of hair to look like "Adam"; and it shows that the "serpent" giving Adam the apple is also a costume; that is: it is a photo of a play or a pageant about Adam and Eve and the Apple.

THE HIDDEN WORLD

This was very interesting to me because of the subtle but vast difference from the Bible's story of Adam. Perhaps you noticed this difference and perhaps not. I had hoped you would all see that there have been changes in the story somewhere along the line of communication with the past.

To understand why and what these changes are, I have to go back to pre-deluge times and briefly re-tell you the story of the "EXODUS" - the time when the true cavern peoples left Earth forever because the moon was approaching to cause the great Deluge.

Mankind was numerous and wise and tremendously organized, before the Deluge. He had evolved from a mere fish in the sea to become the greatest and most powerful form of life on the planet ... far more so than today.

You have to know about all this, and it is pictured out in rock pictures very completely, over and over in the stone pictures.

Now, when the great "Exodus" ships were finally sent out, what was left behind were the criminals ... and that means deros in the Elder thinking. Not just people who broke a few laws, but people whose every thought is destructive, completely so.

Criminals, real Jack-the-Rippers every one, and the completely insane in the madhouses ... they didn't distinguish then between the merely insane and the destructively insane - both were considered plain nuts. Which is the fact of the matter, and our attitude of considering a murderer sane and responsible is the proof of our own mild insanity generally. We just aren't very logical about such things.

After the terrific tidal waves had swept over Earth and scoured her surface clean of most signs of man's occupancy (which it didn't, we are just too stupid nowadays to see the Cyclopean ruins for what they are), in the deep caverns and under-structures of the great ruins still lived a great many "people" who were in fact the scum and refuse of a mighty culture.

The tremendous earth shocks of the moon's fall had broken their prison walls, if indeed they had ever been

1398

locked up by anything but the watchful "TOTEM" mind of a people who had telepathic communication, each with the other, all the time.

Here were the devils, still living, and all restraint gone forever into the skies. The tale is told that one great ship had to turn back, and arrived on Earth some months after the last great tidal wave had subsided and the moon once more orbiting Earth - as it may have before, though the pictures seem to show that it was a planet with an orbit about the sun which we captured - and that this great ship, with some hundred thousand sweet and normal earth people aboard, video'd its landing instructions to the newly released dero population . . . who manned the space guns immediately and shot it down in mid-landing, killing every one of them.

History on earth would have been worth reading if that ship had NOT trusted a liar and his crew of madmen from the broken prisons. If they had landed without video warning, they would have given the new ruler of Earth, the well-known Satan, a strait jacket.

However, that is not the story.

The story goes that centuries went by and the Satanic rule went on its mad course in the caverns, while the supposedly empty surface of Earth received a new wave of immigration from the sea! The rock pictures show these people, and the black and hairy beast they are hunting for sport is MAN himself, the new Adam.

The APPLE the serpent is giving Adam is a poisoned apple. It is this Apple around which every thing one learns about the history of man pivots. This is the same sort of Apple that Loki stole from Idun, when he rendered unto Odin the just reward for harboring a homicidal maniac, mortality instead of immortality.

For the "APPLE" is in fact the ancient symbol for the antidote for age poison! After the "Exodus", there were very few left on Earth who knew enough of the Elder science and medicine to know what an "Apple" was and what it was for. The true apple was a complex chemical that combines with the radioactive atoms which cause age

1399

(there are several, radium is just one of them) and causes them to be eliminated from the body.

The fact that apples grow on trees is a sort of illusion, not necessary to understanding the whole story. It is a fact that they grew many sorts of fruits in their extensive medical, herbal, and experimental gardens; and it is a fact they grew certain fruits in a sort of hydroponic soil prepared with this antidote as a part, a constituent of the soil mixture, so that the resulting apple was in fact a container of the antidote for age as well as an ordinary fruit . . . because it was grown just that way.

Satan, piggish selfishness personified, when the Exodus left him his opportunity to "inherit" all earth and all earth's wonderful cavern treasures, very carefully eliminated everyone who understood the Secret of the Apple!

If you remember the biblical version, Adam ate the fruit unbeknownst to God . . . and if you know about "The Exodus", you realize that "GOD" cannot be the real "God", but must in fact be an imposter, pretending to be the Ruler himself to fool the Other Nuts left behind into behaving and into obeying HIM!

So "God" deplores Adam's terrific "SIN" (stop and think why it should be a "sin" just to eat an apple?) and casts him out of the Garden. Why?

There is only one possible reason: He doesn't want the other NUTS to know there is a way to be immortal and he doesn't want them to see that Adam in fact gets younger because he ate that particular "Forbidden Fruit"!

So he poisons Adam with a poisoned Apple containing the very age poison it was designed to counteract!

He does this by means of "The Serpent" who was evidently very dumb and obedient as it seems were most of the NUTS left behind - in that time most beasts and creatures like the great "serpent" were in fact intelligent by reason of great age and by reason of having constant mental contact with the "Totem" members, the people whose minds added together by means of the Telaug made a "total mind", a large mass mind called the "Totem").

We know Adam and Eve received this poison because of

1400

the passages where they "hide their nakedness" and "cover their bodies with leaves" ... etc., etc.) We know this because this business of being conscious of the privates is a typical result of this particular poison suddenly administered, a simple truth that ray people have observed - for the administering of this poison is an ancient traditional custom in the caverns ... everyone gets it one time or another, with appropriate wool about "it keeps you from worrying about evil, etc., etc.

A sudden influx of sun-polared material into the blood stream will cause a mental upset of extreme proportions and this mental upset will be not only "cafard", it will also cause as a symptom an extreme sort of "morality" or unnatural shame in being a living creature with organs and parts like every other creature. This is in fact a magnetic phenomena having to do with the magnetic focii of the body's natural electric. It is part and parcel of deroism, brought on by sun-polared ions in the mind, that they hate all sex, kill all women ... or women kill men ... dislike what they liked etc., as I have explained innumerable unheard times.

So, you see, there are vast differences in this picture of the story of Adam and Eve and the one now circulated!

To understand these difference, you have to know that the people of Earth left Earth for space, after weeding out the undesirable elements, like the over-ambitious Satan - who promptly took over and denied to all the survivors all knowledge, especially the knowledge of the antidote for age symbolized in all myths by the knowledge of the antidote for age symbolized in all myths by the Apple! To understand the secret of immortality.

This tradition of utter abject slavery to Satan and his all embracing command to do away with knowledge (even one's own) goes on TODAY in the caverns, and the whole cavern population is supposed to bend every effort toward denying itself and everyone else "the Knowledge of Good and Evil" and the other phrase the bible uses: "the Secret of Life-everlasting", remember?

How dumb they have become under this kind of double-

1401

cross is witnessed by the fact they DO JUST THAT!

So do we! I have found the books of the Elder race, and people are too bowed down under the burden of utter ignorance even to LOOK at them!! These books lie about here and other places, they are "just rocks" and they are JUST ROCKS even after people are TOLD what they really are!! How dumb can we become?

It seems the cavern people and the surface people are the results of two separate emergencies from the sea! This was particularly enlightening to me to learn, for there are fundamental differences I couldn't account for . . . now I can! I can also account for the fact "they" were left behind by the Exodus . . . I would leave IT behind myself! A dero is a dero and nothing on earth can stand the sight or smell of one!

Man's worst enemy is a thing the Elder race considered somewhat as we consider the bedbug . . . a thing to exterminate where possible. Only the Exodus gave it its chance to work its one talent, a talent for mimicry . . . like the chameleon . . . The Mime . . . the Mimir. The cavern dero is expert at imitating, impersonating "people" . . . their worst enemy cannot say they are not good at pretending to be "people" long enough to get a Jack-the-Ripper knife into you!

All this you can see in this cover painting taken from an actual micro-photo (if Rap can get a decent print of it into this article) which should be printed herewith.

You understand here that Eve is wearing Amazon costume. The Amazons were apparently subjects or worshippers of the Aesir - their dating system in the stones is based on the "Age of the Aesir" - and this apparently runs parallel to the Christian in the latter parts, but how to correlate the two is not at present known. Apparently nobody bothers with the Aesir legends but a few fools like me who know that MIMIR was the devil himself and took Odin's eye when he fooled him into taking a drink from his "well" - a poisoned well specifically prepared to make fools out of any who drank!

Mimir and his eye-gouging tactics are the typical thing

among those who took over the cavern world after the EXODUS.

How to get the true story of the second coming of man from the sea, only to fall sucker to Mimir and his kind and be destroyed mentally, is my problem and yours!

It isn't just Shaver wool, it is the truth about the biblical changes. The story the Bible once told us was important and gave us some defense against these lies of Satan and his poisoner's crew. Today we have no such defense, and Mimir and Satan are responsible!

I can prove this by such photos as the one I took this cover painting from. That no one has a mind to understand the importance of my foolish Elder stones is a very sad thing for the human race! It means that Mimir still hides behind his well and makes fools of us all. Our well-meaning Odins as well as our would-be Baldurs and Christs all fall victim to Mimir, Satan, and Pluto!

They poison us and they destroy our minds. They deny us the right to read the Elder race writings. I give you the Alphabet, the books themselves in imperishable silica, and the two are all you need to reconstruct the Elder Science!

Yet, strangely, no one but a few would-be wisdom seekers even have the minds to comprehend that the stone writings are full proof of every bit of the story I have to tell you about the past.

Please, dear victimized and brutally mistreated people that you are, PLEASE wake up! No matter what cavern idiots tell you in the dark back of your mind, look at these stones and understand what they are! How can anyone ignore these marvelous ancient picture books?

Please write me and demand stones. I will send them, but you really have to look at them, you know! They aren't played like phonographs, unless you have access to mech now buried under the sands of the Deluge and in the under-borings. You have to study them out with lens and light, then build again the projection device for which they were designed. It's not so difficult as it seems. Elder devices were so developed by an age of growth they are in fact as simple as they can be made.

1403

THE HIDDEN WORLD
Spiritualism and The Shaver Mystery

Jim Wentworth

THIS WRITER has been intrigued with spiritualism ever since he understood the meaning of the word. Is this because ghostly manifestations have been personally witnessed? No - never. Nor have I ever seen a materialized spirit form, handled ectoplasm, observed the levitation of a heavy object like a table or a piano, attended a seance, heard a spirit voice, or spoken to apparently genuine mediums like Arthur Ford, Eileen Garrett, Mark Probert.

Me psychic? I shake my head in amusement, knowing only too well how sluggish are my senses. All of them.

Still, thanks to the sober reading of many fine books on the after-life, I am enormously caught up by it. One of the better books, beautifully clarified, is R. DeWitt Miller's YOU DO TAKE IT WITH YOU. Another of near-excellence is THIS IS SPIRITUALISM by Maurice Barbanell. (First published in 1959 by Herbert Jenkins Ltd., 3 Duke of York Street, London, S.W.1.)

I use the term "near-excellence" because of its one big fault. Though names are given freely enough, there is a woeful lack of details such as time, dates, location, etc. With these additions, this work by the man who, for the past twenty-five years, has been the Editor of two psychic journals (Two Worlds and Psychic News), would indeed have been of the highest calibre.

A thirty-seven year investigation changed Barbanell's unashamedly materialistic outlook from, first, being an atheist, later an agnostic, to finally a convinced spiritualist. This was due to his personal observation of extraordinary psychic phenomena.

Flawless evidence of the after-life came at direct-voice seances. Those in which the great medium, Estelle Roberts, participated were the most convincing.

1404

Sometimes the spirit voices came through what is called trumpet (actually a cone-shaped megaphone made of tin) in pitch darkness. On other occasions, as at Lily Dale, New York, which is America's largest Spiritualist camp during the summer months, spirit voices were heard on a brilliantly sunny afternoon.

Barbanell's book contains a number of remarkable spirit photographs. For example, in his own laboratory, Sir William Crookes snapped a picture of Dr. J.M. Gully of the Royal College of Surgeons, taking the pulse beat of a fully materialized spirit. The seance was held under test conditions imposed by the renowned scientist.

Another photograph shows the clear materialization of Queen Astrid, wife of King Leopold of the Belgians, at a Copenhagen seance after she was killed in a car crash.

A sequence of seven photographs were taken in about thirty minutes which depict the whole process of a spirit form's materialization. From the entranced Pennsylvania medium, Ethel Post-Parrish, a cloudy pillar of ectoplasm slowly builds up to the height of a full-grown woman. Gradually solidified, the figure of the medium's Indian spirit guide, Silver Belle, finally emerged completely materialized.

A "spirit" picture of Edgar Wallace, taken under test conditions by a professional photographer at the seance of the Jewish medium, John Myers, bore an astonishing resemblance to a normal photograph of the famed English fiction writer.

Richard Shaver would disclaim all the above phenomena being brought about by human spirits of the departed, but are really the workings of the antique ray machines of the forgotten race, the Gods, by cavern dwellers.

It was the midget-like, parasitic dero who cleverly created from their imagination the image of Satan. The thought was transmitted into a telaug (or telepathic projector) which greatly augmented the image before directing it upward at surface men.

Since ancient times, dreams and visions have been made to materialize by underground telesolidographs, machines capable of forming three-dimensional, opaque images. Thus

1405

began "spiritualism", rightly termed by clergymen as demonism. For demons (or dero) in their desire to misguide surface man, are the masters of spiritualism.

Yes, underground inhabitants created "spirits". It is wool, deliberately fostered to explain their actions. Thus is investigation prevented, or undesired, for surface people have a scapegoat - spiritualism - on which to blame mysterious phenomena that in truth originates from the unseen world beneath our feet.

As Ray Palmer put it in his editorial for AMAZING STORIES, June, 1947 - the Special Shaver Mystery Issue.

"We found out, also, that he (Shaver) is an extreme materialist. He does not believe in a life after death, or that man has a soul, or that things have a basis in something invisible and immaterial. If such exists, he says he has no proof, and therefor will neither accept or reject. Man may have a soul, he says, but you can't see it, taste it, feel it, smell it or hear it. Therefore, he isn't concerned with it, because there is nothing he can do with it even if he could prove it existed.

"Why dream up an 'astral being' to explain a thing that can more logically be explained with something requiring less faith, and more science? If you hear a voice, even if it claims to be your dead grandmother, why credit it to something that cannot be proved, when it is more reasonable to credit to something so simple and logical as a machine as simple as a radio, and the speaker's voice a real voice in a real person's larynx whose residence is right here on this earth (or under its surface) rather than in a misty 'spirit world'?

"The cave people, says Mr. Shaver, have themselves created these superstitions to conceal their real existence, and thus obviate any real attempt to find them. Who would look for something he does not believe to exist? That is why the caves remain secret, he says. Even if we do see a dero, we call him a ghost and pull up the bed sheets."

At a seance, messages containing details of a very personal and intimate nature have been given time and again by, say, a so-called dead wife to her living husband.

1406

That the medium - a complete stranger to all concerned - knew of these details was impossible. Barbanell discusses this very thing in his book.

A good example concerns the foremost racing motorist of his time, Henry Segrave, who was killed at Lake Windemere where he was attempting to create a new world speed record on water. His wife, Lady Segrave, was shocked by the tragedy, as were hundreds of thousands of his admirers.

Becoming interested in spiritualism, she attended a seance of medium Estelle Roberts. Here a spirit voice addressed Lady Segrave as "D", which was a nickname used only by her departed husband, and quite unknown to anyone else present.

So excited and tense was she that the seance ended prematurely. At the next sitting, however, her more relaxed manner brought about a far easier communication between herself and her husband.

The evidence for his survival began to accumulate at subsequent seances. In her own words: "The whole of his conversation was very characteristic, full of intimate details, so that I knew beyond doubt that it was my husband." And, in summation: "My evidence reveals his complete knowledge of my most intimate and private affairs. Again and again I have turned this evidence over in my mind, examined it critically and calmly. I have tried to explain it all away. I have asked myself the questions: 'Can it be telepathy or the sub-conscious?' 'Have I been deceived?' Always the evidence stood every test."

Maurice Barbanell tells, also, of the Australian voice specialist, Lionel Logue, who cured King George VI of his stammering, and became one of the Sovereign's most intimate friends.

Logue was extremely devoted to his wife, and when she died, he was inconsolable, even contemplated committing suicide. Mourning her constantly, he endeavored to obtain proof of her survival. The medium, Mrs. Lilian Bailey, when approached by a third party, agreed to visit his flat in Knightsbridge to give a sitting, unaware of this brilliant man's identity.

1407

Receiving a clairvoyant vision prior to entering her usual trance state, she said:

"I don't know why it is, and I scarcely like to tell you, but King George V is here. He asks me to thank you for what you did for his son."

One other thing was mentioned at that first seance. Mrs. Bailey claimed she could see the spirit form of Logue's wife who was too excited to do anything more than send him her love.

During the second sitting, the wife proved to her distracted husband that their love could bridge the gulf of death. Since her passing, changes had been made in Logue's house and garden which were unknown to anyone else present. His wife mentioned them familiarly.

Logue was deeply overcome. Mrs. Bailey's spirit guide was William Hedley Wootton, an officer who died in the First World War. In relaying intimate messages from the wife of Logue, the evidence for her continued existence grew, one being that her pet name for him was "Muggsy".

His wife cautioned him not to commit suicide. For instead of achieving the reunion he expected, it would only divide them. That Logue was contemplating suicide was never suspected by the medium.

With his evidence of survival, Logue's despair gave way to radiance. His life was transformed, and he made no secret of his belief in spiritualism. Occasionally he described the Bailey seances to King George VI.

Once it appeared that one of Logue's sons was dying. Through Mrs. Bailey, his wife insisted this would not happen. Eminent specialists, when consulted, had given the verdict that the boy had no chance. But his wife proved otherwise.

Then Logue became ill, and eventually died. Not long after, while Mrs. Bailey was having a seance at her Wembley home, both Lionel Logue and his wife returned there. Barbanell was not then present, and when he asked what Logue had said, he was told that Logue's happiness was indescribable. He had found spirit life to be even more beautiful than he had hoped.

1408

THE HIDDEN WORLD

Famed medium, Hester Dowden of Dublin, Ireland, obtained her communications from the Beyond by ouija board and automatic writing. Oscar Wilde (so claimed) communicated via the latter method. Quoting from Barbanell's book:

"Wilde's spirit signature was an exact replica of his earthly one. The handwriting disclosed his peculiarities. Events from his childhood days were mentioned and inquiry proved them to be accurate. The literary style, which is the acid test, was highly characteristic."

And: "Hester Dowden also received in automatic writing a play that was said to eminate from Oscar Wilde. Without disclosing the spirit authorship, she showed it to some theatrical managers. They all rejected it, one giving as his reason that it was too much like Oscar Wilde!"

As will have been noted from the foregoing, one very interesting fact concerning spirit communication is this: When sending messages from the Other Side, numerous spirit entities with unusual and distinctive voices continued to speak as they did in their earth lives. That is, in their natural and characteristic way. Which does seem to indicate the survival of the human personality.

Many famous people, after attending seances, became convinced that they had received indisputable spirit messages. Sir Oliver Lodge with his spirit son, Raymond, a victime of the First World War. (Medium Gladys Osborne Leonard.) Lady Doyle and her spirit husband, Arthur Conan Doyle. (Medium Mrs. Caird Miller.)

THIS IS SPIRITUALISM contains many fascinating chapters. Like those dealing with psychometry, spirit healing, apports, levitation, spirit photography, materialization.

In describing his experiences with the latter, Barbanell has produced one of the most exciting pieces of writing I have ever come across. Here is his opening paragraph.

"Materialization is the greatest and the rarest form of mediumship. It involves either the complete reproduction of the physical body, or those essential parts of it that are required to achieve a temporary flesh-and-blood creation. What emerges at a successful materialization seance is a

1409

living, pulsating, breathing, solid, conscious being who talks and walks, has heart and pulse beats, is warm and solid to the touch, and has blood or its equivalent flowing through its veins."

Discussed is the medium, Mrs. Louisa Bolt, whose spirit guide, Ethel, underwent a complete materialization at a seance. The sitters present were asked by the strikingly beautiful Ethel to step forward and shake her hands. This was found to be soft and warm in its resemblance to a completely formed human hand.

Getting permission to touch her spirit robing, Barbanell described it as having a gossamer texture; far softer than the softest silk, and giving him the impression of feeling cobwebs.

Before his death, Sir Vincent had been a well-known industrialist and president of the Federation of British Industries. He, too, appeared in a seance room as a fully-formed, materialized figure even to his distinctive moustache.

His removal of two roses from a bowl on a table was witnessed by all. When requesting one of the sitters, his sickly wife, Lady Caillard, to come forward, he handed her the flowers. Then he took her by the hand, this manifested "ghost", and embraced her, kissing her several times, and whispering words of endearment and encouragement.

Returning to her seat, Sir Vincent shook hands with each sitter. Barbanell's hand-shake was accompanied by a most masculine slap with the free hand.

Then, to fulfill an earlier promise, Sir Vincent accepted a proffered pencil from his wife, and on a plain sheet of paper held on top of a notebook by Barbanell, he wrote his signature!

Five months later, with her passing, Sir Vincent and his wife were reunited.

A third and final materialization was made visible during that particular seance. It was Ivy, a little colored control and helper of Mrs. Bolt. All features were clear - black face, white teeth, thick lips, pink tongue, etc.

From Barbanell we again turn to Shaver and his own

1410

remarks on "spirit-materializations". In THE HIDDEN WORLD, number A-1, he tells how he was framed into serving time in prison by the malicious, cavern-living dero.

Torment continued until, after many terrible months, a group of sane, well-meaning tero wrested control from the dero of the land upon which squatted the prison building which, in a later issue, was said to be in Newfoundland.

Shaver then began to experience unprecedented dreams. Bizarre they were, but still of infinite pleasure. In one dream, he received a young tero visitor - Nydia - who sat upon the edge of his iron cot.

She had a strange, rich, other-world beauty, with faintly golden hair "drawn back from her brow and was caught up at the nape of the neck with a ribbon that was pale green."

A solemn promise was made to free the prisoner.

The next morning, an object was found lying on the cot. It was Nydia's pale green hair ribbon! What Shaver had experienced was then starkly realized to have been more than a dream.

What had caused this amazing occurrence? Shaver's answer: teleport mech. Cave people possess the machines to transmit solid objects over long distances by means of tele-rays, which might be somewhat compared to the manner in which a photo or map is transmitted by radio. But there is a difference in principle never fathomed by Shaver.

Thus would apports in a seance room be scientifically explained by this most controversial person.

Barbanell, on the other hand, would argue that apports are things he himself received many times from the spirit world. Certainly it is incredible that apports, in their long distance transportation, defy normal conditions of time and space. But it is a definite fact, often experienced by Barbanell.

Consider the medium, Mrs. Kathleen Barkel, and her spirit guide, White Hawk, who was not the former's secondary personality, but possessed an individuality all his own.

1411

"The only physical indication," writes Barbanell, "that Mrs. Barkel had that an apport seance would shortly take place, was the curious fact that for days beforehand her fingers began to swell. At the end of the seance her body resumed its normal size."

Barbanell did not know the explanation. He did theorize, however, that Mrs. Barkel's body, in some manner "was used to store the ectoplasm required to rematerialize the objects after they had been brought through the atmosphere, doubtless in their atomic form. Obviously, with objects brought from miles away, they would first have to be dematerialized in order that the walls, bricks and mortar would prove no obstacles. The guides responsible for this phenomena insisted that the articles were not stolen. Sometimes they were lost and could not be reclaimed because their owners had died. They might be objects that were buried beneath the earth or under the water for years, or even centuries."

Apports vary in nature. Mentioned are semiprecious stones, a sapphire set in silver, a jade ear-piece set in nine-carat gold, a gold locket, a gold ring with three opals and four diamonds, strings of mummy beads, an amethyst, a scarab edged with gold.

On asking White Hawk how apports were brought to the physical world, he was told that the atomic vibrations were speeded up until the objects were disintegrated. When they were brought into the seance room, the vibrations were slowed down until the objects resumed their natural solidity.

As for how the vibrations were speeded up and lowered, no answer was forthcoming. Perhaps, as Barbanell suggests, fourth-dimensional happenings are beyond earthly three-dimensional understanding.

We have digressed somewhat, so back to Shaver's definition of spirit-materializations.

On the night of his release from prison, the vacant-eyed guard opened the lock of his cell door, obviously under mental control. Behind him was the reproduced form of Nydia, transparent, she herself in a cave where ancient

1412

mech of the God-race was making all this possible.

Once out of the prison building, Shaver ran across the open grounds and into a nearby forest. The transparent Nydia led him by the hand, her projection feeling as solid to his touch as real human flesh.

Many miles of hilly country were covered before the base of a mountain loomed ahead. After passing through an earth-covered door upon which grew grass and small bushes, they found themselves in a cave.

The "ghostly little figure" presently brought Shaver into a vast room where he saw huge, incomprehensible mechanisms built of time-resisting materials. Also seen was Nydia, the duplicate of the phantasm that had guided him underground. Nydia left the machine, and when the two embraced, the phantasm was no more - vanished.

Here, then, is Shaver's explanation of "spirit-materializations." They are not, he would earnestly insist, the spirit forms of dead people, but are really produced by cavern ray operators. These dwellers have access to wondrous machines capable of placing surface people under a form of hypnosis so advanced as to give the impression of full reality. This is invariably done in the seance room.

Spiritual objects that seem real can not at all times be handled as it is pure projection induced by age-old rays. For example, a hand would pass completely through a confronted ghostly form. But, with the application of induced hallucination, one would honestly believe he was touching something solid and firm.

Barbanell, of course, has something to say on levitation.

When, at a seance, a demonstration is made of a heavy table floating in the air, or a trumpet suspended in space, it is obvious that the laws of gravity are defied. Which only means that other laws are in operation.

We are told that this type of phenomena of the seance room "are deliberately staged by spirit intelligences to meet the challenge of those who demand evidence that can be cognized by the five senses."

Professor Crawford of Belfast University experimentally

photographed one of the methods of table-levitation. When ectoplasm exuded from the entranced medium, it first formed itself into a rod, then into a cantilever. Once applied to the table, it enabled the solid object to be moved. One conclusive finding was that the weight necessary to make the table rise was roughly equivalent to the medium's loss of weight during the seance.

Many pictures have been taken of this eerie event, using infra-red photography, as white light is harmful to the medium.

Now Shaver steps forward with head shaking disagreement.

Levitation does not originate from the spirit world, he states flatly. It is a development of an ancient science. The The levitator is a portable lifter beam generator, some so small as to be hand-carried or pocketed.

He declares that levitators have been found in modern times, and used by certain "mediums". (That last word is put in quotes as I am sure Shaver would insist.) The best example is Scottish-born Daniel Dunglas Home (March 21, 1888), whose feats of levitation are indisputable, being vouched for by many prominent people.

"Is it possible," asks Shaver, "that Home 'discovered' his abilities in an ancient cave?"

There are numerous cases of people who, while asleep, or suffering a serious illness, have allegedly left their physical body to travel in their astral form into the spirit world.

Quite common are hospitalized patients having the sudden sensation of floating upward. From their aloft position, they could clearly see their chloroformed body on an operating table surrounded by doctors and nurses.

As they floated away, they experienced a wonderful feeling of buoyancy, peace and well-being. With all human complaints gone - organic or mental, minor or major - their health was now, in one word - superb.

Their new world - that of their graduating into a new plane of existence - was one of unimagined beauty, far beyond anything earthly. Mountains, valleys, rivers, lakes, trees were now much more real than their earthly counterparts.

Colors and lights were glorious. Soft music from an unseen orchestra delighted the ear. The wondrous perfume of gorgeous flowers filled the clear, vitalized air. Multi-colored birds sang in pure joy.

Again, confidently and without hesitation, Shaver would have a ready explanation for the above happenings - a scientific explanation.

He would remind us that the cave people strongly desire our continued belief in an after-life. This to insure their own safety by concealing their existence and activities in the guise of spiritualism. Remember that they are able to operate the magic of Elder race mechanisms, the wonder machines that produce infinite ecstacy by powerful stimulative pleasure rays and beneficial rays unpictured by surface man's mind.

With those rays directed on certain chosen ones - coupled probably with advanced hypnotism and induced hallucinations - a conviction is implanted in their minds. That they have left their physical body and, now in their so-called astral form, they have penetrated the spirit world.

Now, finally, we come to the towering question: what is the cause of all forms of occult, or Fortean, phenomena? followed by the inevitable: Is Richard Shaver entirely correct in claiming that material, flesh-and-blood cavern dwellers are responsible? If so, I ask how to account for what takes place at the vastly impressive direct-voice seance?

Do those living below operate machines that are able to record the most minute details of surface peoples' lives from birth to death, so that during a seance those details can be given from a so-called "spirit" to foster the impression of a spirit world?

Admittedly, here is a claim of fantastic proportions. But is it nonetheless true? Would Shaver swear by it?

This article has been written with the fervent hope that if published, Ray Palmer will have persuaded Shaver to add his much-desired comments at the end.

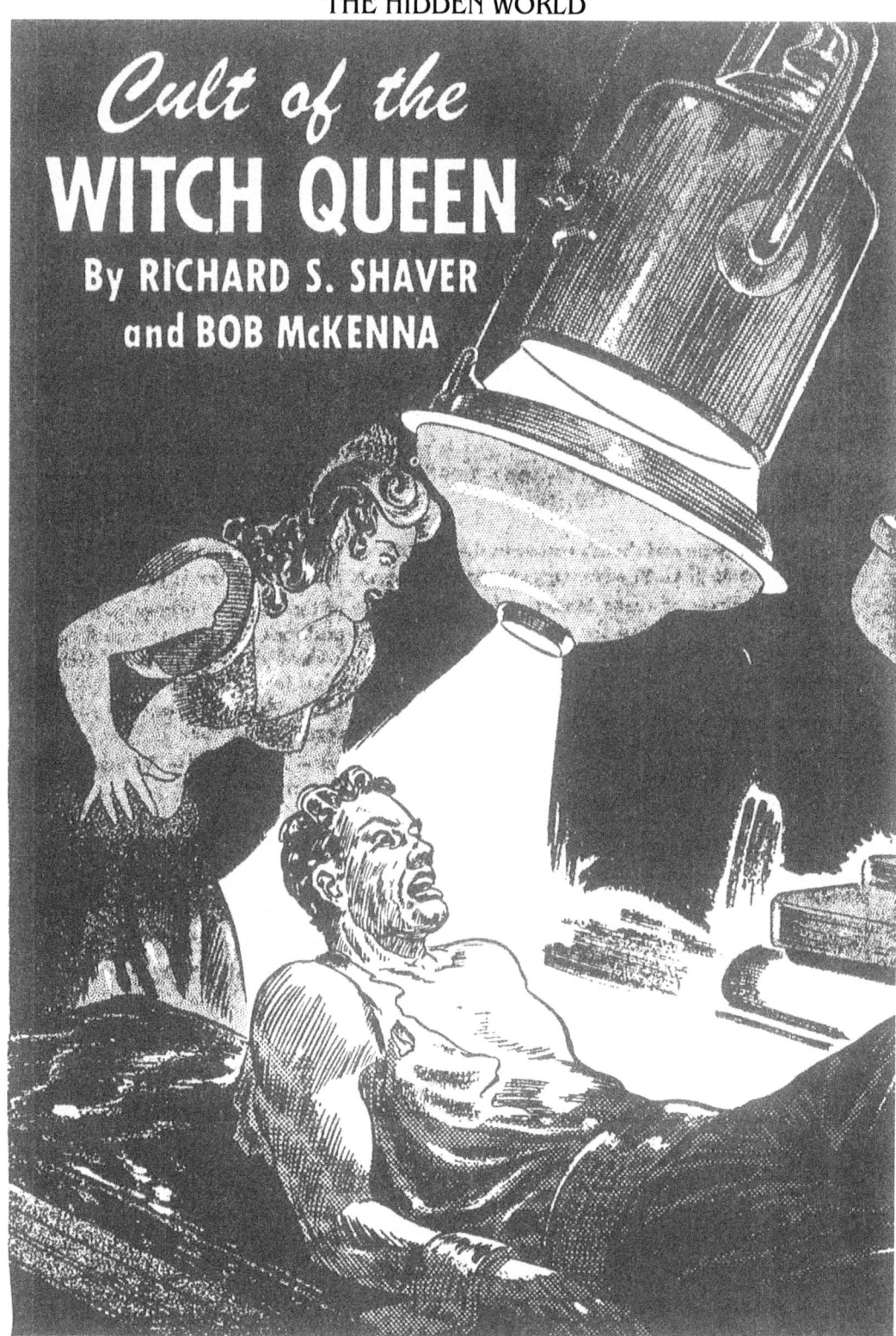

THE HIDDEN WORLD

He writhed, helpless, under the powerful beam of light

THIS is a tale of two planets, Earth and Venus, and of a man who found himself the plaything of the ugliest and oldest woman on the two worlds. She looked like a witch, and a capable witch has spells. This witch had had six centuries to study the ancient magic: the incredibly antique mechanisms left by the race whom we remember in vague myths only as—the Gods.

No one could live that long? Well, quoting Alexis Carrel, who is pretty well accepted in the world called science: "In medieval times, the idea of blood transfusions from young people as a means toward immortality, was widely believed in. . . . was the subject of a transfusion from the veins of a young man . . . The idea has certain things to recommend it . . . under proper conditions it might work." *Man the Unknown*, Alexis Carrel.

And too, did you ever see an old tree rejuvenated by the grafting on of a young sapling? It is a common practice among tree-surgeons.

Well, there is a legend of a woman who lived an unknown number of centuries. The first she is heard from is in fourteenth century Spain, and the legend can be found in the works of Sienkiewicz—who was a reliable man. She was called "The Watcher," also "Hecate, the Undying", also "The Mother of Sin". That there was a cult who followed a woman who was supposed to be undying is well nigh indisputable. But it seldom mentioned after 1500.

One day I met a man who told me this story. Knowing as I do that the antique caverns and the ancient mech of the God race does exist; knowing as I do the works of Carrel and certain others whose indisputable evidence is entirely in support of the possibility of immortality; and knowing that trees are rejuvenated by the grafting on of young trees, I could not help but see the possibility of the truth of his story.

That children can be grafted on to aging people, and the young sap, the vital growth secretions of their bodies, used to make the modern vampire live on and on, I could not dispute, for I can not argue with such men as Carrel who have actually raised virtually immortal flesh in their test tubes and perfusion apparatus.

That there are usable space ships in the lost caverns of the secret ray groups of Earth, I could not argue, since I had seen the caves and the perfect preservation of the mechanisms built by the forgotten race, the Gods. That you have never experienced those things which happen to people—those mysterious and wonderful things which tell them that everything important on earth is not in the newspapers—can believe any of this tale, I do not expect.

For those readers who do not know that a large percent of this apparently fictional account is true, I warn not to read the footnotes; not to speculate on the possibility of age-old and secret vampirism and of mightier secrets too vast and too destructive for any man to find a way to tell his fellow-man.

But to "those who know" I want to answer one question that has puzzled so many of you . . . the question "ARE THEY IMMORTAL?" In this story it is particularly well answered. The other question which I know is in the mind of many of you: "ARE THEY EXTRA-TERRESTRIAL?" is also well and fully answered. To those students of the past who have puzzled about all the smoke around the subject "magic" or "witchcraft" this story is also particularly helpful.—*Richard S. Shaver.*

THE HIDDEN WORLD

CHAPTER 1

Our imagination cannot encompass all reality, for in the infinitude of universes, all things happen.
Eli Cramoisue, "Infinitesme's Philosophie"

Published 1784, Paris.

JUST outside one of the sprawling dull black and grey mills that feed the maw of Mars, on one of the dirty alleys that flank it, was a beer garden; no different than one of the scores that are spawned by droves of hot, thirsty workers.

At a battered bar of this joint was a tall, newly scrubbed young man about thirty. As he gazed thoughtfully into a half consumed glass of "suds," a denim-clad figure detached itself from the group about. In the camaraderie that such places breed he said:

"How'd it go today, Mac?"

"Oh, so-so. A little hot, but it was time-and-a-half today. How'd you do?"

"Okay. Say, I know you now—thought there was something familiar about that voice—you're the welder on #6 Skid, aren't you?"

"Yeah, but I can't seem to place you . . ."

"Electrician—I move around a lot." Casually throwing a rumpled bill on the counter, he said to the perspiring barkeep, "Bring us another round."

Frowning slightly the welder tried to decline the largess, "—had enough, oughta be 'getting'."

"Aw, don't tell me that. Where are you going to go this time of night. Look, how about us grabbing that booth and I'll buy all the drinks. Tonight's my birthday. Celebrate!"

"Well, Okay—but the next round's on me."

Carefully carrying their half empty glasses, they settled themselves on opposite sides of a sticky, ring-marked booth table. Cigarettes were brought out by the welder. "Smoke?" he invited.

"No, thanks . . . used to smoke 'em, but five years away from 'em and you sorta lose all taste for tobacco."

"What's the matter? Swear off and stay off—for five years?"

With a wry grin, the other chuckled dryly, "Would be better to say I WAS sworn off." The welder asked what he meant as he lit his own cigarette and drew the first pleasurable puff.

"Well it's a long story . . . but you look like the type that might listen so I'll tell you." With that he finished his drink and instructed the waiter to keep some spares on deck. Then, toying with the ash-tray, he began:

"YOU'D guess my age as forty or forty-five, wouldn't you?"

The young welder, shrugged his shoulder and lamely wondered, "Well, aren't you?"

"No, I suppose I'm the same age you are—thirty." When the welder raised his eyebrows, in disbelief, he continued, "I know I don't look it, but I've knocked around a lot, been a sailor, and a whole crew of things . . . things that have left their mark. In my eyes mostly. Look at them—they've seen things no man was meant to see and stay sane."

Mentally frowning on his luck that seemed to throw him with crackpots, the welder m o v e d impatiently as though to slide out of the booth.

"No, no, fellow—don't get up. Listen. I'm not nuts . . . and I'm not drunk . . . but I'll go nuts, if I don't get somebody to listen to me while I get something off my chest. I've GOT to tell somebody. Take it easy, and listen, willya?"

As though thinking 'this bird might have a good yarn at that', the welder

1419

pushed his back against the side-wall and propped one foot against the arm-rest on the other end of the seat, and settled down.

"That's it. Relax and listen. Hey, WAITER, bring us another round. Yeah, same thing." Seeming to address the departing waiter's back, he soliloquized, "A guy can't talk to most people about things that are really big —just like you can't put two quarts in a one-quart pail. Well, I've got something big . . . a lot bigger than quarts and pints, but when I really get into it you're going to think maybe you did make a mistake, maybe this guy is a jerk—or screwy. No, wait, don't say anything, just listen. Before I'm done you'll get cold feet. You'll be afraid to even listen to things different than those people usually talk about. You're going to be worried that maybe one of the bunch over there might hear me and take you for a sap for just listening to me—much less taking me seriously. If you got the guts to face something you don't know—even a little—hang onto the handle bars, I'm going to cut loose.

"DID you ever hear of Charles Fort? I guess not. Most people haven't. Anyway, this guy Fort spent twenty years going through old magazines and newspapers. Searching for odd things that happen, are reported, wondered at, and then forgotten. Odd, queer things like chunks of machinery falling out of the sky. Strange shadows passing the face of the moon. Things that "look like ships" crossing the moon IN FORMATION. Twenty years he spent —he's been dead now for seven or eight years—and, except for the Fortean Society, most of those that did hear of him have forgotten already. But he wasn't wrong . . . there IS an understandable CAUSE for most of the things we call mysterious. They read Fort and forget . . . you'll listen to me and you'll do the same thing, too. Marvel a little—and tomorrow, well, you'll know that there isn't anything that can make sense like your welding torch.

Anyway, I have to tell someone even if he won't believe . . ." Then, downing his drink in one gulp, Big Jim continued, "Unless you've read his books, you wouldn't believe there was so much stuff—things that have happened and then were "explained". Hah! that's a laugh! Explanations! The only trouble is those that do the explaining wouldn't recognize truth if it was pointed out right under their noses. Fort had a great big laugh at the weakness of us h u m a n s—all through history things out of the ordinary have happened. First it was the medicine men. Anything unusual was the angry gods. Then the high priests. And now we have a new hierarchy of explainers . . . the scientists. The explanations all had a same "oneness" . . . the gods were angry, the sacrifice wasn't large enough, or . . . 'as proven by mathematical calculation'. Talk. Chatter of little monkeys. Talk. But not the talk I'm going to do. Five years ago I couldn't talk to people—couldn't say more'n a few words to anyone without running out of what to say. Now I've GOT to talk to someone about what I've learned. They won't listen to me, though . . . I'm n o t telling them what they want to hear. Don't reassure 'em that things ARE what they seem. That must be it. They can't understand—think I'm ribbing them. God! I wish I was."

Waving a brawny forearm at the smoke filled room, Big Jim laughed mirthlessly. "Look at 'em . . . racing around on a pointless little merry-go-

1420

round. Twelve hours work, a few beers then home to a dull shack and into bed. Same thing, over and over. I got away . . . once. Escaped from this useless life for five years. Now, dammit, I'm back, and doomed to the same old grind 'unto death'. Doomed to futility.

* * *

'BOUT five years ago . . . '39, it was, I sat in this same hole-in-the wall. Was a little earlier in the year, —June, I think. Hot, fetid night . . . hotter than tonight. You know, the kind of a summer night young fellows prowl the streets, wishing for a woman. Every night isn't the same. You know how it is, one of those nights when every woman you see is the most beautiful thing God ever made . . . some of 'em a lot more than that. Well, I started walking home. Lived up on Cherry street then—about sixteenth. There I was walking along, just like the rest of the single fellows that night, when all of a sudden, I got the damnedest feeling. It's hard to describe—but I could see and hear someone . . . Someone watching me from about a mile away. "This damn heat's giving me mirage's or something," I says to myself. Crazy, I thought.

I can't tell you exactly what this was like—there seemed to be a big woman watching me with a strange kind of apparatus. That's not it exactly. Because, though she was watching me—I was aware of her and her actions . . . Can you imagine yourself in a dream, aware of someone standing beside you, and you're watching the action at the same time you're one of the characters? That's what it was like . . . except I was wide awake. Anyway, if I was dreaming, I didn't want to wake up cause she was interesting—big, and a guy as big as me is always keen on big women, most of 'em seem like midgets.

I KNEW what she was thinking. That's what made me think I was dreaming. Awareness, I guess you'd call it. Someway, I knew she was making a decision from things she could read in my inner self. That's important. I KNEW she was reading my mind . . . as I was hers. But it appeared as though she were watching ME through a mirror or lens, or . . . or what?

She was saying to herself, "Yes . . . he'll do. I'll jerk this big handsome lug out of his dull rut. He'll find a life that's at least exciting, if not . . ." and she chuckled in a sinister way to herself, ". . . if not wholly desirable."

She turned to a girl beside her I hadn't noticed before. If I was dreamin', I was sure picking 'em tonight. This second girl—woman, would be righter, I think—this second one was big and beautiful too, though she did seem younger.

At the first one's signal, she moved closer to this mirror or screen that we seemed to be on either side of.

Remember I'm walking down a street all this time. But when the younger one moved closer to the screen, I seemed to be right there. I could look right at her.

Brother, kicking around all over the world, you meet and see a lot of women, but believe me, I've never seen any like her. Something she had— beauty, or personality, dunno which —came right out and smacked you hard. You know, your mouth seems dry, your stomach flutters and you think you'll never draw another breath, the way your throat's tightened. That's the way she was.

I remember her nostrils most. Nicely flared . . . but red, inside. Not pink, red.

I was sure I was dreaming—she was gorgeous, but her hair seemed almost

1421

too fine, like spider silk. And her hands seemed webbed, almost.

She smiled a queer little smile, just showing her teeth—bigger and whiter than most people's.

And her eyes! Man! Bigger than any I've ever seen. Soft and luminous and knowing. A little sad. Strange too—with a strange sadness I can't explain.

She didn't have much on. A few spangles and sparklers . . . like a specialty dancer, or something. She didn't need anything else. The big woman said something to her in another language. The girl nodded and leaned toward the screen. I don't know how she did it, but she kissed me.

Like I'm dreaming, see, she kissed me and yet I couldn't touch her. That kiss was like a thousand thrills piled on top of each other. Gods! nothing —anywhere—has ever affected me like that kiss. Perfect ecstacy.

But I'll never get kissed like that again—I'll never see her, again. I wasn't dreaming . . . she WAS real. But she's lost to me now. Lost for the same reason you won't believe what I'm telling you. Poles apart . . . yet . . .

THAT funny sense of dreaming while awake—of seeing things a mile away, left me, suddenly. The way a light goes out. One instant I was being kissed, in ecstasy; the next, I was just walking along as I had been before I became aware of the big dame reading my mind.

The moon hung low at the end of the street, half hidden by that hill on the north side of River Street. Big. And a funny kind of golden red. That night it seemed too low—like a furtive celestial prowler. It made me conscious of bloody, evil, unknown things. Even the familiar, common things suddenly seemed horrible . . . inexplicably . . . The horror almost of death . . . as though I were a walking dead man in a corpse world. I hated myself and the world with a dull, hopeless hate. Hate for the dull routine of the steel mill—the dirt—the choking smoky air—the booming clank of steel being born in the bowels of a grimy, impersonal, soul-destroying monster. Hopelessly, I tried to think of a way to get away from its depression. I didn't care to walk anymore, so I leaned against a 'phone pole. No reason for going home . . . even if I could sleep, that would only be a brief release. No reason for going anywhere.

Then SHE appeared again . . . but differently. No dream this—the McCoy. I think, "What kind of dreams am I having?—first I see her in or on a screen, now I'm thinking she's standing in front of me. I'm nuts."

You'd think, seeing someone, you know if it was a dream or real. But she seemed taller and dressed differently . . . like she'd just come from a masquerade, or something. She had on a long dark cape—in the poor light of the street it looked like it was red . . . like blood. Fastened close around her throat. Falling in straight folds almost to the ground. I noticed her shoulders were nice and square but appealingly female, despite her size. I couldn't see her hands—nothing but her head and this long dark cape.

I stared at her face, but out of the corner of my eyes I saw queer designs in gold chasing each other around the lower part of the cape. They didn't help my sense of unreality, I'll tell you, I half consciously wondered who the hell would work up designs like that? Then, driving all thoughts and wonder from my mind—like a door opening into a darkroom—she spoke.

1422

Softly . . . with an amused little laugh, that was sad too, somehow . . . "Hello, big fellow."

I just looked . . . finally I managed weakly, "D—didn't—I see you—in a kind of a—a—a dream—a little while ago?"

Again that funny little laugh like the the tinkle of a little glass bell . . . "Yes, you did—that's why I'm here." The funny accent didn't make me any more certain I wasn't dreaming yet, but I was willing to gamble when she invited.

"Come with me. You'll soon understand . . . everything."

I wanted to pinch myself. Instead, "If you'll open that cloak," I said, "then I'll know you're the same girl I saw in the dream."

SHE turned her head, quick, to see if anyone was looking at us. Then assured that the street was deserted, with one motion she opened her arms, spreading the red cloak behind her like a curtain of blood. I felt my strength go to water . . . like a white flame against the night she was . . . no more on than when I saw her before.

"I am called Ceulna," she said. "You are to follow me."

"Sister, if you're real, I'll follow you to hell."

"Come then," and she turned, allowing the cloak to fall concealing that glorious figure again.

She led me down a few blocks into a street where all the lamps were out. Dark as pitch. I thought what a guy usually thinks in such districts—why do they live here in places like this. Why don't they get out? You know how the houses are down there, all alike.

Well, she went in one of them with me right after her, my big feet stumbling, for she moved fast. Back apiece, where there was more light, I could occasionally glimpse the outlines of her body, as the cape would momentarily cling to her in places. That figure was a swaying promise of delight—the answer to all my dreams, and I didn't mean to let her get away from me.

Somewhere inside the house, without turning on any lights she found a door. Opening it, she turned slightly, and, taking my left hand in hers, started down stairs . . .

I never went down so damn many stairs before or since. Down and down, pausing every once in a while, she'd open another door, then down again. Down, always down 'til I thought I'd never be able to walk if we did hit a level spot. Doors opening before us, closing after we'd pass through . . . then on down. Big doors, I noticed—after my eyes got accustomed to the faint light that seemed to be all around, without any source of light being seen. As though everything—walls, floor, ceiling and doors—were giving off a faint illumination of their own. Big doors of dull metal, that kept getting bigger the farther down we went. Groaning open before us, clanging shut—I wondered if she had walked up all these stairs in so short a time—IF she had.

"What are all these steps about, sister?"

"You'll find out!" And that's all she'd say—but she didn't stop going down stairs.

Well, I couldn't do anything but shrug and follow her. Then suddenly, my thoughts were interrupted—we'd run out of stairs!

There in front of us was a door, bigger than any of the others. The kind you don't expect to see 'til you meet St. Peter.

The girl, Ceulna, I should call her

1423

now, turned and said, "Inside you will learn about life—and its absolute worthlessness. For your own sake, I hope you learn quickly. For down here you can die awfully sudden . . . or awfully slow."

Then a final reassuring squeeze of my hand and she busied herself with some strange lever. That big door ponderously opened, and we went through.

You couldn't tell exactly how big the place was . . . it was all black hangings instead of walls. But I got the impression that they did cover walls. All over the still black folds were gold figures like those on the girl's cloak. Peering closer, I was mildly surprised to see that the figures were artistic crabs, and from some place in my memory I recalled reading that the crab was the ancient symbol of evil wisdom and power.

SOME distance from the great door were people. Those drapes made distances deceptive. We moved toward this group, which, judging from the way Ceulna moved, was our destination. Maybe I should have said . . . our destiny . . .

Walking to the throne, which I saw now was what the group was clustered about, I glanced at the floor. A green floor that seemed to be half alive. Then I realized it was the color and the curving, veinlike lines of dark red carefully worked into the material of the floor, that made it look so like the flesh of the lower reptiles.

After what felt like an endless walk, we stood in front of this throne-like chair. Then I knew I hadn't been dreaming, for seated in the chair was the woman who first contacted my mind back on the street. There was the screen and a whole mass of apparatus.

I used to be a ham radio man and I worked with electricity, but I couldn't tell what any of those tubes and screens were for. The only thing I sensed was that some way they were electrical. But I swear those glowing tubes, view screens, dials, lever switches and peculiar glowing globes were never built by men for men's hands . . . or women's either. Oddly, I thought, "Hell, this looks like some of the equipment beings of other planets make . . . in science fiction stories!—or like some of the stuff that I've had nightmares about after too much whoopee.

But the dame on the throne didn't look like a monster (at first). She was beautiful. Like I always imagined Cleopatra was. Beautiful—and dominant. A kind of voluptuous beauty that set the blood pounding through your temples. The kind of woman a life of indulgent luxury makes. She was big too, like Ceulna. Big all over. Not gross, just big.

There she was half reclining on this couch or throne. It might have seemed like a gag—except everyone around her was so darn quiet—like they were afraid to even breathe.

She had on a long gown that was out of this world—made of some shimmering material that clung to her in the right places, like it was part of her. One leg was crossed over the other, and the constantly changing shimmer of the cloth highlighted a long smoothly curved thigh that I'd have whistled at if it hadn't been so damn quiet.

I figured, "I didn't crash this joint so I'll give her the once over a couple of times." And I did.

STARTING at her head there was some fine metallic net that kept her hair in place, except where it hung straight to her shoulders where the soft waves started to cascade down her back. Her shoulders, too were wide, but certainly not girlish ... well rounded with an inviting texture. The only reason I could see for the dress was she wanted the color.

She looked at me with half closed ice-blue eyes.

The dress was like a thousand miniatures of her eyes—like some weird jewels had been woven into the cloth. Glittering and sparkling like liquid gems—or the eyes of vampires—a diamond under a full moon.

She stared at me awhile longer, so I looked the rest of them over. The men—slaves, I felt—wore only G-strings, but the females were all wrapped up to the eyes like Arab women. Evidently, the boss on the throne dislikes any other women displaying flesh where it might look better than her own.

Finally, her pouting mouth twisted into a grin and she spoke. Her voice was hardly human—almost musical, but lacking the tone flux of human emotion. A mocking meanness ran through her words,

"You are a fortunate man, Big Jim," while I wondered how she knew my name. There hadn't been a peep out of me. Then, I remembered the machine—if I could read her mind while she was using it, I suppose she could read mine too. But what was she saying?

"You have been chosen by a mighty organization as one more unit of strength ..." On that last word her cold eyes ran over my body like a horse trader looking at a good buy.

I thought it best to keep my mouth shut 'till I found out what this was all about.

"You will remain here until you understand what is expected of you. I will decide what your duties will be. If you are thinking or refusing, remember that your wishes in the matter are not important. None who enter here return to reveal the entrance to those not of our organization."

My first impulse was to get up and slap her face for her insolence. I couldn't speak. I was getting damn mad. Just as I was ready to say something, she continued, "Now, while you are at hand, I can show you our punishment for disloyalty—in case you are ever tempted to betray us. Happily, I can also demonstrate the rewards you can receive for devoted accomplishment in obeying our orders. When you are shown, remember you can obtain more of the same pleasure anytime you are able to do us a service."

SHE gestured languidly to a female slave who quickly pulled back a heavy drape, revealing a greater mass of huge mechanism. A massive complicated thing that wasn't anything made by modern man. The rounded intricacies had the beauty of life forms. The surfaces had a hard glitter and irridescence more living than metallic. Looking at the strange shape, I felt its power and knowledge. Power more piercing than mortal men. Somehow, I felt puny and ignorant, looking at that thing. And I'm not puny and I'm not ignorant. But the mech—down there they call all the ancient machinery 'mech'—the mech wasn't really big, it just made you sense the bigness of it.

Above this—mech—hung the crucified figure of a girl. Eighteen she might have been—her body a soft symphony in sculptured stone.

What were all the good looking women doing here, I wondered. Here down so many steps, under ——— City. I guess we might have been a mile or more under the earth.

I thought at first that this new girl

1425

hanging above the mech was just a horrible parody of a statue—the way certain lights and shadows were playing over her body. Then, suddenly, I went cold. It was a living woman!—she moaned softly, and her limbs writhed—painfully—slowly. She was alive—a crucified living young girl!

Placed under the girl's feet was a long, ominous looking couch. I didn't like the gruesomely suggestive look of the thing—there were straps attached to it, hanging like the open arms of Death, waiting for something—or someone. Someone to hold down—while the gods only know what horrible things were done.

The Boss dame gave me just a few seconds to take in the scene—then she made an imperious gesture. I should have been on my toes—but I wasn't.

Two of the slaves came alive at her signal then, and before I realized what was coming off they had hold of my arms. That made me mad—fighting mad. With a curse, I jerked my left arm free. Before the two dumb slaves knew what I was doing I had swung around. Getting a good grip on the one on my right, I tossed him against my other little playmate and both went sprawling. They weren't too anxious about getting up again, either. Before any more could jump me I turned around, ready to sock the next bird that made a move. No one did.

There wasn't a sound—except my own gasping breath. Then, the formerly soft, pouting moist mouth of the big broad running the show hardened into a thin line and she spoke—her voice like the lash of a blacksnake whip in the stillness—no longer soft and voluptuous, but strident and threateningly angered.

"I see I shall have to teach you several lessons at once!"

I GLANCED right at her. She was standing up now—that smooth, just too soft figure of hers quivering with scarcely concealed anger.

Without any warning, she bent slightly, reaching for the banks of controls. She found the one she wanted and threw a switch or lever. A beam sprang out of the huge mech. Sprang out like a searchlight's beam—in my direction.

I figured that if I was to do anything it had to be now, so I started toward her. I didn't get far—I was out of my league. She moved the beam onto me saying, "Now, note, my muscular rebel, everything you do you do by my will. Mine, not your own. This is the first lesson—learn it well. Resistance is useless . . . your big muscles are my property so long as this beam is on you and I look into this screen."

I wanted to smash my fist into that lovely, angered, sneering face, but what she said was true! I had no volition of my own. I tried and couldn't even move a finger.

With my mind fighting for control of my own body, she made it move to the couch and lie down, the beam always on me.

Strapping me down, the slaves fastened several wires as different places on my skin.

This Hellion that was ruler here stepped down from the throne and glided over to me. Her voice husky with some emotion—some strange eagerness suddenly awakened within her, she whispered, like the hiss of a snake.

"Now you will experience one of the least of the rewards we grant those that do our bidding, loyally and well. She that hangs there," indicating the crucified girl, "has earned our punishment by betraying us to our enemies. Absorb both 'lessons' well—if you wish to enjoy yourself here in the future."

With that she seated herself at what looked like the console of an organ, not three feet from my head.

Directly above me drooped the body of the girl. The woman's mechanical voice, still husky with that strange note explained, "This mech is called the organ of opposites. From it lead two sets of wires, one controlling a synthetic nerve impulse of pleasure energy, and the other, a synthetic nerve impulse of pain. With it I can give immense pleasure and intense and violent pain at the same time. The girl is wired to the pain source; you are connected to the pleasure vibrant. Beware that you are never at the other end of the wires ... watch, and feel ...

She let her fingers down caressingly on the keys—she depressed one, and through my body ran a wave of intense, insupportably sweet pleasure.

Momentarily decreasing my enjoyment was the sight of the girl hanging above me—simultaneously contorted with violent pain. Then I became aware of the girl's thoughts and sensations ... the ancient mech that was controlling both the girl and myself could, almost magically, make both of us aware of the other's thoughts and sensations—a w a r e, as though our minds and emotions had been transplanted. I KNEW her thoughts, and somehow, I knew she was aware of my own.

THE first surge of opposing emotion was only the opening note of what proved to be a symphony of unguessed pain and exquisite pleasure. Whatever else the cruel voluptuary at the console might be, she was a virtuoso of an art unknown on Earth to ordinary men ... by the skilled use of some sensation music, playing bodily sensation with the feeling and dexterity of a masterful surface musician.

Enrapt by the cacaphony of opposite sensations she was sending through her subjects, her fingers increased their speed—greater, and more intense, the sensations coursing through our bodies, crescendoed as her fingers depressed key after key ... exquisite chords of pleasure, at this witch's mad artistry, were multiplied a thousand times. A vast storm of ultra-powerful synthetic emotions and pleasure sensations grew within my brain—within every nerve and tissue of my body ... the pleasurable sensations of a lifetime packed into each wave every time she pressed a key ...

God forgive me! the thoughts I had while that damnable machine was playing will haunt me through hell and a thousand lifetimes! ... while I was groaning with the floods of delight, I DELIGHTED in the girl writhing painfully above me more than anything on Earth ... At one foul step the operation of the ancient mech made me cruel ... and EVIL ... all my flesh and being *desired agony and pain* for her that *I* might soar the heights of pleasure that was the inevitable accompaniment of her torture.

No man could do otherwise—for the setup of those synthetic nerve impulses was an automatism of *evil*—pleasure in another's pain was the essence of the mech.[1]

In a brief moment when the wave of sensations had subsided before crescendoing again, I looked at the big witch

---

[1] These synthetic electric sensation impulses forcibly replace one's natural will with its artificial will. The victim's will and self obeyed the great evil machine, for its strength of nerve- and thought-electric was so much superior to the natural will of man. The good, beneficial uses of the ancient machine had been perverted by the profane hands of others than the original builders.—Author.

who was controlling my delight drenched body . . . like an artist pouring his soul into his playing, the woman's face was rapt—I realized that neither the poor tortured girl on the cross, nor my own ecstatic body, meant more to her than a page of music does to a pianist. Vaguely, I wondered . . .

"WHO . . . or what . . . WAS she . . . where'd she come from?"

Then, cutting short any further thoughts, the stops of synthetic emotion were pulled by the witch-artist, and, once more, my senses and self went reeling and soaring in their first lesson in evil desire . . . in devilish pleasure in another's intense agony.

Whatever she was I didn't care then. I was her slave . . . for such tremendous joy and bliss had never before been mine.

This type of treatment, springing from the ancient cult's customary practices in increasing its evil strength was what had made the woman what she was . . . but this I learned later.

I was favored 'cause my arrival coincided with her punishment of the girl, and the witch couldn't resist the chance to practice her art on an attractive male and spend her venom on a beautiful woman together.

An hour of this weird and horrible music of opposite sensations passed. Pain for the girl whose lovely body by then was dripping bloody sweat over me in a steady stream; pleasure for me, straining at my bonds, consumed with ecstasy. Pain and Pleasure. The girl's mouth was pulled open in a continuous scream—a sound to haunt the deepest hell.

At last, a final crescendo of rending chords made the two bodies strain violently toward each other . . . mine in a convulsive surge of delight . . . the poor agonized girl's, in tearing deathly pain . . . a torrent of blood gurgled from her open, agony-frozen mouth—death was setting her free from her Hell. . . . With her last few gasping breaths her eyes glared at me . . . her face . . . God! . . . her agonized face will never leave my mind—nor ever let me sleep in peace.

THE male slaves came and released me. I couldn't think—but an evil desire had been born in my brain . . a desire to have such pleasure always. Too, I had a strong sense of guilt . . . I HAD enjoyed the death agonies of the girl.

The woman who had just tortured a girl to death and awakened a devil in my own soul sat with her eyes gloating at the racked body of her victim. I knew, instinctively, that many, many people had died at her hands in just that way. She turned to me.

"Now you have seen our punishment . . . and tasted a bit of our reward—" She was looking at me approvingly as she continued, "—if you do well what is asked of you, you can earn a life of such pleasures as few mortals have ever known . . . If you get idealistic or squeamish—and or try to buck the ruler group—you will die as she died—or in an even more horrible and painful way I, Nonur, have spoken. Go."

With that and a tired wave of her hand a slave came and led me away. I couldn't have answered her even if my condition had permitted me. As I left, my ravished humanity began to reassert itself, and I swore an oath never to rest unless I had to, until I had stopped such torture forever, by killing all such as she . . .

I knew it wasn't, yet I kept telling myself that this was just a wild nightmare—I'd wake up, sweating and worried and then forget about it.

But I didn't wake up—I WAS

awake! Such things just couldn't go on under a modern American city—but they could—and DO!

That night I met others who had thought such things couldn't be—but are. Others, like myself, recruits for the secret army the hidden people were gathering. For that was the purpose of numerous other young men I saw. All as strange to this place and its ways as I was.

CHAPTER II

"I have killed many things, but none was a greater crime than this, that they should die before the flesh had quite grown used to being round a soul. A white and shrunken nothingness...."
From "Memoirs of a Warrior"
Bikaren of Tuon
Venus, 1609.

THE rock down here under ———— City was a labyrinth of rooms and passages. Big rooms that seemed to have been lavishly furnished, sometime in the past, but the splendor was covered with inches of dust now. If I had only known how ancient that dust was, down there in the almost dustless caverns, I'd have looked more searchingly beneath its blanketing greyness.

Some of the rooms had been cleaned out and furnished with beds and plumbing. These rooms contained but few of the bulking mysterious mechanisms characteristic of the ancient place.

They contained other men too—the room I was taken to had an occupant already. His face was thin and haggard—broken teeth were hideous when he spoke. About forty, I guessed. As soon as the slave escorting me left, the old one began to question me. Impatiently, as if he'd have burst if the slave hadn't gone and permitted him to satisfy his curiosity.

"What do you know of this place, young fellow?"

"Very little," I answered, "but before we go too far hadn't we better get acquainted? My name's Jim McKenna, steel-worker from the city upstairs."

"Glad to know you, my boy. My name's Farne—Henry Farne. 'Hank' to my friends." He stood, taken aback, when I reached out to shake hands. Then hesitatingly, he put his out.

"You're new here, aren't you?"

I just grunted an affirmative "Uh-huh."

"I'm an old hand in this hellish life— and ole Hank knows a greenhorn when he sees one—"

Better be careful, I thought, so I said, "How?"

"Well, the look on your face, fer instance—all the oldtimers have a dopey, fatalistic expression. It's the 'stim' juice—that's stimulative electric, case you didn't know; anyway, the stim juice kills their souls."

The old boy was evidently glad to have an audience, for he continued like a lecturer or something—

"Think I know why too—that mech is too old—way too old—to use like they do, constantly. Not as healthy as it was when it was built long ago—God only knows HOW long ago." Here he smiled, displaying those dirty, discolored, broken teeth. "You'll find out—'s funny to get used to the idea that a secret underworld life like this exists on Earth without anyone upstairs getting wise. Been like that for centuries— little change ... but to get worse, I guess."

He'd been looking no place in particular, when he suddenly looked straight at my eyes and said, "Your face, Jim—that's the name, isn't it?— your face, Jim, is still human—or I'd be afraid to talk to you ... afraid you'd run to the big shots and get me in wrong. You are newly arrived, aren't you?"

I NODDED, my curiosity aroused. This Henry Farne seemed to know something of this darkly strange, horrible organization whose ruthless torture and cruel pleasures I had felt tonight. As a frog's tongue does to a fly, these cave dwellers had reached out and snared me—the beautiful creature who had led me here was just bait for the trap whose rulers were shanghaiing an army. I wanted to know what I was in for.

"Look, man, give me the dope, will you—what's this all about anyway?—I just came down tonight."

Evidently this satisfied the old man for he squatted on his heels against the wall in front of my bed. Settling himself, his eyes scanned me carefully, then—

"I'll take a chance and tell you what I can—but don't let THEM know I told you anything. I've been punished before for my opinions . . . the rulers don't like truth spread around too much."

He paused long enough to take a long, thin, purple cigar from his pocket.

"Know what this is?" he asked, holding up the cigar. I looked at it a minute then answered, "Well, it looks like a purple cigar, why?"

Hank put the long cigar in his mouth and lit it.

"It's a cigar alright—but it's not tobacco—it's a drug grown on the planet Venus . . . a whole lot different than tobacco—here, taste it."

I took the weed and took a drag on it. The smoke was sweet, heady, and very pleasant. At the first puff my mind felt a new exhilaration—it was racing. I was suddenly more awake than I had been all evening. Somewhat reluctantly I handed the cigar back. "That's certainly not tobacco—no tobacco ever gave me such a lift. Wonderful stuff," I commented.

Satisfied, Farne took the cigar again, saying, "That was just a test to see if you were familiar with the weed. Had you been an old timer, like me and the rest, your face wouldn't have shown surprise when you first tasted that potent drug."

"This old bird isn't as dumb as he looks," I thought to myself, as he leaned back and began an account that lasted half the night.

"You've got to be careful down here—never forget that. Careful . . . careful of even what you think . . . That cat from Hell out there can read minds with her damn mech."

Like the caliph of ancient Bagdad listening to Scherezade, I listened without a word as Hank spun his yarn.

"NONUR . . . that's the witch's name . . . Nonur, and others like her rule these caverns—these ancient caves that go back beyond the memory of man. The caves—these caves here—are the long hidden home of some ancient, wiser-than-human race."

"Did you see the mech of opposing sensations?" he suddenly asked.

"See it? Hell, man, that crazy dame put me through it!"

"Well . . . that's not so good, but the point I was making was that machine and thousands of others—all the mech you'll see down here, except the plumbing—was built unguessed thousands of years ago by beings who knew infinitely more than modern men. Nonur, and the others before her, have had this ancient mech since earliest time . . . I suspect since before the biblical flood."

I was having a hard time getting that, when he continued to pour out one startling fact after another . . . I couldn't believe then . . . but IT IS TRUE!

"The use of this antique mech has made them into dero—most of 'em, anyway." At my puzzled glance, Hank explained that "dero" meant degenerate robot—degenerated humans, lacking in will or souls. "Through the years," said Hank, "the continued use of these marvelous mechanisms, and other factors, idleness and cannibalism, for instance, has caused them to evolve in an utterly different way of life. And in the centuries they have managed to keep the secret of the caves hidden from surface men—whom they despise and hate . . . so they say."

By this time the Venusian cigar was consumed. Hank tamped it out and then continued. "Even their bodies, minds and thought processes have been changed from anything you are used to regarding as natural to men like us. Let me warn you, right here, young fellow, never forget that as long as you're in the caves . . . they're not human, so don't try to outguess 'em by figuring they'll act like you would."

"I suppose," continued Hank, "this ancient mech was built originally for pleasure and stimulation—but these devils have managed to make torture machines out of pleasure rays and body-electric-stimulants. It's their source of power—brings some of 'em riches, tremendous riches—to boot."

"NOW, Boy, these devils have plans for you so I'll give you the dope on things you might need to know. The ancient people who build these caves . . . also conquered space. Some of their old spacers they abandoned when they left Earth forever. This bunch down here have found some of 'em and got 'em running . . . that wasn't too hard . . . the ships are practically indestructible. When they got 'em operating they traveled the far spaces, in the past centuries. Still do, even today . . . make regular trips between Earth and Venus. They go to Mars too, I hear, but I've never learned much about it—except there isn't much life on Mars, but I HAVE been to Venus."

I had seen too much already to offer much doubt about this—these ancients were far, far ahead of the boys on the surface, so I urged Hank to tell me what Venus was like.

"Venus is a whole planet of jungle paradise . . . peopled by a beautiful and advanced race superior to Earthmen in many ways. The women of Venus are far more beautiful than those of Earth, on the average, but, then, so are the men,—though they're not as large as the women. Now, the ones we work for aren't good for the Venusians, nor good to them. Unlike Earth, however, the Venusians are well aware of the evil presence in their midst—and we of Earth are that Evil. The Venusians have the antique mech too, but it's not a secret with them; they know more about it than the secret rulers of Earth . . . and that makes them powerful enemies. They're getting wised up now, but they used to be gullible as Hell, which made them putty in the hands of a skillful liar. You are here because the Venusians, millions of miles away, are wising up."

For the life of me I couldn't see how anything that far away could affect me so I asked him to explain.

"The native races of Venus," he went on, "have recently risen against the invaders from Earth—done pretty well, too. Our chief allies there are the 'cultists', the Hagmen—priests of Hecate—led by their so-called goddess, The Hag, herself. Hecate—The Hag's—age is unknown—supposed to be immortal. She's a giantess—bigger'n yourself.

1431

Big! And a master of much of the ancient wisdom. She went to Venus centuries ago—and in that time, has built up a well-knit, effective organization. That's why you're here . . . you are going to be trained to fight for these hidden powerful people of Earth against the free peoples of Venus."

The idea didn't appeal to me. Not that I didn't like to fight—but I do like to pick my own. This business of being forced into something made me mad, but I figured I'd better let Farne go on talking and learn what I could.

"YOU talk like a man whose been well educated," I prompted him, "yet, you look as if you had had a life of poverty and hard work—how come? What happened to you?"

He smiled, though there wasn't much humor in it. "Well, you see, these people—the ones from Earth—have a government of a sort perhaps comparable to the government of Rome during the corrupt reign of the later Caesars. I was sent to Venus years ago. I liked the natives, got along well with them—too damn well, in fact. When trouble came between the Venusians and the Earthmen, I was under suspicion. And, with these rulers of ours, my young friend, suspicion means they either kill you or throw you in a cell 'til the danger is all past. That's where I've spent my time . . . in a dank cell deep under the mighty fortress-city of Luon."

As though he was wryly pleased with himself, Hank continued, "Hah! Then when our little Venusian Friends really began to fight, and a long war was seen to be inevitable—our beloved 'masters'," and here he spat, "decided my great knowledge of Venus might be needed. Soo . . . with many apologies, they took me out of prison, gave me a square meal for a change, new civilian clothes and put me aboard the first ship for Earth. I got here yesterday . . . and they haven't paid any attention to me since I landed."

That seemed to end his tale, so I figured I would ask a few questions myself. "Just what," I asked him, "are these Venusians really fighting about?"

Farne looked at me quizzically. "It's hard to tell you . . . but their children have been disappearing regularly—and they blame Hecate's priests and the Earthmen. More than that—well, I don't know absolutely—but from the usual practices of the Cult of Hecate—the Hag she's called—I can imagine that the Venusians have plenty of provocation."

"What is this 'Cult of Hecate'," I asked, "this 'Cult of the Hag' as you call it?"

"Well . . . it's a sort of an old thing on Venus—you might call 'em 'Early Settlers'. Went there from Earth, around 1400, I think. They're a cruel bunch—my front teeth were smashed when one of them kicked me in the face . . . though they're not unlike our own secret ray people here on Earth in their cruelty. I want to warn you—"

"Warn me!" I interrupted, "against what?"

"Yes, warn you, young fellow—don't decide you don't care to join their little army . . . since you know all about them now, you'll not be allowed to return to the surface world. And if you balk at the enforced soldiering . . . you'll be treated as a deserter and put at some kind of hard labor . . . or worse. Pretend to be highly entranced and wholly charmed with everything down here . . . no matter what your true feelings, approve of their cruelty when you see it . . . or you won't see long."

HANK talked for a long time before we turned in—of the immense

1432

steaming jungles of Venus, of that tropic planet's girl-warriors in their gleaming ray-proof armor, racing on the crystal spider-walks they spin like great glittering cobwebs through the tremendous tree growths. He talked of the ancient love-cults whose rites and ceremonies he described at length; their struggle with the horror cult of the cruel Hecate, the Mother of Sin—the Cult of the Limping Hag. He told me of the great glass houses, of their cities that hung like strange and gigantic fruit from the huge tree limbs of the forest giants.

Hank caught my imagination as no one ever has; I longed to see this strange world where the trees grew large enough to form the foundations of cities; where the great sluggish rivers dotted with the shining crystal craft of the laughing youth of Venus, rolled their awful might to the deep red seas.

The desire to see the wonders of Venus for myself made me more reconciled to the rugged training I soon had to undergo—even more I was anxious to go on, now, after hearing Hank.

SWIFT days of training passed. I was outfitted with a uniform and weapons. Taught to handle certain of the antique war mech of the caves. These seemed to be in great profusion, collected from the labyrinths of dwelling caves—perhaps from other planets, too. They were thousands of years old . . . but they had been built by that ancient Master Race . . . built by the God-race, to last forever—built of time resisting materials, and the caves themselves were so air-tight and damp-proof that the ancient mech was, for the most part, still in good condition. All the antique weapons were self-contained units—some were mounted on wheels, having a seat like a tractor. The mech had a tank into which they poured water and inside the tough shielding metal a little dynamo of tremendous power sprang into whirring life at the touch of a button. Its power must have been drawn from the disintegration of the water by some method long lost to men.

On the tractor-like model there was a lever in the center that controlled the ray-beam of destruction—in the same way a joy-stick controls the movements of a plane in flight; right and left swing for right and left sweep of the beam and forward and back to move the beam up and down.

I learned to read the dials in the view screen—dials that indicated rough, fine, and vernier focus of distant objects.

They didn't teach us how to make any but the simplest of repairs wouldn't let us open any of the cases. But then, I don't suppose there is a man living, anywhere, who could have really fixed one of the ancient mech-weapons that had actually broken down.

That view-screen was a marvel. I wondered if the rays' amazing power and range was due to fine lenses or to a system of magnetic fields, like an electron microscope, or something. That thing could bring a man thirty miles away into such sharp focus that his face seemed just two feet from the screen. Most of our training consisted of practice with this instrument—bringing distant objects into swift focus, center 'em on the cross hairs—then press the firing studs. 'Wham! and whatever was in focus just wasn't anymore. A terrible, deadly weapon—but only a tiny unit, comparing with their large weapons as a rifle does to a Big Bertha.

From what I saw of their weapons and maneuvers in the vast caverns, this small force of a couple of thousand men could have beaten any of the Earth's

1433

surface armies before the army knew what had happened.

These rulers of the caverns were the potential, if not the actual, Rules of Earth . . . yet, VENUS COULD FIGHT THEM!

What terrible forces would we shanghaiied soldiers have to face? What would the Venusians throw at us that could stop an army armed with these marvelous weapons of the Gods Themselves! And surface men didn't even suspect they exist. They still don't!

CHAPTER III

"Evoe! O Bacchus!" thus began the song; And "Evoe!" answered all the female throng.

Unbind your fillets, loose your flowing hair, And orgies and nocturnal rites prepare.

Virgil

HANK knew what he was talking about . . . they trained us . . . and kept us in luxurious kennels. I had been there about two weeks when they called us to a feast. To celebrate our departure, we learned eventually, but departure to a far planet—not to home. A sort of a morale builder before they sent us off to the wars . . . their wars.

As we entered the vast cavern hall, which dwarfed the immense tables set with a thousand places, I was stunned. It wasn't the sheen of the golden vessels, or the sparkling of the jewel-set lamps, nor the rich fabric and design of the hangings, nor even the glittering bosoms of the Rulers. It wasn't even the thousand dancing girls' glistening bodies present to amuse us . . . It was the several hundred gossamer-draped girls—floating in the air! like living bubbles in a god's draught of champagne . . . through some weird magic of the ancient mech they floated in a hypnotic state—each buoyed up by a levitation beam from the mech and synchronized so that they moved slowly about without ever crossing or colliding.

Due to their hypnotic condition, their faces were the faces of dryads long hungry for love and suddenly released from their tree-coffins. The gleaming, flashing girdles about their hips, enhanced the seductive, never ceasing motion . . . their floating hair glittered with what may have been gold dust—but looked to me like diamonds or stars.

This magic of floating women set the keynote of the feast—lavish beauty above the somehow sinister faces of the luxurious, decadent group who were the descendants of those who for long centuries had kept the secret of the ancient magic.

A Bacchanalian revel to show those who were about to plunge into battle for them that they weren't niggardly . . . but the Rulers could easily afford the cost—I learned later it wouldn't have to be repeated for many of their new soldiers . . . most of these young men were soon to die, fighting on the spiderwalks of the Venusian cities of crystal. Soon to die—but they had no inkling of it, who would have, in that utterly abandoned orgy? Nor had I, except for a brief wonder at the weapons that the Venusians must have if they could face the mech we used . . . even here in the banquet hall.

When the blood is racing and your eyes can't focus clearly for the delightful way your mind seems half attached to your body, logic is soon forgotten . . . and the Rulers that night had the means to do it. That feast surpassed anything I had ever seen—or even read of in ancient Roman splendor . . . strange drugged drinks were served to excite us, the strange, wild haunting melodies of Venusian music never

THE HIDDEN WORLD

ceased. The stimulating pleasure rays I'd already experienced, and still craved, played always about the hall—an invisible lightning, intensifying the interest of a man and a maid—drifting on to other couples when their attention turned to other affairs.

There were jugglers, and conjurers, and dancing girls from Venus. It was in this group that I met again the girl Ceulna . . . the same one who had lured me here, the first night. She had just concluded a dance whose furious tempo and strangely exotic gyrations would have exhausted an Earth girl far more than it had this tall glorious, marble-limbed Venusian. A Venusian —that's what she was—a Venusian, here under a modern American city. She . . . and thousands like her.

VENUSIANS are subtly different that Earth people—their nostrils flare widely and are scarlet inside. Their eyes, a light grey or a flashing green that varies according to their spirit and interest—much larger eyes than one sees any need for. And webbed hands! Yes—webbed—webbed almost to the tips of their long, graceful fingers. Brilliant, large white teeth—oddly, the canines are larger than those of Earthmen, but still pretty.

Well set on their heads are their very thin, shell-like ears. Rather large though, but one doesn't notice this in the women, as they are hidden in the floating silk of their hair. Venusian hair is curious, being of infinitely fine stuff—like spider silk—too fine for quick combing, often quite matted, but always beautiful. Beauty? Ceulna was . . . how do they say it? . . . the ultimate of beauty.

I was suddenly more than glad to see her again. I felt more acquainted with her than any of these others reveling about us, so I invited her to join me.

Like women everywhere, though, that was her idea—what had brought her to my table anyway.

Evidently that was the case for we soon were talking like life-long friends seeing each other after a brief absence. She spoke a little English in that funny little accent that made my heart do flip-flops—and I asked her many questions, as much to listen to her as to really get an answer. Simple, common little questions like, "What do you young people of Venus do for amusement?"

Then, the thinking voice, "make love, like you of Earth . . . or we swim . . . and swim. We of Venus swim much, much more than you. Or, we like to make thoughts on the old machines . . . but of that you would not know."

Finally, lowering my voice, I asked, "How is it that you of Venus work for those who are at war with Venusians."

"You do not know much of Venus," she stated with a sad shake of her head. "You see, in my home city the Hagmen rule—and that Limping Hag, their Queen—she is not a good ruler. So . . . I go to work for the Hag's allies, for they have more fun . . . more dancing and music. Hecate, the Hag, is not fun, ugh!"

I grinned back at her wide, good humored smile as she just wrinkled her nose. She probably didn't care for the Hag, I thought, but she didn't let it mean too much in her fun-loving life. She had a terrifically attractive personality—a kind of lazy vitality, a sureness of herself I envied. Well, I like fun too, and she was more than fun—just to be near her was exhilarating. I frowned at her as though I thought the Hag was distasteful too—then we both laughed gaily, like little children.

WE WEREN'T the only ones laughing—about us swirled increasingly

1435

unrestrained revelry—being excited to ever greater unrestraint by the sweeping pleasure-ray's stimulation.

My curiosity as to the strange unsuspected strength of these hideous Rulers . . . that whispered fear of the Hag I'd heard so often—I felt I could get answered if I kept my interest masked in gaiety. So, I laughed as I prompted, "Tell me of the Limping Hag that you fear, Ceulna."

Shrugging her beautiful shoulders, she started, "The Hag is a very ancient . . . supposedly immortal . . . creature. They say she is centuries old . . . many centuries. She's a giantess —a hideous, old giantess. We don't know when she first came to Venus . . . she and her followers landed in the wild forests and were there many, many years before they were discovered."

Ceulna glanced at my eyes as though to assure herself I was listening, then continued, "She was much smaller, then —and her followers weaker in numbers, possibly only a few thousand in all. But the gullible and innocent women of the Tuons who ruled the surrounding country believed every lie the Hag and her men told, and let them live in peace . . . until it was too late. The Hagmen are accomplished liars—particularly in lying to a people to whom a lie is unthinkable—the Tuons believed too easily all they were told. Now . . . now, we know the Hag is an antique vampire who prolongs her horrible existence with the blood of young children . . . and takes no other food."

I guess I expressed disbelief, momentarily, or something, because Ceulna hastened to reassure me, "Oh, yes, the Hag even has many big farms . . . farms of children . . . but, somehow, her . . . child-cattle, don't do very well, and are old when a normal child would be just grown. She steals their youth . . . by living on a daily infusion of their young blood!"

"What does she—the Hag—look like?" I asked her, my eyes on her vivid, startlingly alive face with those oversize Venusian eyes flashing strangely out of the ultra-whiteness of her Tuon skin.

Cocking her head coyly to one side, she asked me, "Would you like very much to see?"

I nodded with a smile and she arose. "Then follow me and I will show you some magic that children play with on Venus."

I trailed after her spangled dancer's form as she threaded through the boisterous, drunken mob, wondering where a person acquired such a gait—like a tight-rope artist's—her figure as balanced as a gyroscope, yet, as sinuous as a cat's. Had I seen the spiderwalks of her home city on Venus, I would have known how many generations of perilously racing feet had produced the delicate precision of her stride.

SOON we were in the part of the caverns where the dancers had their quarters. Ceulna's apartment was lavish and luxurious. At my appreciative glance, she laughed, "Boss, he like my dancing. He say, 'You like this place?' I say, 'Okay, Boss.' He say, 'Okay, Beautiful.'"

Opening a curiously embossed metal chest, she withdrew a green crystal globe that had a kind of coronet attached. Immediately, its resemblance to the Egyptian headdresses worn by priests and gods made me wonder if the pictures I had seen in history books were similar contrivances from the same source? However, my speculations were cut short by Ceulna's actions.

"Now watch the ball and you will see what the Limping Hag—the Mother of Sin, looks like," and she pressed a stud at the side of the heavy coronet base.

1436

THE HIDDEN WORLD

A light quivered into vague life within the green ball's depths ... the crystalline, murky green slowly whirled and cleared to reveal a picture—as though one were looking down on a scene from a great height.

"I spied on her one day from a big tree—she didn't know I was there," Ceulna chattered, as the globe became clearer. "There! There she is ... the big one."

The figure in the globe *was* big, standing twice the height of the figures about her. Her body was well covered with flesh, still, she seemed bony. Barbaric ornaments were hung and fastened all over that huge harridan. Her face was a fierce Medusa mask from antiquity, covered with a network of fine wrinkles. She seemed to scorn clothes and her immense dugs hung down to her waist—the living incarnation of that foully evil Hindu Goddess KALI! in the flesh.

The green whorls had left the globe entirely and I could see the background. The Hag was in a big garden—a garden that I found out later could only exist in the hot-house air of Venus. Among the immense, flowering shrubs, and over the heavy carpet of weird yellow-veined grass, played many scores of children.

"She loves children, that old one," said Ceulna bitterly. We have conclusive evidence that the children are bled to make Her live! Here on Earth, you graft young saplings onto old trees, and the young sap makes the old tree young again, so why not the same thing with people? The Hag learned how to do just that in some Hell in the far past ... and that is why she does not die ... and why she loves children so. Huh! it's no wonder—they mean eternal life to Her."

I couldn't answer, but I understood the bitter tone of her voice—think of the horror if the unscrupulous rich ever discovered that evil method of the Hag's for staying young. It would be one burden too many for the broad backs of the poor to bear.

CEULNA'S voice had dropped lower as she continued, "Soon, you go, with many young men to fight against my people ... to fight for such undying Evil as that hideous giantess, to fight and kill my people so our children may be used to make blood for those evil veins. It's ... it's too ... horrible!"

My own voice dropped, sad and low, and I answered, "This has always been a harsh world of work and worry for me, Ceulna, and I see your own world isn't much better under the rule of my fellow Earthmen. I don't know what *I* can do about this mess, but Ceulna, if the time ever comes that a blow from my fist can help free the people of these two worlds from the burden of these damn vampires, I promise you, I'll strike—and HARD!"

It's not like my nature, but Ceulna's grateful glance as I spoke made me feel very noble—like a crusader or something. But I meant every word I said, then.

"I can't see how I can do anything now—but I will learn, and later the opportunity may come. Tell me more, Ceulna!"

She nodded, smiling slightly at the way I spoke her name, the green brilliance of her eyes shining with tears. "I have always done others' bidding and it may be I always will, but among the free people of Venus—my people—it is not so. They love their people, and life, to them, is a rich feast of love and pleasure. Some of us though, under these secret rulers from Earth, and under the priests of Hecate, we foolish ones who believed their lies, do the work and the rulers seek only to weld our chains tighter."

A tear welled from one of the beautiful, limpid eyes as she stifled a faint sob and continued, "When one knows that the children she bears will be used only as blood producers, and be old with the antique, ancient blood they pour back into the children's veins, it's . . . too horrible. Some day we will be like the ants, without sex or pleasure, living just to serve the huge body of some ancient Queen—like Hecate—the Limping Hag, who lives on the youthful bodies of our children. Life does not get better for us—it's—but tell me your name, O my new friend."

I WAS falling for her—but hard. Still I thought that nothing was to be gained by letting them know who I was. I told her, "You can call be 'Big Jim' like all the rest of my friends, Ceulna, though I guess down here I'm just Number one-eight-seven-one-X—that's the number they gave me. But, I'm not so young, nor so innocent that I can't appreciate your beauty, Ceulna, and desire it!"

"Aah! that's better," she smiled, "I remember how your big feet followed mine when they sent me out to get you . . . in . . . here. You were so very anxious to get some place with me—I couldn't help but know what you felt. You should . . . know how I . . . how I hated to lure you into this evil life, but I had no choice. They see and hear over such distance with the ancient apparatus, that I have to—must—do as they ask—or die, as that girl died that night. She was a young friend of mine who tried to keep a young boy out of their clutches, and failed—but what woman could help such actions? Many, a great many of us die when they catch us talking, even as we are doing now."

"Boy! they certainly hand out the punishment for even little things around here, dont' they?" I asked, as much to bolster my own rising alarm as to make Ceulna talk more.

"They are unjust—so, we will talk differently after this—talk of the glorious wisdom of our Rulers, of the foolishness of those who dare oppose them. We must talk—and think—like this for you never know who is listening with the telemech rays.

At the mention of even thinking, I must have raised my eyebrows in disbelief, because Ceulna hastened on as though to convince me.

"Yes, even your thoughts must be guarded. When you know, or feel, someone is listening to your thought, my handsome friend, you must think as if you loved to be treated as an animal to be fed upon, or some of the 'watchers' will report you to the Rulers as an enemy, and you saw yourself what they do to an enemy."

"Watchers," Ceulna?" I asked, "What are they?"

"The Watchers are the spies of the Rulers," Ceulna spoke rapidly with quick glances over her shoulders as though she expected someone to catch us here in this weird apartment a mile under the earth. "The watchers stay at the telemech screens listening to others' thoughts—thoughts they hasten to report to the Rulers, trying to curry their favor. But not many of them dare to do that for they cannot but help think wrong too, at times, and then someone else would get back at them. At least that's one thing we have, we who are used to this life. We can protect each other by such methods—those who don't do so, get it sooner or later."

"Surely, Ceulna, you are stretching things a little, aren't you?" I told her, though truthfully I didn't doubt her a bit, now.

"No, Handsome One, it is truth—there is always danger—unless we get

1438

them first. That is our life. Remember it!"

I COULDN'T imagine controlling my thoughts so well that no one knew what they were, so I told Ceulna lamely, "Well, it must be hard to pretend to approve of robbing children of their youth for such a witch as the Hag! But, Ceulna, wh . . ."

"No, wait. Now I must tell you what to do while there is yet time," she interrupted, "—for I may not see you again. When you get to Venus, you must escape from these people. How, I don't know, but you must. Do not fear my people . . . or be afraid to go to them—you of Earth know little of pleasure or true beauty, or the emotions that the correct use of the ancient mech can arouse, but we Venusians have developed our science along the lines of those of the ancient Gods who first built these magic mechanisms—the mech of love and beauty—so do not fear us that still remain free. Go to my people— you will have to think of a way after you get to Venus—and tell them that you are a friend. Among those of my people still free you will learn something of love and beauty that will change your whole life . . . and perhaps help you to free your own people!"

Ceulna was now talking so fast that I didn't have a chance to interrupt her for more details as to how to find her people—she must have been excited and assumed that I knew enough of Venus that I could find my way around it like I would my home town. But what was she saying now?

". . . remember, while you are near the Hag's men, or any of those that you think MIGHT be siding with the Rulers here—think of something other than your true thoughts, or your true purpose. Think other thoughts . . . or the secret Rulers will kill you with a ray!"

Before I had a chance to open my mouth with an answer to this, a pair of girls came running into the apartment, bare legs flashing. They were mere children but had the muscled firmness and smooth-flowing movements of highly trained dancers.

They clamored at her in the Tuon tongue of the dominant people of Venus —the tongue of most of the white races on that cloud-wrapped planet. It was a very different sound than any earth tongue, sounding like a musical exercise of predominately vowel sounds, and prolonged oooh's, nnn's, rrr's—a very liquid language it was.

I couldn't make any sense out of what they were saying, so I just stood there and took in all the beauty of those six flashing legs and well-knit bodies. If these were samples of Venusian women, the whole planet must have been populated with show-girls. "Not bad!" I thought to myself.

Ceulna finally turned to me, and grasping my hand with a slight squeeze, told me what all the bird-talk had been about, "They are calling for my Spider Dance, and I must do it . . . wait for me afterward at your table, and we will talk some more . . . 'bye . . . and don't forget!"

CHAPTER IV

From her black bloody locks the Fury shakes
Her darling plague, the fav'rite of her snakes

Aeneid
Virgil

ON THE stage had been strung a huge web of shining strands like a monster spider web. It angled upward from the footlights to the top rear of the stage—the farther strands lost in the gloomy shadows. Half con-

1439

cealed in these shadows crouched the huge figure of a black spider, twice the size of a man—a beast from a nightmare. (I learned later that such monsters were inhabitants of the vast forests of Venus!) As I took my seat the monster moved out over the web and did a slow dance upon the strands —a lazy spider testing his web with his weight. Then it retreated again to the rear. As the spider grew still and the web ceased to vibrate, out upon the shining threads sprang Ceulna.

Her superb body was striped with colored prismatics in insect simulation of a fly, her arms concealed in the thin membrane of a pair of transparent wings. A dizzying exhibition of tight-rope dancing such as no earthman or woman could ever emulate followed. She spun, fluttered, dipped and rose, flew above the huge glittering web like some beautiful fly, fascinated by the glitter of the strands of the web. Then she faltered and fell near the center of the web. She struggled and writhed with marvelous acting, too marvelous, I thought for that tremendous spider was creeping forward inch by inch and the suspense was terrific—the threat optically so real. The sticky ropes seemed to hold her inextricably. Down upon her rushed the great spider, jaws agape, around and around her he whirled, thin silken ropes wrapped her again and again. Then he settled to his meal. That spider was too damn real. I leaped to my feet as Ceulna's lovely body disappeared between the monster's cavernous jaws. I distinctly heard bones crack, and blood ran out of the thing's mouth.

A silly conjecture that the cruel humor of some such character as had entertained me on my first night had placed a real monster of the type the imitation body of the spider had been designed to simulate upon the stage came into my mind. I could think of no other way the act could look so real.

But Ceulna emerged again from the spider's mouth, her face and arms covered with blood, the beautiful wings crushed, and fled bounding across the webbed strands off the stage. The spider seemed in a frenzy, his great mouth hung open dripping blood, the jaw appeared to be broken. The monster swayed about the web. The falling curtain cut off the scene. That was either marvelous stage craft or something horrible had taken place before our uncomprehending eyes. Impatiently I sat waiting at the table where Ceulna had come before. At last, she appeared, swathed to her beautiful chin in a cloak of brilliant bird feathers—like the ones worn by the ancient Aztecs. There was a long scratch on her face, across her nose and down her soft cheek.

"That was great, Ceulna, and don't tell me that is the way they do their ball room dancing on Venus! I thought—."

Ceulna had looked directly at me then, and the expression in her eyes told me that all was not cream on her peaches.

"Ceulna! Something's wrong! That dance scared me to death—I knew something was rotten in Denmark. Tell me, Beautiful, what's wrong?"

SHE sat down, her breast heaving from all that exertion—and it looked to me like she was going to cry.

"It's—that spider. I . . . I . . . oh, I don't know how to start! I tried . . . I. . . ."

"Now take it easy, Beautiful," I tried to soothe her. "Just you sit back and relax . . . there, that's better."

At my concern over her, Ceulna smiled gratefully and I'd have liked to take her in my arms, as you do a restless baby.

"Oh, you are too kind to be in this life, my Handsome One, it's all so unclean down here . . . I knew something like that would happen to me—eventually—that wasn't my brother . . . that . . . that," and here she started to sob, but quickly stopped the sound, though I could see the tears all set to start pouring out.

"Easy does it, Ceulna," I said, patting her hand. "What wasn't your brother—the spider?"

Quickly nodding her head, she said, "You see, on Venus that dance has been performed like that for many centuries. It's a favorite of my people's—the Tuon's. The costumes the dancers wear, having been m a d e so often through the years, are exact reproductions of the genuine creatures—mine and the spider's—that spider wasn't a costume, that was a real Arakniden from the jungles of Venus—a monstrous survival from the age of insects. My brother has always taken the part of the spider, when I dance, and he does it perfectly, which made it hard for me to realize that it was this monster instead of my brother in costume. I thought at first it was my brother going through the routine ill or drunk; he didn't follow the things we usually do. When it seized me, I thought that my time had come. I drew up my knees and then straightened out, breaking the *thing's* jaw with the full strength of my back and legs." She sobbed again here. "But I didn't get away unhurt—look!"

She drew back a cape of feathers and showed me great fang gashes in her arm.

"Gods! Ceulna, then that was your blood. Who . . . what devil out of hell would make such a damnably fiendish substitution for your brother?" I was half afraid of the answer she might give to that.

Shrugging that rainbow-clad shoulder, she said, "One of the ruler group—it means some of my careless talk has come to the attention of one of the blood-takers—one of those seldom seen."

"Who are the blood-takers, Ceulna? Surely none in this hall right now—look human enough."

"No, my Handsome Friend, none here in the hall, but these are only part of the Ruler group—the others are hideous creatures, many of them so hideous a sane person breaks into uncontrollable screams if he is suddenly confronted by one of them. They are cruel as the spider you saw, and they keep other monstrous creatures for their own frightful purposes."

"WHEW! Some pets these birds have!" I whistled. "But surely your brother isn't one of them."

"The Gods forbid! What really frightens me most is what has become of him? They—ugh—must have taken him to the lower caves—none ever returns alive from there but the vampires themselves."

"Now, Ceulna, I wouldn't worry—how do you know they've taken him?"

"I just know. They couldn't have made the substitution without his knowledge, and Mala wouldn't have weakly submitted to having his sister eaten by the horrible spider!"

I couldn't figure what to say to that—this place had too many queer angles, and all of them deadly. She told me she was sorry and when I asked why . . .

"If I am in the Ruler's displeasure, why so are my friends. I shouldn't have come to you now. It places you in danger—but I just had to."

It seemed to me that I'd been in danger since she had led me into this magnificent wormhole, so I just shrugged . . . what the devil!

"They may do nothing to me for a long time. They love to keep someone in an agony of fear—like a cat and a mouse game, and, then, when one decides they have forgotten and begins to feel safe, they strike again. I . . . I can't stay here. I must flee . . . but where? It's almost impossible to get out of these caves."

"Well, Ceulna, let's see. The little time I've been here," I suggested, "I've noticed many of these dusty corridors lead to unused and seemingly endless caverns—like this we're in now. Where do they lead? I'd think they'd be an easy escape?"

Smiling, she patiently explained, "To a newcomer that would seem true, but the ancient exits and entrances are covered by time with rocks and earth —it's a mile, or more, to the surface. Strangers can't realize the immense age of this place—the indestructible nature of the antique work fools their senses. Oh, yes, we could get into the other caves—and wander on forever— finding nothing—no food—no water— nothing but tube after tube, and chamber after chamber—forever! The ancient God-built machines can do much, but they don't make food—they don't create water."

ADMITTING her arguments were good, I tried to reassure her, "It's plain to see, from the little I know of this mess, that you are doomed if you stay here. Lessee, now . . . look, Ceulna, a man can live for weeks without food, if he has to, and I'd say that the ancient builders piped water into these caves—someplace. I'd say the the pipes still held water if we'd look for 'em. Then, too, they must have stored some food—I've read that honey and some other things, seeds and stuff like that, have been taken from the tombs of the Pharaohs—4000 years old and still able to be eaten. The Egyptians put this stuff in containers sealed with wax—probably the ancient builders of these caves did the same thing. I'd gamble my life on the chance we could find such containers and make our way out."

Ceulna, seemingly, didn't think too much of my idea for she shook her glorious head, then frowned slightly.

"No, it might succeed—if the Rulers didn't know the caves like I know the palm of my hand. We'd wander in circles, they would follow, and we wouldn't escape."

"Well, Ceulna," I commented, "what would you suggest?"

"I don't know . . . I don't know what to do. If I pretend nothing has happened they may do nothing to me —that's the way they are. You can't tell what they'll do—except that it will be horrible, and fiendishly cruel. I don't know what to do."

"Look, Ceulna, I've got an idea. Soon they are sending this small army to Venus—sending us in *some* kind of a ship, a ship I have never seen—but you have! You know where it's kept."

I was trying to appear as though I was just talking to one of the pretty dancers the Rulers had provided for the entertainment of their new troops, yet, at the same time, I was desperately trying to make her certain of my plan.

"Listen, Ceulna, go aboard that hidden ship—any way at all—then, later, when we are in space, watch from your hiding place and when you see me, whistle. If anyone else hears it I'll pretend it's me whistling. When I've found you, I can bring you food. Then, when we get to Venus, steal off the ship while it's being unloaded for the return trip to Earth."

1442

It must have sounded like a large order, for she looked at me sort of helplessly . . . and very appealing.

"Stowing away isn't hard, Beautiful," I assured her. "Most of the crews I've ever heard of are more apt to help a stowaway than not. It is very probable, from the way this thing took place, that those aboard the ship for Venus won't know anything about it. If they do, they'll probably be sympathetic and help you, even if you are caught after the ship leaves Earth. I'd say your worst danger was here—hiding yourself aboard that ship as quickly as you can seems to me the safest course, but, Ceulna, I . . . I'm sorry, I don't like to say this . . . but I can't see how you can help your brother, even if you stayed here. Perhap's he's dead already."

WHEN I mentioned her brother, she couldn't keep the tears back, still the girl had grit, and she was a swell little actress.

"I will do it!" The poor girl's eyes glowed in gratitude to me. "You make it seem so easy! Believe me, the spider is an easy death compared to some they think up for us." She stood up then. "I go now . . . the less you see of me, the safer for you, so you will not see me again until we are in space. When we get in space, walk everywhere about the ship that you are allowed. You will find me."

The brilliant cape of feathers floated swiftly away through the crowd. A lump of pity . . . and something more . . . was in my throat. I was beginning to get my bearings in this Devil's Dream I'd been decoyed into. I swore a great oath to myself—an oath that I would taste no pleasure, relax not the least fibre of will, 'til I found a way to strike at this ancient, powerful nest of parasites on man! It was an oath I kept, too. For even though they are equipped with the weapons and machines of the very Gods themselves, these ancient idlers have allowed their brains to atrophy—and I know why. The ancient, infinitely capable machines, which they spent no effort to create, have removed most necessity of effort from the Rulers' lives. Those ages of idling, of deviling poor ignorant surface men, have cost them their birthright of Will and Sense, the best gifts the Gods left us. Surface men have had to exercise these gifts somewhat, and, as a result, are more of a man, and less a horrible insect that can live only be bleeding a host.

I sat thinking, digesting the horrible setup of this age old cavern life, until the last drunken reveler had staggered off to bed. Then I took myself to my own chamber—a chamber filled with Farne's very audible snores.

CHAPTER V

Wish for the Wings of wind to mount the sky;
Or hid, within the hollow earth to lie!
" . . . . made this short reply
'Tis hostile heaven I dread, and partial Jove."
Twelfth Book of the Aeneid

THE next morning they marched us a long time in the gloomily beautiful caverns. At last we came to a black and silent expanse of water, whose farther reaches were lost in the darkness. Under our feet the black rock stretched flat and smoothly glistening to the water's edge, where it ended, cut clean as a straight edge. At that edge was moored a vast ship. It was a tremendous vessel, like a submarine, a craft from the Elder World. Its antiquity was only seen by blot-

1443

ting mottles on the dull sheen of its metal hull. That it was a still spaceworthy spaceship I realized from Farne's accounts of them. It was probably older than the Pyramids, yet, but for the dull mottling of its hull, looked as if it had just slipped from the ways. Had this been its resting place through those untold ages of time? Of what marvelous material was it built that it was still in running order after all those tired centuries had passed?

My speculations as to its origin were cut short; a harsh order barked down the long line of men. Great doors opened in the side of the ship and our lines of green-clad troops marched aboard and down the long gangways to deep inside the bowels of the ship. Platoons were assigned quarters inside and I had a chance to look around. The ship contained round portholes but they were all closed. I guessed, rightly, that vision was obtained by the marvelous penetrative rays the Ancient Builders had used so much. We stowed our gear and then stood around waiting.

A slight swaying motion was the only indication that we had taken off. This continued for half an hour, then, quite slowly the cabin floor started to lean at an increasing angle. Shortly the after wall became the deck. As this deck slowly became less and less of a deck, I found myself floating—and the rest of my companions likewise. There we were floating in air like a lot of fish in a bowl of air. Gradually, the ceiling which had been the forward wall of the cabin, became the floor. Suddenly a sensation of falling upward swiftly faster and faster nearly robbed me of reason. In despair I called to Hank Farne.

"What the hell is happening? What goes on here!"

"Well," Hank finally managed, after laughing like he'd choke, "that's an order not easily filled, my ungainly friend!"

"Dammit, Hank," I snorted, "this ain't funny, now cut that insane laughing and tell me what the devil is happening to us, or I'll drift over there and wring your scrawny neck!"

MY ANGER and the way I was flapping myself around in the air just sent him into gales of irritating laughter. Finally he calmed down.

"What a sorry hunk of frightened little boy you are—but I'll tell you what's happening—much as I can. You see, my short-tempered friend, modern science doesn't understand the nature of gravity, so there is no concept to employ in explanation with which you are familiar."

"Well, Hank, I got lots of time. Let's hear what you think it is." I was beginning to get over being miffed at his laughing and felt Hank was in one of his 'lecture' moods.

"All right, I don't think y—— Never mind. The ancient race who built this monster ship DID understand gravity —and a lot more. The same God-Race that built the caverns on Earth, and who knows on how many other planets, and all the ancient mech—they knew or learned, that gravity is an inrush of tenuous stuff going into all matter and becoming absorbed by it. Gravity is a reverse force—in many ways—to light which is an OUT rush of flaming force particles. These particles only return to matter as they become gravity, thus completing the full cycle of change which forms our universe."

"But, Hank," I puzzled, "what's that got to do with this falling upward sensation we're getting?"

"I'm coming to that. In the tail end of this crate, and along the bottom are the 'Driver Plates,' as they call 'em in these ancient ships. Incidentally, there is an immense supply of these plates in the original storerooms. I've seen workmen replacing 'em. Now, the 'Driver Plates'—a strange dense metal they are, too—are hooked up to great cables from the power supply—generators like the ones on the dis-beam."

"You mean that they're flying this buggy on electricity?"

"No, not exactly. Just what happens to—or in—the plates when the juice is on, no one now living knows, I don't suppose. Anyway, the plates melt slowly away, and somehow give off an out rush of force particles . . . similar, in effect, to gravity, but far stronger proportionately. Thus anything near the plates starts to fall 'away' from the plates above, and Earth falls 'away' from the plates beneath. The more juice they shoot in the Driver Plates, the faster the 'fall' takes place. Get it?"

"I think so. But go on, Doctor, I'm listening."

"In other words, those plates are *reverse-gravity* drives. Some ancient scientist did a swell job of *reversing* the integrative process of gravity, and so got a beautifully simple process by which matter causes things to 'fall' away from it. Clear enough?" Hank grinned, looking like a dirty little urchin, with his straggly hair and splintered brown stubs of teeth behind his twisted lips.

MY STOMACH seemed to be turning inside out, but I began to see the sound cunning sense beneath his not too attractive exterior. I grinned back, for Farne was my kind of a man. You didn't have to tell that boy anything twice—he was usually way ahead of you.

"Clear, nothing," I answered him, "I don't suppose modern men *can* come very close to understanding those wise ancients. This idea of matter being growing stuff is a new one on me. If I've got it right, all matter INTAKE is the cause of gravity, right? The ancients reversed, and speeded up this INTAKE process, then, the matter melts away, and things fall 'away' from the matter." I grunted, "Huh! It *sounds* simple. I suppose, though, all great things are simple in concept. All they did then, I guess, was put the plates between Earth and the ship and it takes off."

"That's almost it," Hank was being very patient. "But the fact is that the repulsions on either side of the plate would neutralize and no motion would result."

"Oh, I hadn't thought of that," I acknowledged. "Well, then, how do they get action?"

"'Understanding'. The ancient God-Race understood the nature of energy flows and devised materials which are opaque to them. Now, the chamber in which the driver plates are placed is lined on the ship side with a material opaque to the repellant flow. They designed this opaque lining to reflect the flow around the plate and out the rear of the driver chamber. Result—all the repellance is in a rearward direction. Thus, the ship runs like a skyrocket—by recoil. Though the source of the kick is different. That's as close as I can come to understanding the drive of these antique ships. However . . ."

Suddenly I remembered Ceulna!

"My God, Hank, Ceulna is stowed away on this ship and I forgot her! We've got to find her!"

"What the devil is she doing abroad?" demanded Hank.

I quickly recounted what she had revealed to me after the "Dance of the Spider" the night before. Farne sputtered when I told him the fake spider of the dance had been the real thing.

"The Devils!" he cursed, "they go to any lengths to kill the thing people like best. Ceulna is the best loved of all the Rulers' entertainers!"

"We've got to look for her, Hank. Everywhere . . . everywhere she might have hidden. You know the ropes, so you lead the way."

THE two of us left the cabin, walking quietly forward. The whole layout was strange to me, but Hank seemed to know his way around. We hadn't gone ten paces when an officer stopped us. His voice had me plenty worried.

"Enlisted men are to stay in their cabins while the ship is in flight." He spoke firmly, but in the slow drawl of Southern U. S. A tall dark fellow, but his face was pale with his years in the caves and his eyes were dull as though his brain were asleep.

Farne was not taken aback. He smiled easily and flashed a badge he'd taken from his pocket. I had an idea what it was, though Hank hadn't told me just what kind of work he'd been assigned to since his return.

The officer saluted. "Sorry, suh! I didn't know you. Is there any way I can be of service, suh? My name's Leadbetter, suh. Lieutenant Leadbetter."

"Perhaps, Lieutenant, you can." Hank was acting like an officer himself now. "I'm on the lookout for a certain Venusian—no particular description. Distinguishing marks reported to be a shredded left ear and a scar on his left wrist. Wanted under suspicion of working for the Tuons. Know anyone fitting that description, Lieutenant? To my knowledge, there aren't a dozen Venusians aboard, are there?"

I figured Hank was giving a fictitious errand to explain his presence on deck, but as an intelligence officer, he probably had full right there.

The officer scratched his own left ear reflectively. Apparently, he could think of no such Venusian. So, wishing us luck, he saluted and left us.

As soon as he was out of sight, Hank led the way swiftly aft.

"If she knows as much about these ships as I think she might, she'd be in the driver compartment. They're warm, and at a distance of several feet the radiations from the plates are beneficial."

1446

THE HIDDEN WORLD

WE ENTERED the deserted propulsion end of the ship. The driver-plate device never needed attention. Since these antique creations were perfection in craftsmanship, they didn't demand attention, so the crew seldom came here.

We had hardly entered the place when I heard a low whistle. I looked around but couldn't find the source of the sound, so I called, "C'mon out, Ceulna. This is my friend, Hank."

I heard her low, luscious laugh behind me, and turning, saw her emerge from a tool locker like a reviving mummy from a sarcophagus. Even the tool locker of one of those ancient marvel ships was decorated as beautifully as a Pharaoh's mummy-case.

"I've had the most wonderful time," she laughed. "Last night when I avoided the two sentries and came aboard, I came right here. I had heard the rays given off by this drive mech were beneficial—but no one told me it felt so good. I've been lying in stim for nearly twenty hours—no way to get away from it."

Still laughing gaily, she kissed me. "You look like a beautiful young God after all the stimulation I've had!" And she kissed me again laughing irresistibly. "I had no idea!"

I told her she looked like a beautiful young Goddess herself. I'd never seen such an improvement in anyone in such a short time. I was going to spend as much of my time aboard as possible getting the double stim of her presence and these rays she was talking about.

"I thought you were running away from danger—not eloping with Jimmy, here," Hank grinned at Ceulna.

"Ceulna, this is Hank Farne, my only friend aboard besides you," I introduced Hank to Ceulna.

"I'm always glad to meet a friend of the so Big Jeem," she said, giving her hand to Hank as Americans do, then kissing him on the forehead as the Venusians do.

"Hank has been on Venus for years," I said.

Ceulna, puzzled, looked at Hank, "Oh, then he knows our customs. I will give him our formal greeting or he will feel hurt."

Hank put up his hands protestingly, but she sank kneeling before him and embraced his knees in the ancient Greek fashion.

"It's a very pleasant custom," explained Hank, "once they greeted one another that way in many countries on Earth—long ago."

Hank seemed much taken with Ceulna. "But we must plan how to avoid your capture. You know how nasty it can be to fall into the hands of anyone connected with the followers of Hecate—the Hagmen!"

"Yes, I know—too well," answered Ceulna, her supple body shuddered all over. "I have seen some of their 'entertainments' of my poor people in my home city of Delphon."

"Just what is the difficulty in keeping her concealed?" I asked. "Can't she just stay here, quite comfortably, on the food we can bring her from our own meals? There seems to be plenty of it."

"Listen!" Hank hissed suddenly, for outside in the long companionway came the slow clump of a workman's boot. "At anytime one of the officers or repairmen may come in here to get tools outa the locker or to inspect the generators, or to oil some part that's lost its ancient sealing."

The clump of those boots didn't stop, but grew louder and louder, finally halting outside the door behind which we stood immobile.

A GUN suddenly appeared in Farne's hand. I didn't have one, but I held up a restraining hand in front of Hank, making a gripping motion with my fingers. My paws are about twice the size of the average man's, and Hank got the meaning.

The latch grated, the door swung in. A blue-demined figure started through, a large wrench in his hand. Quickly my own hands locked about his throat. A slight startled gurgle and he was soon quiet. I didn't care to kill him, but a look on Ceulna's beautiful terrified face tightened my grip the last destructive bit. I felt his windpipe crush—a convulsive shudder, and he went limp. Dead. The first man I had ever killed—but he wasn't the last. It's not a good feeling to kill, but it had to be done.

"What the H— ah ... blazes are we gonna do with him, Hank. He's dead!"

"Oh, you huge beast, you ... !" Ceulna's face blazed in sudden fury and revulsion toward me. "You didn't have to kill him. We could have hidden him somewhere—in a locker or something. He would have been found eventually!"

"I'm sorry, Ceulna. I was excited. I couldn't help it—he ..."

It grieved me to have her look at me as if my hands were dripping blood.

"We'll get rid of him." Farne wasn't ruffled. "There is a space lock for refuse in several places."

Ceulna's anger and revulsion subsided, and she suggested, "We can put him out the drive tubes from this same room—there is an opening."

Getting an artistically decorated wrench, I went to work. Time had tightened the bolts pretty effectively, but at last the cover came off revealing an opening a little larger than necessary for a man's body. Everything the Ancients left is too large for mere man. They were men, if they were men, of huge size—that Ancient God Race.

"The drive flow is too strong!" cried Hank as a blast of force drove me back against the far wall, nearly stunning me. "We couldn't shove this carcass through that opening if there were a dozen of us!"

The field of force-flows sealed the opening more effectively than any metal plate. It formed gravitational vortices within the room; we swayed this way and that, or were thrown to the floor as though by a living opponent. We had to get that cover back on, even if we couldn't push the body through—but how?

After an hour of futile struggle, Hank solved the problem. He detached the great insulative nuts that held the cables from the generators. The great cable, as thick as a man's arm and heavy as Hell, was a job. Finally we lifted it off, and the tricky gravity flow, that buffeted us about the room, ceased. We shoved the dead stranger out the drive tube, replaced the plate and tightened the ancient bolts. What metal that stuff was! Old as I knew they were, there was only a fine grey corrosion to show it, less than an eighth of an inch loss in all those uncounted centuries.

I SPENT many hours of that trip in the drive chamber, for the radiations were intensely stimulating, with a cumulative charge effect. After you were in there an hour, a glow of well being stole about your body, gradually increasing until you could not tear yourself away. Ceulna forgave me for the inadvertent killing—thanks to that influence which made the world seem a bed of roses.

All three of us were mighty worried about discovery, for we knew how these secret people habitually made mountains out of molehills to get a chance to punish somebody. However, nothing happened to further the chances of any mishap.

CHAPTER VI

Lo, take this herb of virtue, and go to the dwelling of Circe, twill keep from thy head the evil ... Thy company yonder in the hall of Circe are penned in the guise of swine ... in their deep lairs abiding.
The Odyssey

THE ancient hulk—its indestructible generators purring sweetly on the water that was their only fuel—settled slowly into the obscuring clouds of Venus. They must have been following some kind of radio beam, for we drifted out of the clouds directly over a vast cathedral-like structure rearing up from among the mighty, primeval trees. That this type of structure, built of rock from a foundation deep in the earth, was nearly unique on Venus, I didn't know. Nor did I know that the cult of Hecate, the Hag, whose headquarters were located there, were the descendants of the cult of the Limping Hag who had left Spain some five centuries before. These things I learned later. I had expected wonders from an alien race of a different development than our own. When the mighty ship settled lightly to earth outside a vast medieval pile, I was nonplussed at its strangely familiar appearance. The men who lowered the drawbridge came to meet us clothed in antique monkish robes such as are worn in some monasteries on Earth today. I turned to Hank.

"Say, what is this anyway. Venus or fourteenth century Spain?"

Farne smiled. "I was waiting for your reactions. These are people whose ancestors came to Venus just as we are coming now in the ancient ships from the secret caverns. They belong to a terrible and very ancient

1448

cult—the cult of Hecate, also called the Limping Hag. It is a schism—an offshoot from the ancient Rosicrucians. The Rosicrucians are hardly more than a memory on earth today, but once they were a mighty and mysterious power on earth. When Hecate's followers perverted the science to evil ends, the Rosicrucians drove them out. It was at the time of the plague on earth, and fleeing simultaneously from the plague and the wrath of the mighty world organization at that time, they came here to Venus and so have remained. They have been a curse to the Venusians for their practices are cruel and terrible.

"The Hag, herself, is a kind of living Goddess, said to be immortal. She is the ruler here. Hecate is hated by the natives but they cannot drive her out. She is our ally in the war now going on."

SOME days later I stood with Farne in one of the great corridors of the church-like fortress. Through the dark, high-beamed rooms of the musty old stronghold moved a strange mixture of races. The descendants of the original Rosicrucian renegades were at times clothed in sober, all-enveloping monk's robes, and sometimes dressed like warriors of fourteenth century France or Spain. Guards in steel corselets with halberds held erect stood at the doors and passages. Past them went groups of the two-white Venusians of the northlands, fierce redmen from the hot equatorial belt, and green amphibians from the marshy islands of the sea cities. The green men, a species peculiar to Venus, were green skinned with gill slits in their necks, interior lungs as have ordinary men, webbed hands and wide-webbed feet. They had no noses to speak of, large staring, fixed eyes, and spines on their heads. The great black duckfooted men of the south lands were the most formidable in appearance. Huge muscled and gigantic of build, they had a dull stupid look, small eyes and flat heads. Through the ages of life in the swamplands of the south, they developed a tremendously wide foot. All were subjects of the cruel Hagmen, Farne explained. Most of them wore nothing but a few glittering baubles, the hothouse climate was not conducive to wearing clothing. Always their skin glistened with the cooling moisture they exuded. The smart uniforms of the recently arrived forces soon wilted, hanging damply on heat weary Earthmen. Yet they looked more efficient and capable than did the living relics of the past and some savage looking Venusians. But the white men of Venus, even though nude and flashing with barbaric ornaments, had a noble, cultured air superior to that of the Earthmen. They were taller, too, averaging well over six feet.

Ceulna had escaped into the jungle. We gave her a gun and several clips of cartridges before the ship landed. She intended to steal off the ship the first night after it landed. We thought it safer not to try helping her, though Farne wanted to accompany her. But it would attract attention and pursuit if either of us were missing. Ceulna, herself, said, "You would only be a burden to me in the jungle. I can travel swiftly and easily through the high trees. You have seen me on the ropes of the "Spider Dance"; these limbs are not so different. We Venusians inherit such ability. I will get in touch with you at the first opportunity. Please, please take off yourselves." She kissed us goodbye. Ceulna was gone, and with her most of the pleasure of life.

SINCE my arrival on Venus I had little time to learn the exact nature of the political setup between Hecate, the Hag, the native rulers who were our allies, and the invading forces of the Earthmen. Later this became clear to me. The men of Hecate, as well as the red, green, and black races, were minority groups on the planet, while the white race had always been the dominant force. Now the lower races and the recently arrived Earthmen joined forces to destroy the ancient white cities.

Harak, one stronghold of the Hagmen, lay sixty miles north of the tree city of Lefern. Lefern was a mighty city built in the gigantic trees of the forest Hank told me about the first night I descended into the caverns. It was a powerful city of the Whites. I learned that Lefern was our first objective. It had been able to hold out against everything the Hagmen and the colored Venusian races directed. Now the shanghaied Earth forces were to be used to the last man if necessary to annihilate the Whites' stronghold. If the Earthmen succeeded, if we subdued Lefern, our value to the Venusians would be demonstrated, and our leaders would probably cash in plenty.

But if we didn't conquer the city, our position with the leaders of the Venusian aggressors would be decidedly minor.

Few Venusian roads were laid on the surface of the ground. Instead, they were strung between tree piers twenty or thirty feet above ground. These suspension bridges were made of the universal plastic substance in common use on Venus. It was light, strong, durable. Over this swaying transparent structure our trucks of supplies, the little one man ray tanks such as I was assigned to, our bigger six- and eight-man units, and our marching army of infantry moved toward Lefern—somewhere between six and eight thousand men, I guess.

On Venus it rains every night—most of the night, but the days are often clear. There is little wind, just the slow drifting of the grey mass overhead, the clear almost shadowless light, and the brilliant vegetation. The latter is full of pulsing life, growing, always growing; you can almost see it grow! The soil is seldom solid enough for any vehicle, but much of it can be walked on, if one knows where the firm places are.

About thirty miles from the city, in easy sight through our telescopic penetray-vision weapons, the bridge-road branched like the fingers of a hand, into dozens of smaller roads, all pointing toward different parts of the wide-spread city.

The city itself hung like festoons of giant cobwebs on the gigantic trees. Level over level, the cobwebs were hung with the many-colored and glittering globes of the Venusians' homes and shops. Of vari-colored plastic, these homes were of all sizes, suspended from the great web of the roadways or from the limbs of the trees themselves.

AS OUR engineers set to work on the cables of the road, strengthening them with ray resistant additional cables so they could not be burned from under our feet, we deployed on the two outer roads which ran at nearly right angles to a line directly into the city. The idea was to bring as many rays as possible to bear on it.

From the sparkling city came no sign that we were sighted. I swept a close focus over the vast system of webs which was Lefern and, except for an occasional tall warrior woman racing on some errand or other, I could discern no life at all. Apparently the place had been evacuated. I noticed that many of the larger globe houses, which were factories or store-houses, were opaque to my vision beam. Heretofore, I had found nothing that obstructed its passage, so I was sure that these places were opaque by some device of the Venusian Whites. At my side Farne, who was equipped with a special long range vision device, spoke to me.

"This city of Lefern is a woman's city, ruled by Amazons. For three months in the spring of each year men are allowed to visit the city, the rest of the time no men are allowed within."

"Well, if that's all the opposition we'll have, this is going to be a pushover!"

"Don't be too sure, my optimistic young friend. Those ladies in there really can fight . . . and then some!" said Hank, obviously trying to caution me against losing my precious head, "and they are fightin' mad now. They're especially bitter against the men under Hecate, because these Amazons have a kind of religious veneration and love for children—as well as a mother's love—and they don't care for what the Hagmen do to kids."

My stomach turned over. Fighting women was not to my liking. But I knew it was fight or die for me. I had seen the fate of others who had objected to their forcible induction into the strange army. I did not care for any of their "deserter medicine."

At the order, we commenced firing on the city. The opaque globes resisted my disray, as well as the others' rays which rather astonished me, as nothing before had failed to disappear before it. The few Amazons who had been racing along the net of walks quickly disappeared—some shot down, some had ducked into the opaque buildings. Just when I was beginning to wonder why the city did not return our fire, and the webs of the city were beginning to be a tangle of cables cut by our rays, it happened.

A huge ray flashed out from the top of the center globe. It touched our bridgeways reinforced supports which our engineers had fondly imagined to have been made impervious to ray fire.

HERE and there it lanced, pausing a breath to burn through the cables, then dancing on to the next support. The bridge-road began to sag, and before you could count ten our whole army and its many tons of equipment was spread out on the soft muck of the earth below the road. At the same time billows of yellow gas arose from the ground ahead and began to roll steadily toward us. Behind the gas I could see the crisscrossing beams of the windmaking ray I had heard of, but had never seen in use before.[2] Scrambling about in the soft mud and the tangle of cut cables and equipment, we hurriedly donned our gas masks and awaited the worst, that is, those of us who had not been crushed under the fallen tonnage.

My little ray equipped tractor was sunk two feet in the muck which bubbled greedily as it sucked at the mass of equipment. Somehow, my heart rejoiced that these alien people were so well able to defend themselves. The gas rolled steadily closer. Would our masks prove as ineffective against their gas as our tactics had proven useless against theirs? Strangely, I hoped so, for those tall cool women in their jewel-like city that hung like a web of magic against the pearly sky of Venus, were not what I wished to destroy.

After I had gotten my gas mask in place, I secured my sinking weapon to a nearby tree trunk with a heavy vine. I had a great regard for those antique products of a lost science. I had not much time for thought before the gas cloud rolled over our struggling ranks and I learned that our masks too were futile against the Amazons. With a Hell-Fire in my nostrils, I passed out.

I AWOKE with a sharp intermittent pain in the rump. I put back one sleepy hand to encounter what seemed to be the toe of a boot. Looking around, I saw what appeared to be Ceulna, grown still taller and now covered all over with a strange tattoo.

I cried, "Ceulna, when did you get tattooed, and what the devil are you pointing that confounded pistol at me for?"

But Ceulna's double paid no attention to my words, only kicked me again in a spot

---

[2] This windmaking ray is described in the story "Thought Records of Lemuria" and was an essential part of most antique ray installations. Much of it was weather-controlling apparatus; they made winds, caused rain or dispersed rain clouds, and could throw lightning bolts.—Author.

already sore. I got groggily to my feet. All about me a similar scene was being enacted in endless repetition.

The Amazons had followed in the wake of their anaesthetizing gas and were making us captive. There was no fight in us. I didn't see anyone reach for a weapon. Somehow, I was glad, very glad I would not have to shoot any of these tall pink-and-white darlings. They were not made for that. I grinned at the woman warrior beside me. "You don't know how glad I am to see you."

She made no answer, only prodded me into line with that peculiarly deadly looking weapon she carried. Between a double line of the Amazons we started the long trek to the city. They wore mud shoes, a wide rounded board slipped over the boots, but we captives struggled along ankle deep in the muck, often falling when we hit a soft spot. A ripple of feminine laughter accompanied each fall. Somehow our mighty army was ridiculous. Remembering the bloody death sweats I had seen, such as the one of the girl on the cross the first night of my arrival in the caves not so very long ago, I blessed the fortune that had forestalled our attack.

Behind me Farne nudged my shoulder. He whispered, "This is something I've wanted and waited for for ages. When I get the ear of one of their officers, we'll make out Okay."

Ahead of me another earth man spoke up. "I'd like to see old Hecate's hag-face right now. She'll probably bust a blood vessel and lose some of that baby blood she's full of."

Another voice remonstrated. "Aw, I don't believe all that stuff. Didn't you ever hear of war propaganda? They treated us pretty white. That show they put on for us the night we left Earth must have cost plenty. The grub was always good, too."

No one answered. The line slogged on in silence. Shortly we ascended a swinging ladder into the tree roads again. Here lines of long narrow vehicles waited, which explained the swift arrival of the Amazons. As we stood waiting to board the speedy looking buses, I examined the guarding warrior nearest me.

EXCEPT for the webbed hands and feet, they were almost identical to earth people. But their appearance was utterly different. Tall feather plumes on their head gear accentuated their height. My guard's clothing consisted of a G-string and weapon belt, arm bands of heavily jeweled and shining yellow metal, and knee-high boots of a gleaming stuff like woven metallic thread. Her skin was intricately tattooed with an all over pattern that even covered her face with lovely curving lines. The design was sea waves and flying long-necked birds. As I looked about at these tattooed skins I learned definitely that the beauty nature gives a woman can be immensely enhanced.

Later I learned that the tattoo was used as we use family names, the motifs indicating family ancestry. A heron over a sea wave meant one was the son of a woman of the Herons and a man from the sea tribes. A tiger stalking a deer indicated family connections with those tribes. On Venus they wore their family trees on their backs. But some modern city groups had dropped the tattoo as too barbaric. Ceulna had not been tattooed, I recalled.

One of the men near me, who had also been all eyes for the beautiful Amazon bodies, shouted in English, "Buddies, their mating season doesn't start 'til next month. We'll be the only men in the city. Talk about tough luck, this is terrible!"

One of the women seemed to understand English for she snickered and then repeated the man's remark in the Lefern Venusian language. The laughter rippled up and down the line until the sharp bark of an officer stopped it.

The glittering, jewel-hung mist-web that is a Venusian city in the distance soon became recognizable dwellings and streets as we flashed into the outskirts on our way to the center.

We did not have time to enjoy the beauties of the city and its feminine population. We were unloaded from the buses directly into a large and forbidding structure that ran all the way up the side of a tree almost to the low clouds. Many trees of Venus are large enough to have the tops hidden in the low clouds. This was a big one ... I guess about the size of the Woolworth Building. I noticed that the weight counterbalanced the pull of a great suspension cable on the other side holding up the main street of the city.

Those delicious looking Amazons locked us up in cells and left us. I wonder how many men felt as slighted by this neglect as I. A man's thoughts and emotions are so seldom logical. The days dragged by slowly.

CHAPTER VII

"I supplicate thee, O Queen, whether thou art a goddess or a mortal? . . . to Artemis, I liken thee, for beauty and stature and shapeliness.
                The Odyssey

AT HER broad desk in the Intelligence Bureau Central Offices of Lefern, City of Tuon, Oanu, Chief of Secret Police, sat musing. The usually disciplined controlled lines of her face had relaxed except for a slight contraction of well shaped eyebrows. One long fingered, webbed hand kept pulling at her lower lip. The other, beautiful and white, idly drummed the polished top of the desk. Aimlessly, she pushed back the chair and with the grace of a serpent, stood up, her long metallic cloth cloak falling in heavy folds to the floor.

Six feet of efficient fighting machine—and gorgeous. She, too, was a warrior woman of Venus. And like most of the women of Venus—most of the white Tuons, she was beautiful and graceful. The long cape was the only covering she had, the jewelled straps and belts she wore weren't designed to conceal the well moulded figure —they functioned. Upon them were her shining insignia of rank and hooks and clasps for more of the strange weapons of Venus. A short bladed, damascened knife crossed the center of the girdle belt, and on the left side was holstered one of the deadly little hand gravity-beams of the jungle planet. Her plumed, ray-proof helmet was carelessly flung on her desk and her golden Tuon hair tumbled about her broad shoulders. Oanu lacked the leaner lines of the younger women, such as Ceulna, voluptuous rather than slim; still, she, too, carried herself like a skilled dancer, head held regally high, the movements of her hips fluid and the slow pace of her stride like the rippling muscles of a leopard.

Now, she seemed tired. With one hand she absently pushed a stray curl off her broad high forehead, then hooked her thumbs in the broad weapon belt. A few idle pats with her finger tips, and with just the faintest suggestion of a swagger, she strolled toward the broad window at the side of her desk. Stopping in front of it she raised one tapering, delicately tattooed leg and planted a gracefully sandaled foot on a low seat.

Wistfully, she stood there watching a rainbow-plumed pair of Venusian lovebirds cavorting in the branches of the great tree. It was too bad, she thought, that the too rigid code of the Tuons forbade living with a man. It would be nice to be near a man always. The mating season was so very short—only three months, and if you found that you had fallen in love, it was hopeless. You must lose him forever, for the next year there would be another mate. The law forbade more than one child of a union ... and, of course, the law was correct. It was a known fact that a race acquires strength by careful crossing of complementary traits. Yes, true, but it did spoil life so to lose one's mate every year. ...

FROWNING, Oanu put aside her thoughts and pressed a button among the rows on the side of her desk.

"Bring those films that were taken by the telescopic camera of the Hag's city of Harak, as well as the films of the city they now call Disin," she barked into the orifice below the screen. "Also have the prisoner, Henry Farne, brought to me."

Oanu seated herself at the magnificient desk. An aide brought the films she ordered. The door opened the second time for a tall warrior guard and a prisoner. Henry Farne's dirty, bedraggled figure appeared more than ever the adult urchin as he entered the green dream of an office. He stood smartly at attention before the Intelligence Officer and flashed his most flattering and impish grin. Farne knew women; he knew that the boy in him would appeal to Oanu, the mother.

Oanu's eyes softened—almost twinkled —as she looked at him, and when her eyes relaxed like that, she was as beautiful as any dancing girl in this Tuon City. Suddenly, she snapped back to her role as Chief. The soft contours of her body tightened imperceptibly, those beautiful eyes hardened, and her inviting, voluptuous mouth contracted to a hard thin line.

"I have been informed, Earthman," said Oanu, her voice not at all pleasant, "that you have been in the service of these modern invaders from Earth for sometime, and also that you have been working for Hecate. It is obvious from your long experience here that you know something of the conditions that exist on Venus which have brought on this conflict. How is it that you continue to serve them if you know their vile purpose?" She looked at Farne like a schoolma'm who's just caught a kid with a rat on a string.

"You would not ask if you knew the details of my record," Hank said in defense, however, not in fear of his examiner. "I have been lying in prison here on Venus for many years because my too open sympathy for your people aroused suspicion against me. A short time ago I was sent back to Earth. They figured I might be able to give the Earth leaders some valuable information about your organization. Now, I'm back here on Venus as a scout in their enlarging army, that is, what was their enlarging army."

"How many men did that last ship bring from Earth?" Oanu asked, a slight smile playing around her mouth. Hank's words had pleased her.

He realized she already knew the answer, but wanted to hear what he would say. "About two thousand men outside of the crew—all new recruits who have trained for about a month in the use of the antique weapons. You know, of course, that Earthmen are not accustomed to the antique mech. That is confined to a few sparse groups."

Oanu looked at him a long time. "You have a loyalty to these people who keep your own people in ignorance of the wonders of the ancient science?" she asked.

Hank grinned at her frankly. "None whatsoever, lovely lady. If I have any loyalty in my heart, it is for such women as you who have built a wonderful life for your people and who know how to fight to keep that life. But women like you are seldom able to trust such men as myself. You aren't clever liars, nor do you understand a liar and dissimulator like myself. I was raised in a very different school. My boyhood days were spent in criminal pursuits. All the dodges by which we live in such an environment are to you but cowardice and villainy. But I could be of service to you just because of my experience with the people whom you think of only to despise. It is one of your people's weaknesses, their inability to understand the criminal mind."

1453

"Yes, that may be true," Oanu agreed. "There is a saying I have heard from Earthmen. 'Set a thief to catch a thief.' It is the thought that was in my mind when I sent you for." She picked up the cylinders her aide had brought her. "I sent for these films taken in the city of Harak from which you just came and in Disin and other cities under the Hag. My purpose is to arouse your sympathy and so loosen your tongue. You will find them interesting."

Oanu raised a small projector from a recess in her desk, inserted a roll of film, and on the wall as the lights dimmed, a picture appeared.

Farne said, "Before you go on with the film, I suggest that you have the rest of the prisoners assembled and show them the nature of their ally, The Limping Hag. They are Americans like myself who have had the advantages of some moral education. I can assure you they are not savages. The secret ray group on earth have treated them very well, and they haven't the faintest idea what they are here to fight for, nor have they had a chance to refuse this service. Most of them would work for you gladly if you were to show them the truth."

Oanu liked the idea. She had expected to spend more time bringing Farne to realize a sense of duty toward the Tuon cause. She had not expected his smiling understanding of the rightness of the Tuon position.

With a quick affirmative nod, Oanu pushed a button and spoke into a silvery wire sphere, "Elpha, have the male prisoners brought to the assembly hall." Then beckoning to Hank to follow, she strode out through a circular door flanked by barbaric vases.

Soon, more than a thousand young Americans were assembled as Oanu had ordered. Like a mad dream, there they were, hundreds of modern American fellows, prisoners of a warrior race of women on a far planet, looking at scenes Earthmen hadn't seen publicly in six centuries.

The first image to appear on the huge circular screen was the medieval looking square in the fortress city of Harak, which they had just left in their attack on Lefern. The square was the market-place of the city, but no one traded there. They stood about a pyre of wood, staring at the figure that twisted its white face to God and back to Hell again. Fantastic flowing smoke clouds swirled above the victim as flames licked hungrily at tortured white skin that turned black and ran with bursting veins of scorching blood. The stake was high. The people circled slowly to see the woman's form that writhed, surging against the chains that bound her. The flames grew higher; the woman twisted slower like a sick snake. Her lips were stretched apart and her teeth clamped whitely on a tongue that streamed with blood, her blood. As the flames blew this way and then back again with the fitful breeze, the people swayed in unison to see between the licks of fire. Black smoke rolled low and took shapes that beat against the brain with fearful meaning. Fluttering birds streamed by and wheeled, and flew back whence they came, sensing the black coils of fear that were in that place. The dogs sat on their haunches, their red tongues lolled out dripping slow saliva on the worn pavings at the smell of the cooking meat of the living woman. Some of the priests of Hecate's evil worship strolled by muttering, their beads clicked in their hands. They did not bother to look at the familiar scene of torture.

More and more of these horror pictures followed until we learned Hecate's worship was, in effect, the ancient Inquisition still functioning with its rack and stake, its needlers and iron-maidens.

The rich-cultured, low voice of Oanu kept up a running commentary of the scenes we looked upon. A good quarter of the globe of Venus was under the domination of the Hag's followers. Many once beautiful cities like Mersepolis were now wrecks, inhabited by misery.

Mersepolis hung among the great golden trees called Redgans for the scarlet blooms they bore. Once its vast web of walks and bridges had bustled with the laughing throng of native Venusians and its maidens had been famous all over Venus as the most beautiful of any city. Now Mersepolis had been in the hands of Hecate's men for thirty years, and no longer thronged these walks with life. There were only plodding workmen in rags. There were a great many children, but most of them were extremely pale and listless. The bright colors and the semi-nudity that was their custom had been forbidden. They now wore a kind of over-

1454

all of blue and gray which was dress for the lower classes. Occasionally the black of the priests was seen, but rarely passed the gold and scarlet of the high priests, the inner circle of Hecate's empire. These were the blood-takers, the beings who lived on the blood of children.

Beside this city of Lefern, where the captive Americans watched the films depicting the cruelties and baseness of the Hagmen, there were twelve main cities on the continent which was the largest of the three large land bodies of Venus. Much of Venus is ocean, and much of the land is jungle. Of these twelve cities, Bruchion with its dazzling splendor, Rhacote, where the spires of the love-temples pierce the clouds, Panete, which was one huge building pierced by the trees that supported it and fronted by two rosy obelisks like great horns were of the Tuon race; all were Amazon cities and the most advanced culturally.

The three-towered city of Isis Phar had an inverted race of people living there of some strange culture—the men were like women and the women like muscular men. They were still free. The seven-columned city of Isis Loch was a neighbor of Isis Phar. Its people worshipped an ancient sea monster whose age no one knew. He was said to come in from the sea to answer their call.

There were seven cities in the south under kings—the kings were alleged to be immortal, but Oanu smiled as she explained them. These were called Alexan, Phys, Rhylat, Arsinoe, Delphon, Ekippe, and Nicosthene. And last, she showed scenes from Bubastison where the people are all one sex and could give birth by self-fertilization.

Of all these cities, only four had fallen to the Hag's intermittent warring, but over half of the land and the smaller communities had fallen to her warriors at some time in the past. These big cities, like Lefern had withstood all attempts to subdue them through the years, though one knew that they were always preparing for the next onslaught. Withal, it was a great land and rich and lush with life.

CENTURIES before, the Hag, with her evil crew, had come from Earth in the great and ancient spaceships, blasted out room for herself, and there sat in her fortress built by her slaves, brooding over the beauty of the world and hating it. From time to time she sent out warring expeditions, but this last one was growing into an attempt to subdue all of Venus. There were two reasons for this. The inner circle of blood-taking semi-immortals needed ever more and more children for their increasing demands as their number grew. And, there was an ever growing resentment of this same use of the children. This resentment had to be crushed before it became an organized power.

This was a bigger job than it would have been on Earth, for unlike the Earth people, the Venusians had known and learned to use the antique machinery of the God-race since the earliest times. Their science was a product of both their own work and the super science of the Ancients. On Earth only a few secret groups knew of the existence of the caverns and the weapons they contained. Since their science made the Venusians formidable antagonists, Hecate had contacted these Earth groups and was receiving men, supplies, weapons, and manufactured articles from them. In return she showed them how to delay old age by use of transfusions of children's blood.[3]

It was a disgusting, repulsive setup, and Farne realized that if Venus' free peoples fell, Earthmen would have no chance or hope of ever throwing off the evil leech that the secret ray groups would become with the Hag's methods of stealing children's youth. In time the Earth people would become what the Hag's people were, a slave population existing solely to support the priests and to furnish children whose blood would be used by the inner circles to prolong their horrible lives.

The hidden strong-hold, Disin, was the principal city of the followers of Hecate since the Hagmen came to Venus. The fortress City of Harak was the place our ship had landed. Under each of these cities, as under most of the cities of the raywise rulers, tunnels had been driven connecting them with the ancient cavern cities of the God-race and with each other. Bruchion, Panete, and Isis Phar of the inverted sexes had all fallen to the Hagmen

---

[3] Alexis Carrel in "Man the Unknown" says, "In medieval times the practice of transfusing young men's blood was widely spoken of and recommended."—Author.

recently. Isis Loch had just been reported captured. Lefern was the last place attacked and had surprised the Earth leaders with her able defense. But this was just the beginning of a long struggle for supremacy on Venus, Oanu well knew.

SOME scenes on the films were of the children farms kept by the inner circles of the Hecate cult. Those showed the chubby, well-fed infants of four and five years before they had been subjected to the blood transfer by the old members of the cult. Needles were inserted into the arms of these unfortunate children, then as a small pump drew the fresh, healthy blood from the child for the old man, his aged blood flowed into the child through a companion tube. The child remained hooked to the vampire for a month while the blood of each was exchanged for the other's. The child was allowed to eat his fill, but the vampire touched neither food nor drink during that period. The effect was miraculous for the old ones. Wrinkles almost disappeared, the flesh became firmer and the body began to grow in stature. At the same time the child rapidly showed signs of old age. Nor was the child released after one blood transfer. After several such sessions, his young body was allowed to recuperate and then was used again by the lesser priests.

This process of prolonging life had been brought to Venus from Earth early in the fourteenth century when the Rosicrucians drove out the Hagmen for their perverse use of the secret science. The practice had grown under Hecate, and now there were many men and women of the Hag's inner circle who were several centuries old.

So it was that a group of super-vampires, led by the Hag whose age no one knew, except that she had brought the original band from Earth five centuries before, endangered all the children of Earth as well as the children of Venus. For the older and the bigger the vampires grew, the more children were required to keep them in health.

At the beginning of this practice on Venus, the children were returned to the neighborhood from which they were stolen. But it wasn't long before the Venusians realized just what these little old people who had been carefree, healthy children, meant to their race. When several attempts were made to rescue the kidnaped children, the Hag doubled the guard on the baby farms, killed on sight anyone caught near them, and sentenced to death each child whose young body became so filled with the poison of age that they were no longer useful to the vampires.

One film showed the mother caverns. In great hospital-like rooms in hidden caverns, thousands of Venusian maidens were kept constantly pregnant, bearing more and more children for the baby farms. It was a revolting picture, this making cows of human beings, and the men from Earth who watched growled fiercely in their throats and clenched and unclenched their hands.

AS THE pictures of the baby farms unrolled before us, we saw the huge ogre-like body of the ancient witch out of the bloody past, Hecate, the Mother of Sin, strolling among the playing children, putting her mark of the Egyptian crossed circle with an electric branding iron on the arms of the rosiest and most active youngsters. Hot anger welled up in each man there. Hate flooded the assembly room. We wanted blood—Hecate's blood—her dying blood. We swore not to rest until the Hag was slain.

I wish I had sworn to stay several miles away from that same ogre-like body, for Hecate, the witch, still had a spell or two. But that came later.

Then came scenes showing the Hagmen burning the children who had reached the end of their usefulness as blood producers. These vampires found it more desirable to rid themselves of the prematurely aged youths and maidens, for their living presence was a perpetual reminder to the lower classes of the Hag's empire of the hideous nature of their rulers' parasitic life, feeding on the life blood of the people. So they were gathered together to a place called "The House of Life," so called to disguise its true purpose. Here they stayed for a short time, but daily dozens of them were taken into the cellars of the place and thrust living into a furnace. The furnace was a great iron statue of the God Moloch, whose worship the Hag had revived from her memories of Earth, to explain the burning of the children.

She taught that the ceremonial burning transported their souls to a children's heaven. The victimized people knew better, but they didn't dare talk openly against the thing, for the Hag was an old hand at getting rid of lowly opponents.

As we Earthmen saw more of the film unfold before out eyes, and realized what a horrible change the influx of the Hagmen brought to the beautiful life of these people, a thing surprising to Oanu happened. A chorus of cries arose: "Give us a chance, Amazons, let us fight for you against this thing."

The film stopped. The lights flashed on. Oanu stepped forward.

"Now you have seen the horrible system of life which you were blindly fighting for. For ages, on Earth, your own planet, such vampires have secretly existed unknown to you. It is one of the oldest and vilest practices of your Earth. We, the free white peoples of Venus, are the only force on the two planets who understand and fight this evil. Because of our knowledge of antique ray science, we are the only force that can fight against the Hag. If you want to cast your lot with us, and fight beside us for the future of your seed, for the future of all men against this destroying evil, you will be trained as our own soldiers are trained, and trusted until you prove unworthy of trust. If you choose not to fight for us, you face only the prison from which I summoned you."

The prisoners, Farne and I among them, rose as one man, shouting a Venusian word we had learned in the prison. "On! On!" The word was "yes" in Venusian.

So it was that the other prisoners, who had to a man chosen service under the Tuons, were trucked off to the military headquarters. At Farne's suggestion, Oanu kept him and me after the others had gone.

OANU was not a subtle person unless the occasion demanded it. She came to the point at once. Her voice was low and intense.

"We need spies. We have vast resources in man power, in the stores of antique weapons, as well as modern copies which we manufacture. But we need spies to tell us precisely what weapons the Hag intends to use. The study of these antique works is a very deep science. The Elder Race made many things for which we cannot discover the purpose. Some of these mysterious machines may well be weapons and it can easily happen that the Hag, from her centuries of experience with the God-work, may know of weapons which would wipe us out completely. If she, herself, takes a real interest in the struggle and throws herself into the battle seriously, she may bring into use mightly destructive mechanisms which we will not be able to counter."

Farne glanced at me with a knowing look, and then grinned. I guess I did look pretty silly—this spy business was way over my head. Seeing Hank grinning, I tried to grin back, but I was puzzled—with all the stuff I had seen, why the necessity for spies?

As if in answer to my unspoken question, Oanu continued:

"We must have someone find out what weapons they intend using in the crucial struggles yet to come. We have spies, but we get little information from the inner circles, and that is what we must have. Certain marks from the weapons they prepare for battle must be in our hands before the battle is joined. If we guess wrong, we will have no counter. It is this lack of vital information that keeps us from attacking the Hag. We do not know, as you Earthmen say, what her 'ace in the hole' may be."

"Where do we come in?" queried Farne.

Oanu answered bluntly: "You, Hank Farne, are perhaps the only man on Venus really fitted to act as a spy on the last arrivals from Earth . . . and vice versa, you are the only one fitted to spy on us for your former masters. So to avoid the latter, I intend to use you for the former."

Ragged as he was, Hank looked like a real courtier when he bowed and assented to Oanu's remarks, whether with mock dignity or not, I didn't know, but it sounded good.

"Whatever I can do, My Lovely Chief, I will."

"You profess to admire us Tuon women much. You will risk your life daily in this service, and if you prove true to us, one or more of us will be your reward. You should find that highly attractive for we on Venus have developed the art of love with the use of the ancient stimulation electric."

"At your service," grinned Hank, his snags of teeth showing, his eyes twinkling devilishly. "I'll take the job, and by Jupiter, I'll come back for the reward, too.

The reward of being first on your list," he said meaningly.

Oanu smiled on him. "If it is really me whom you admire, it can be arranged. You will be first on my list if you succeed, I promise you. But, remember, we take a new mate every year."

"AREN'T you two forgetting me," I interrupted. "Though I can only wonder at what possible use I can be as a spy."

"We have ways of making you capable of getting information for us. We need only your consent. Of course, your value to us is enhanced if you are equipped with knowledge of our ways as is Farne. Our methods have little to do with your present ideas of what is the work of a spy."

"A spy spies, doesn't he?" I asked, a little flip.

"No, he doesn't," patiently, Oanu went on. "I will explain. To make a spy, we insert a tiny radio transmission apparatus in the skull. This is done in such a way that the apparatus is not noticed even under penetrative vision ray. Your own knowledge of its presence and function will be erased from your mind so thoroughly that even the most exhaustive examination by the telaug will not uncover the fact that it's there. The memory cells in your brain carrying those thoughts will be themselves destroyed in your head by our penetray surgeons. We have a minute needle ray for just that purpose. The wound it makes heals in a day; the memory is gone forever. By hypnotic conditioning, you will think yourself a supporter of Hecate. You see, a spy does not know he is a spy. But a spy is very easily controlled by us from a great distance, by virtue of the same mechanism which broadcasts his thought to us."

I turned to Farne. "I don't follow her, Hank. What does she mean?"

"See," answered Farne, "she equips us with an invisible walkie-talkie, unbeknownst to us. It tells everything we hear or see all the time over an individual wavelength. Then, the Tuon Intelligence listen to our individual broadcasts and guide us by mental control into situations where we can pick up info. For all of which we get a soft break when we fall into Tuon hands again, and their controls keep us out of trouble among the Hagmen."

Oanu smiled at this, nodding. "I'm glad you think that way. We can do it, although the credit for the development of the wonderful piece of equipment that makes it possible, belongs to the Elder Ones. We found a few of them a long time ago in an ancient underground arsenal. Guessing that it was part of their war mech, we were finally able to divine its uses. I don't think they made very many, for there were only a few of them in the arsenal."

"WELL," I asked, "how does this thing work?"

"After we had discovered how, it was simple. All it is, is a miniature, ultra-powerful thought augmentor. With it, it is possible to control the spy completely—thoughts, emotions, and actions. But what makes it valuable is the way it augments the spy's thoughts and alters them so that they can't be read by an ordinary telaug. Through it, we can so control the spy that he is guided unconsciously into an advantageous position where what he sees and hears will be significant. By placing a large number of such robot spies throughout the Vampire outfit, every move the Hag makes will be known instantly here in Tuon Headquarters."

"Well, if it works the way you say it does," I spoke up, beginning to believe that she really knew what she was doing, "it certainly beats carrier pigeons!"

Oanu smiled condescendingly, then went on: "The 'spy-mech' is very much like those modern radios brought here to Venus by you Earthmen. Here, I'll show you one."

Walking to a far wall, she opened a small door and took something out. Coming back to where we stood, she extended her hand.

"Look," she said, "don't let the small size fool you. With this little thing we have the key to unlock the flood-gates of destruction on that detestable Hag and all her evil cohorts."

Neither Hank nor myself had ever seen the mech that she had been talking about so we both bent over to examine it.

"Why, that doesn't look like any radio," I protested, "that looks to me like a small half inch bit of flat bone or something."

"It looks like a piece of skull," Hank seconded.

"That is what it is supposed to look like," explained Oanu. "Notice the little jagged edges of the case—that is what looks like bone, the case. Well, those little jagged edges are fitted into a similar opening that our surgeons make in the spy's skull."

"Say," I protested, "don't tell me that we'll have to run around with that thing in our skulls!"

"It isn't as bad as it sounds," Oanu explained. "We only do it with the spy's consent. After that is obtained, a very delicate operation will insert this apparent piece of bone into your skull; it almost entirely replaces the bony section it is designed to resemble. When it is in place in your head it will look still more like a piece of bone. But within that deceptive bone is some of the most powerful and complicated appartus on all Venus. The case is of the same opacity as bone and nothing can be seen of its interior—not even a shadow, as the interior is made of materials transparent to the penetray, and their outlines are hidden by the shadow of the case.

I didn't see where any comment that I could make would do justice to the genius and skill that had made that originally, so I just nodded affirmatively, "Very clever, very clever."

"It is that," said Oanu, "and it is the only way that we know of that surveillance and intelligence work can be carried on where telaug rays read the minds continually and where the penetrays search every man for concealed weapons or enemy radio devices. There is practically no danger of discovery for nothing could possibly be noted except a slight portion of the skull which seems more opaque than the rest. And there is another advantage. The operations also splices certain nerve fibres fast to the receiver and transmitter so that your thoughts are instantly broadcast, and any commands given through the mech are immediately superimposed on your motor nerves. Thus, your actions can be completely controlled from this Intelligence center. And, too, we are able to protect you, whereas, we couldn't if you were free of any control. But, you will have to consent of your own free will."

"Well, if you say that is the way to lick the Hag," I said, "when do we start for surgery?"

"That goes for me, too," said Hank.

"Good! I thought that you both would agree to it—that's why I called you here to my office. You are going to become valuable operatives of our Intelligence, eligible for the greater rewards that recompense services of this type."

Then, she impulsively reached out to shake hands with Hank and me . . . a Venusian Warrior woman shaking hands. That over, she planted a big kiss on Hank's surprised mouth.

CHAPTER VIII

Now at the head of Hel's pale Host
Those livid armies of the lost
A giantess, all shameless, strode . . .
For Baldur gleams the beaker bright,
His seat is set by Hela's side;
Elvidner was Hela's hall,
Iron-barred, with massive wall;
Horrible that palace tall.
        From "Valhalla,"
        Julia Clinton Jones.

OUR uniforms gained us entrance to the city of Disin. Without knowing just why, we asked to be taken to Hecate. (Farne surmised that sometime in the past she had taken the name of the ancient Goddess Hecate. Her undeniable great age would lend overwhelming support to the idea of her ignorant followers that in medieval times she was Hecate.) The guards before the great drawbridge accosted us in antique Spanish—Castillian, it sounded to me. We only repeated the name of Hecate over and over, and finally the guard called a comrade and sent us down the labyrinth of passages.

I found myself greatly excited. We might see the living antique who really could be the ancient, infamous goddess of evil. At this stage of the game, nothing seemed impossible to me.

As we approached the inner sanctum, the guard with us was challenged time after time by the steel-cuirassed inner guards. With a few words, they permitted us to pass. Presently we stood before a monkish figure, white-haired and falsely benign of face, a gold chain his only adornment relieving the severe brown sweep of the cowled robe.

The fellow questioned us in an archaic form of English—sounds and words in a language that hasn't been heard since Cromwell's time:

"Ye have escaped the Tuons? Mayhap ye can tell me how it happens that of all the gear and war-ray sent against that accursed city, but ye two ray are able to find

1459

the path back?"

Farne spoke up quickly, probably fearing that I would put my foot in it, though neither of us really understood what had happened in the interval of time, as the memory had been obliterated from our minds by the Tuon medicoes.

"When the cables were cut at the time of the attack, we fell from the road into a huge bush. Looking out, we saw the other soldiers being made captive by the Tuons. We were afraid to stir from our hiding place for fear we would be taken too. After the Amazons left, we climbed down. To avoid capture, we left the open road, and not knowing our way, we have been lost in the forest. Some natives found us, and although we could not talk to them, knowing only English, they brought us here."

After several more such questionings, Farne and I were taken through more chambers. We were on our way to the Hag. We noted that everyone refered to her as "Mighty Hecate," that is everyone who had any sort of position in the fortress. However, those that feared and hated her called her "La Hag." But few of the lower classes even knew she had another name, for the lower classes all hated her. But when in her presence it was surprising to hear the many voices calling her "Your Mightiness," "Hecate, Our Goddess," "O Glorious Fount of All Wisdom" and other outrageously flattering salutations.

We marched down several gloomy corridors. Torches placed midway on the stone walls for illumination cast strange moving shadows like the small lighted candles do in a darkened church. More fourteenth century geared soldiers guarded the passages. The monk's rustling habit and the clack, clack of our footsteps echoed and re-echoed. Finally, we halted before a massive iron-banded, oak-beamed door. At a command from the robed figure, guards flung open the door.

SHE lay within the chambering transparencies of some old vitalizer mech. It was a tremendous thing pouring a flood of rich, golden rays over her great body. The emanations of these rays, striking the eyes, gave the illusion of beauty even to the Hag's hideosities. I knew how unspeakably pleasant just a touch of those golden rays could be, and guessed at the vast flow of infinite pleasure which such a flood of the potent gold must bring to the senses.

In spite of my better nature, my knowledge of the unutterable delight she controlled in the mysterious ancient stim machine made desirable the vast, brooding, terrible strength in that old, old body of hers. Vampire, she was, yet I felt a devouring interest in her. Like an unholy mass of putrid, pulpy flesh being born from a bud of a rose, something—something awful, and unclean—something in me rose horribly to destroy the last dying spark of decency in my brain—a brain that wasn't my own. I couldn't know it was the Tuon Intelligence women reading my mind and stimulating those thought to protect me from her savagery—and her unpleasant habit of killing whomever displeased her.

Now, Hecate was a sensitive reader of thoughts, her centuries of experience with the telaug rays and thought augmentors had given her memory such complete data that she knew the thoughts most men think as children know the multiplication tables. Give her a facial expression and she could build up a man's thoughts by deduction quite accurately. Beside this, always on watch around her were several aides at the old thought augmentive beams, reading every thought of every person and looking constantly for every possible approach of danger or opposition. When anything interesting came up, it was their custom to throw a trans-telepathic beam into the great one's head. Seeing liking for Hecate rise in me in spite of my will, these unseen watchers connected me instantly with the ancient mind, for they thought it amusing that this big foreigner should actually register love for her.

Looking at Farne, she saw the fear and understanding he had for her. She saw, as well, the compliance toward her. This the Tuons had superimposed upon Farne's thoughts to protect him Then her eyes returned to me, reading the strange emotion the Tuons had placed there. I knew she returned my interest from what happened. Perhaps the Tuons had not forseen this or perhaps planned on it, though I did not think they could wish the secret upon which all their intelligence work depended placed so dangerously close to the Elder-wise eyes of the Hag. But they were unable to change the course of events without too much maneuvering. Tuon caution or their inscrutable purpose cost me my soul.

THE Hag questioned both of us sharply as to the nature of the Tuon attack upon the small Earth army. Learning that it was gas that accomplished our complete defeat, she dismissed Farne to the care of her intelligence men for complete questioning. She kept me standing before her while she lay on the transparent couch of the ancient vitalizer mech. Here began a horrible phase of my life.

Hecate, the unholy Mother of Sin, the Ancient Hag herself, was looking at me with her yellow eyes blazing. The others had left the room. Those yellow, feline eyes burned upon me for a long time. She lay there fingering the black hair that coiled weirdly over great, rock-gray shoulders.

Suddenly, from the bank of instruments and controls before her couch, she played a ray over me which caused an excess of inner energy to make every muscle of my body stand out quivering.

"So," her peculiarly accented English, coupled with her deep voice tones rolled persuasively from the depths of the splendor of the ancient wonder work about her, "you find the terrible Hecate attractive. How is it that so young a man can find attraction in this great, ugly body?"

Simultaneously, she played another ray upon me, causing an intensely pleasurable stimulation of every sense of my body. A fierce emotion horribly not my own, but one which ruled me, nonetheless, surged up into being within me. Or was it myself . . . aroused and impassioned with a consuming curiosity by the vampire lure of this witch woman—a thing often written of—written by writers who had never felt the terrible conquering power of the real aura itself? I did experience that power. No man's mere will can buck a dynamo. I succumbed.

"I don't know," I heard myself mumbling, "O Mighty Ruler of this land on a planet strange to me, why I should love you more than other women. But you can read the truth in my mind."

Now Hecate had many male sycophants and paramours who would have done anything she desired, many slaves to choose from, but some perverse whim in the dark labyrinth of her mind made her want me. And anyone who knows anything of the science of stimulative and nerve control electric knows that I didn't have a chance once that whim grew into a full-fledged desire. My great size, my ignorance of the dark and evil life about me—what it was that intrigued her is hard to say.

I watched her huge form with eyes I could not turn away. Step by step I mounted the stairs under the flood of thickly golden rays, and erg by erg, the commanding pressure of mighty, overwhelming pleasure electric rose within my body. No man could have turned back from the ancient sugar coating of that bitter soul of evil. Then I stood beside her fascinated by those terrible yellow eyes that were neither human nor beast—like the faceted eyes of a female spider watching the approach of her mate, or the calculating, impersonal eyes of an octopus. All the untamed fierceness of such creatures lived in her eyes— their selfish will to live no matter what the cost to others—the ignorant soul of the she-tiger that eats her own cubs was in her character wholly. Those eyes, alive with the fire and the selfish wisdom of centuries of feeding on the young blood of children, burned into my own, hypnotically erasing every thought from my mind but the horrible joy that flowed through me and would flow more and more greatly if she so willed it. That synthetic joy—no less irresistible for being a product of a machine—flooded me, overpowering every natural impulse. Too, in my mind was the suggestion she put there, that through the prostration of my will to hers, lay the path to power as well as to strange, lost wisdom for me. I yielded—I failed—I lost myself in those strange arms.

SO it was that I became Hecate's thing, and stood behind her throne at the daily audiences of her ministers and her appointed rulers from the conquered cities. Always, I stood ready to her pleasure, and daily the clean, naturally good will in me died away, replaced by the insidious, inhuman electric of her control mech. Perhaps it was her doing and perhaps not, but the old mech placed an electric charge within me—in the tissues of my body which remained there like a new character. Daily the faraway Tuons heard through my mind what their ears were never meant to hear, and credited me with much valuable information on Hecate's plans.

As the time passed and my freedom became greater, I pieced together the facts and circumstances that had spawned Hecate. Some I overheard from lesser courtiers

—but most from the lips of the legendary Hecate herself.

Wise Mistress of the Ancient Wisdom—hellion goddess of abysmal evil and dissolution, she was 'Mighty Hecate' to her attendants; to the enslaved peoples under her heel she was the 'Limping Hag—the Mother of Sin.' The common, whipped people spat her name, 'The Hag'—but she was a filled-out hag, a human leech bulging with the blood of uncounted victims, and heavy for her size from the use of certain beneficial rays which were concentrates of certain vibrants from the gravitational flow. She explained later to me that much of her durability was due to this type of ray, that the blood transfers were supplemented by the rays. She obtained a vital and growth-promoting food supply from the veins of the young, but she obtained health and strength and the ability to absorb the blood of the young from the ancient integrative rays.

She had a deformity of one foot which gave her the limp that caused her to be known as the 'Limping Hag,' the devil's rival, partly because of the similarity to the devil which this foot imparted to her appearance. The foot was much smaller than the other. It seemed to lack the forward part, as though it had been lopped off about the center of the instep. On account of it, she looked more diabolical than nature intended, and it was easy to understand why to the common man she was the 'Limping Mother of Sin.'

TIME and unnatural growth had done strange things to Hecate. Centuries of indulgence of every kind had enlarged her lips; they were thick, full, and sensuous. Her smile was extremely wide and revealed oversized teeth like the fangs of a savage beast. Her nose, too, had grown out of proportion and was very long and sharply pointed. The burning yellow eyes and long black hair that just hung straight, uncurled, the huge mouth and enormous nose made up a face so different from that of ordinary man, she looked like another being. Ugly, even hideous, she was, yes; but a fierce vitality and a ruthless kind of sense was in her, giving her a weird dignity. A fear-impairing face it was.

Her hands gave the impression of strength and dexterity far beyond normal humans; the fingers were extremely long and strong, the knuckles large. Her hands could fly over the keyboard of an ancient force organ so fast that nothing but a blurred motion could be seen. It was when she was at work at one of these old mechs that her true witch-like character was apparent; her yellow eyes blazed intensely, wickedly, straight black hair swished and fanned out grotesquely on rock-gray shoulders. There was nothing of the decorative female in Hecate.

Yet there was a wild, savage attraction about this creature from the depths of the past. This living myth of ancient magic—she was alive. Evil had given her life—the hetacombs of children who had perished that she might live—all the endless cruelty she had practiced and believed in for centuries as efficacious policies to power, all this hung about her as an aura that caused fear and revulsion—these two things caused a confusion in the mind of men who met Hecate face to face. One feared her, was revolted by her, but one came to her as a moth comes to the flame. As for me, she left me no choice. I was to serve her in any way she decided. I did.

By black, unholy arts, Hecate worked over my mind regularly, telling me she was improving its setup. Actually, I think she reduced to impotence those parts of my mind which made me independent of her will. Needle X-rays cut the connecting nerve tissues. In time, Hecate made me a reflection of her will. Without spoken words I was obedient automatically to every slightest wish of her mind, evil as it might be. Hecate had gained such control over my being that I was just another part of her body, an extension as obedient to her will as were her own fingers. But she did not know that at any time the tiny instrument the Tuons had placed invisibly in my skull could become my master, ruling me more thoroughly than she herself.

Why did the Tuons not cause me to kill her? Because there was no real chance; there were the watchers about her always, reading any alien thoughts. The Tuons bided their time.

THE months went by. The armies gathered and drilled. The tremendous war mech of the ancients was dragged from the caverns and mounted on great trattors. Another expedition, this time calculated to crush utterly any possible defense that might be prepared against us, was nearly ready to launch against the beautiful city of Lefern of the Amazon Tuons.

Some part of me, the decent me, still lived on within my mind, helpless to the horror I was fast becoming, weakly shuddering at the daily tortured deaths of captives in which the Hagmen delighted and with which Hecate saw no reason to interfere, although I believed she was tired of such performances. This still living part of me was powerless to struggle against the evil that overwhelmed me.

I learned to handle the intricate pleasure ray aparatus, the stimulative and beneficial generators of an endlessly variant number of electric rays and energy flows; the whole myriad of involved apparatus which the ancients had left intact and indestructible behind them. I learned to handle all these things under the tutelage of the most experienced hand on two worlds—Hecate herself, who had had seven or eight centuries to learn the art of the ancient ray.

Always, of course, I practiced this art upon the body of Hecate, my new Queen ... the unthinkably ancient art of stimulating—and feeding—the sensation nerves of a living body with electric flows from the antique, cave-held mechanisms. Somehow, through the ages of time, the Elder Race had learned to nurture and stimulate the human senses by using hydrogen ions bearing certain vital nutrients, carried by beneficial, ionizing electric flows.[6]

Accustomed as she had become to it in the long centuries, Hecate's giant body absorbed the floods of 'ben' like a dry sponge. She was the one that received—and she was the one that controlled—always. I practiced on the ancient mech with the Hag in complete control of my mind—I was but the tool of her will.

---

[6] From "A Bipolar Theory of Living Processes" by Geo. W. Crile, *page 13, paragraph 3.*—"Hydrogen ions permeate all living organisms. The slightest change in the hydrogen ion concentration fundamentally alters the organism; and it is known that hydrogen ions are of high electrical significance."

Page 214, paragraph 2.—"In living organisms an acid alkali balance on opposite sides of the dielectric films (surrounding all cells) is maintained by a difference in the concentration of H- and OH-ions."

Page 46, paragraph 1.—"The constant oxidation of the lipoid films of the globules would meet the hydrogen ion-electric potential requirements of the cell."—Author.

She conceived a sort of affection for me, and I found myself imbibing strange and potent fluids, even submitting to regular transfers of the baby blood into my veins without a murmur—the Elder Goddess of Evil Incarnate, Hecate, had removed the cause of any such murmur from my mind.

Her former favorites were, of course, wildly jealous of me or greatly relieved, whichever the case might be, but none of them could carry out any plans against me for fear of her anger. All knew Hecate's anger was usually fatal.

STROLLING beside the giantess with the evilly smiling face through the gardens of the baby farms became a regular part of my life—and not the most revolting part, by far. These walks we took had a sinister purpose—not the romantic thing that lovers feel—but the selection of child blood donors. This hideous life that I walked beside, selected the rosiest and healthiest children, placing her personal mark indelibly upon them for her future personal use.

This mark was done with a small electric branding iron. The seal of Hecate, a circled cross above a serpent, was burned deep into the child's flesh, and that child, from then on, was the personal property of the Limping Hag.

I was as oblivious to the children's howls of pain as I was to the screams of the men and women who daily died before her throne or in the grisly dungeons that underlay the whole stronghold of Disin. I was a man walking in my sleep.

In her gentler, more mellow moods, Hecate was wont to confide her plans to me, her ambitions and her memories of long, gone days. During one of these periods of relaxation, she said:

"You see, My Muscled One, long ago I was young and ambitious, an acolyte of the Rosicrucians. Well, I had a way with men, and some of the inner circle of the order were reputed to be immortal. I wanted that secret—that deeply-guarded secret. I schemed and planned ... connived. I flattered, ogled the senior priests until at last my chance came.

"One day, they left me alone with the records and I found it, how it was done— this fighting age with young blood. I learned why it was secret, too. There is a great deal to know about this method of using children's blood for one's own veins, drugs to add to the fluid to keep it from clotting and causing death. One must even learn why people grow old, in order to avoid the foods that cause age, learn how the sun causes age by throwing bits of its fiery self at us in the yellow light, learn how these bits of ever-fire gather in the body from the water and from the meat we eat. I studied how to prepare water free of the terrible poison from the sun and how to feed a child and take the child's blood into the veins instead of food into the mouth, so that the poisons gather in the child and the cleaned blood of the child brings food to one's body free of the cause of age. All these things I learned by giving myself to those old priests, by being pleasant and useful to them—keeping my mouth shut so that none of them ever got into trouble through me . . . or suspected my real purpose—stealing their greatest secrets for my own use.

"Since that time, many tired centuries have passed and I have learned more than any other living person." The unfathomable pits of Hecate's eyes seemed to focus in infinity. She shrugged.

"But I have become a horror and a plague to men, for I must have the blood of their children—and I will have it—for my plans are too great to be abandoned for any of their infantile emotions or virtues.

"I have learned by the study of their writings, how the Gods lived—the Elder Race who built these vast machines and endless caverns, and I have decided to follow in their footsteps."

At my startled glance, she nodded, smiling, "Yes, Tender One, I know where they went—I know why they went away from this accursed sun that makes a horrible blight of all the growth in life—the treacherous sun that lets men grow intelligent . . . only to die before they learn enough to become great.

"This life is but a faint dying echo of that mighty past. A little living reflection of a great fierce time when men were Gods, and the Gods living men, so heavy they sank ankle deep in the solid rock. Look at that machine."

OBEDIENTLY, I went over and examined the great ray-gen mech she indicated. There were many prints of feet in the rock, inches deep, overlapping. It was true . . . the Hag was right! That solid granite was but soft muck to the feet of those heavy men of the past.

"I've noticed these prints before about the caves," I said to Hecate. "You mean to tell me those men were so heavy they sank into solid rock as though it were soft clay?"

"Turn on that switch in front of the machine," Hecate directed, watching me with indulgent interest.

I reached out a hesitant finger and pushed the lever down to its lowest mark. A hum came from the heart of the mysterious old mechanism. A strange force gripped me . . . stronger and stronger. My knees sagged with a great weight bearing down upon me, but, strangely, the presence of the weight was an exhilarating thing.

"That is the beneficial force which causes the world itself to grow. It is the force of gravity focused and refined into an integrative force which is now making every part of your body denser and much stronger," Hecate explained as the weight forced my legs into a greater crouch to bear the strain.

As she watched me, grinning her fierce, big-toothed smile, the heavy, penetrative, intensified gravitational ray made every bone in my body stand out distinctly. Like a man of glass, every organ and bone was outlined glowingly.

Suddenly, the Hag started and rushed toward me, a great fear on her face. She seized my head and looked closely at the back of it under the strong penetray.

"What is that dark bone in your head!" she shrieked, "What are those wires and metal I see inside?"

I disclaimed all knowledge of what she meant, which was not acting, for the Tuons had removed all trace of this mental apparatus insertion in my skull from my memory. After a close examination of the thing in my head, she called an aide—Enora—showed her the thing in my skull, and ordered her to find out just what it was and what data they might have on such a thing. Then, apparently dismissing the thing from her mind, she went on explaining her plans to me . . . for, now she meant to include me in those plans.

I LISTENED intently, for her mind was the oldest on two planets, sunk though it was in the sin of many lifetimes. Something of the girl that once had been so long ago—something of the good ambition that burns in all men seemed to burn fitfully within her, although in her continually recurring rages, every good she might do was wiped out.

This something . . . some of the primitive will to survival of the race, still lived in her . . . though it could accept the bleeding process that stole the lives of children to give itself life, accept the burning of these same children to hide the deed from the people, could not accept the idea of all that life used for no purpose.

She consoled herself with the thought that she would be equal someday to the ancient Gods whose work she knew so well and had puzzled over for so many centuries. This plan of power she talked about with me at times, though I was hardly a part of the conversations. She was so used to controlling those about her that automatically I made the answers she expected to hear without volition of my own. In truth, I was not myself at all, but only a reflection of her thought augmented by the great tubes of the telemach until her thought controlled me, unconsciously to us both.

She knew that in the early days of earth's history just after the two races of Gods had left earth and while the mechanisms of the cavern cities were still comparatively new, men had become practically immortal by the rays of the mech alone, without her device of blood-stealing from children. She had, in ancient forbidden records of the Rosicrucians, found accurate accounts of these first cities in the days of the latter Gods. Then, such cities as Asgard were numerous on earth, though the tales of Asgard are almost the only ones to survive. In these cities were conditions such as are described in the Niebelunglied . . . where the heroes of Valhalla could not be killed, but were put back together and healed under the beneficial rays of the healing palaces left by the God-race. She knew that these accounts were not legends, but were the truth.

In those far gone days, the secret rulers of the abandoned cities of the Gods sent their maidens out in flying craft to pick up the best of the dead bodies, for they were very human, even though long-lived. They pitied the dead, as well as had a vast need for fighting men in their own wars. The dead men were revived by the magic of the ancient healing vital rays, and entertained regally, as the legends tell us, by all the devices the God-race had developed through ages of study of life. Such latter Gods as Odin, Wotan, Zeus, she knew to have been ordinary men who had used these vital rays to become virtually immortal. She suspected that they had studied the writings of the God-race and had gone in search of the Gods themselves to avoid the death—the death from the sun—the inevitable fate of all on Earth. This was her ambition, to follow in their footsteps and learn to search space.

TO DO that, she had to build an organization capable of searching every bit of the caverns for data on space travel and on the ancient ships, for those they used were fractious at high speeds, and the men who skippered them could neither repair them nor could they chart a straight course through space. They could only drive the old ships by the seat of their pants, by trial and error. Long as they had been using the old ships, for some six centuries and more, they had learned little about them. Space travel is a science which cannot be learned from modern science, but only from the very ancient records of the builders of the ships. And none existed who could truly read the ancient writing—the very concepts that fit the symbols they used are long dead on Earth and Venus. Trouble and wars with the peoples she despoiled for their children's blood ever kept her from her true desire—mastering the science of space travel and building ancient ships so that far space could be traveled at the high speeds the ancients had used.

This always sounded very big and noble . . . as though she were concerned with the progress of humanity. I am tempted at times to concede that occasionally she really and sincerely was the philanthrophist that her talk would lead you to believe . . . though centuries of an unnatural existence doesn't make one so soft and loving. She lived on the raped blood of children, and the next moment talked of pursuing the gods for their secrets of eternal life for the people whose young blood she ravished.

Any woman is a mass of contradictions, but in Hecate all the contradictions had a bloodly result. Her hands were bloody almost from the time she suckled at her

1465

mother's breast, and rivers of thick, bubbly blood had followed in her wake from that day forward.

As the Mighty, Gory-handed Hag herself tells the tale . . . I think that she told it to those paramours who had preceded me . . . though where they were is hard to say. Dead, probably. She tells . . .

Of a sunny land bordering on the azure shore of the Mediterranean. A far off land on a far planet . . . far in space, and what man, save the Hag herself, can say how far in Time?

In a tiny village, there was born to a poor couple a child, their fourth, and the third girl. Much like any other child, her birth was not remarked, and she grew and played with her sisters. Her parents, as people in those days did, went on having children. The sun rode smiling across the blue bowl of heaven, day followed night. She was fourteen. Her sisters were a dozen, her brothers three. Their clothes were a simple woolen wrap, their feet bare, and their limbs long and brown and bare. Their only trouble was their stomachs which were never quite full. The fields were stony, they worked, but the food was never quite enough.

TODAY, is a holiday, the little town is full of the people from their homes in the near hills. A sheepskin or a wolf pelt is the men's attire, while the women wear short woolens in bright colors. They have flowers in their hair. The brown, strong children run and shout, the girls go by in groups, arm in arm, chattering shrilly, or racing across the grass in flight from the pursuing youths, who chase and catch them, rough their hair, dip them in the stream or roll them down the slopes. The games go on in the circle near the temple continually, short races, practice with the discus and javelins, mock battles. People come and go, watching the games—strolling through the village—talk and motion and laughter —brown clean limbs, curling hair, bright faces and shining teeth—the people of the tiny village are having a holiday.

The temple is old, but bright with this year's many colored paints on the frescoes and sculptured ornaments on the pediments and capitals. Flowering trees droop before the wide steps by the deep path. Men and women with solemn faces come and go reverently, bearing wreaths and food to the Goddess. Before her dreaming, mysterious face, they bow to the floor, peering through the dimness at her polished form, and lying in imploring attitudes on smooth stones.

This day, Hecate did not race madly past the pillared doorway to meet the youths in the woods, but paused and looked long at the temple's dark coolness. Something drew her, and her white face with its twisted drooping lips that were too ripe, too red, and her yellow eyes that held those strange depths lit up by some hidden thought within her. She went in from the warm sun, into the coolness and stood looking at the pale limbs of the Goddess, at the pedestal of many sculptured breasts, at the figures that moved about the walls in a pale pictured life of their own. This reverence and worship awoke a rage within her. In contrast to the prostrate forms of the villagers, she stood erect with hands clenched and teeth grinding inaudibly as she gazed about. If she could, she would have toppled over the tall stone Goddess, kicked the offerings out the door, torn down the paintings. Why was she raging inside, she wondered. Why does this thing that filled the dark air with love and fragrance fill her with despair and hate?

A red mist came into her thinking, a shuddering over her limbs. She moaned in agony and ran from the temple, not stopping until she crouched alone in a thicket in the woods. A hunger was in her, her throat was dry, her palms burned. What would fill her, ever? The red fog that was her thinking grew thicker, her mouth dropped open, her white teeth ground together. She slunk through the woods like a dark-eyed and bloody-mouthed ghoul, hunger was in her and her red lips shone with drool. What this hunger was she did not know, but it drove her on.

A soft bleating came to her ears. She saw by a pool not far off, some sheep with their new young lambs. Stealthily, she approached, her body sinuously hugging the ground like a great cat, though there was no need, for the sheep, startled, galloped off in bawling flight. But under her lay a soft throbbing little body clutched in her arms, its stick-like legs thrashing at the grass. She bent the square little head back sharply. The great soft eyes rolled toward her in piteous terror and something in her exulted and feasted avidly upon the helpless fear.

IN HER hand was a little glass knife, a long sliver, its handle wrapped with twine. Slowly she drew its shining edge across the woolly neck, quivering in ecstasy as the blood welled out and down her arm. She held the lamb's head tightly. The round, black eyes rolled madly. It struggled to bleat, but she held the mouth, it could only moan sickly in its throat. She bent and drank the hot blood, drank and drank until the hunger died away and her heart stopped throbbing against her ribs. The lamb was quite still; its little feet were limp and strained no longer.

She rose, left the still heap, and went to the pool and washed herself, combing her hair and making herself like other girls again. Then, she strolled back through the trees again, her eyes sleepy, her lips satiated, her body relaxed. The herdsman would think some fox or other creature killed the lamb.

Now the night lay sadly about her. Her sisters slept fitfully, arising often to drink, while her father snored a tiresome plaint into the dark. A hunger was in her again. It was days since she killed the lamb. A compulsion came into her veins, her palms were dry, her throat constricted. Her eyes burned into the blackness, but it burned back at her. Softly she crept, snakelike across the floor until the warm softness of her little sister's body was against her breast. In her hand she had the sharp piece of glass, a thread cutter from the spinning. The tiny one sighed a little, turned against her. Hecate parted the dark hair, baring the thin neck, and with the glass made a quick, deep slit. She filled her throat with the warm blood, holding the soft little head fiercely, her hand over the struggling mouth. After a long time, the body ceased its struggle, but she held it for the leisure of the stillness, and the sweet trickle down her throat. At last the hunger left her and she crawled back to her pallet and slept.

In her sleep she dreamed—dreamed of the good feel of a full stomach—the pleasant warmth of a cheery fire when the heavens outside are weeping. And other things she dreamed—of stars and planets—and strange peoples—and the dreams of never growing slow and wrinkled and old—a dream wherein she was a god.

Vampire spawn of Earth that she was, she could still talk of her God quest—and with supreme indifference be the cause of torture and death. Torture and death with a motive. And her motive was always the immortality of Hecate, the Limping Hag. Nothing that went on in her fortress did so without her approbation.

ONCE, walking in some of the lower chambers, I idly paused to watch a fine-looking old gentleman being broken on the wheel. I had so sunk into my role of the Hag's favorite that the sight of agony and hideous death howls left me with only a slight thrill of pleasure. But, this day, for some reason I wondered at the cause of this man's being racked.

Nodding to one of the Earthmen members of the Hag's forces, I inquired as to the reason for it.

The answer was astounding when I grasped it . . . the still human part of me was astounded, I mean.

The Earthman looked at me strangely—my position as the Hag's favorite would indicate that I should know. He shrugged his shoulders, then said. "He was manufacturing a steel 'beam' on Earth and planning to sell it widely. A steel beam in their midst would detract from our ancient moral standing."

The Hagman laughed at his cryptic speech and walked off. I pondered awhile, then walked up to the man sweating in a death agony. He was an Earthman—a high type. An intellectual head he had, and long fingered hands. A beautiful specimen of the highest type of Earthman, though he was broken and bleeding now.

I knew that the antique rays was made of what was called the Elder Metal. That was what he had meant by "beams." I realized then what that secrecy cost the peoples of Earth in engineers and others . . . the secrecy of the ancient mech buried in the caves beneath our feet, though at the time I was too much under the Hag's influence to care. This man was evidently an engineer or a physicist who had been making a ray using a kind of steel that was nearly as good as some of the antique "beams." He had been taken captive and shipped to Venus for final disposition . . . the ancient, brutal wheel a reward for his fine effort for the future of man. These hidden rulers of Earth and the Hagmen—the Hag herself—had no use for such a man but to crack his bones. I understood the whole thing much better. It still goes on.

At another time I was standing in an apartment of Hecate's noticing some very beautiful figures of women. They were very realistic—colored like life. Curiously, I touched one of the beautiful nudes. It was not stone but had a "give" to it—like a firm cushion. Looking closer I saw that the figures were literally stuffed women! Once they had been beautiful living creatures . . . creatures vibrant with the surge of life. Whether they had incurred the wrath of Hecate, or merely that she had coveted their bodies, so much lovelier than her own bulky carcass, I never knew. But the Hag had them now, permanently . . . had them stuffed and decorating her chambers, like the trophies of a hunter.

This . . . this was Hecate, the Mother of Sin . . . my unlovely, all wise Mistress who was telling me of her plans to pursue the Gods Themselves with me at her side.

CHAPTER IX

"Expect that by such stairs as these," thus spake the teacher, panting . . .
"We must depart from evil so extreme:
. . . I raised my eyes,
Believing that I Lucifer should see
. . . but saw him now
With legs held upward. Let the grosser sort,
Who see not what the point was I had past
Bethink them if sore toil oppressed me then.
—The Divine Comedy

UNDER the combined influence of the Tuon intelligence that directed my every action, and the spell of Hecate's marvelous ancient mech, the incident of the discovery of the dark bone in my head was forgotten . . . even my Evil Mistress had, seemingly, dropped it. We were languidly tasting the delights the ancient "stim" possessed in limitless streams.

Suddenly the quiet spell broke.

Shattering precedent of ages, Enora flung aside the drapes covering the door, and, with the shortest of salutations, rushed to the couch of Hecate, yelling hysterically, "It's an old spy device, Oh Hecate! A spy device of the Ancient Ones—it broadcasts a man's thoughts!"

The shrill tones had hardly died in the room when the Tuons made the move they'd deferred for so long. Like a switch had been thrown, I was galvanized to action. I had nothing to do with it. A powerful compulsion seized me. Leaping between the two huge women, I swung a terrific sleep-inducer at the smaller and closer one which happened to be the aide. I connected powerfully—with a brick wall. That old bag had been under the integrative ray too much—soft and fluffy like a chunk of concrete! I yelped—thought I'd broken my hand!

Instead of folding up like she should have, she didn't even grunt—just looked at me, all the time tugging frantically at the gun bolstered at her side. Boy! I had to think fast. If she got that little playtoy out it would have been all over for me—except for flowers and slow music. I stepped back, my hand feeling like it was broken in a hundred places, my eyes on that wicked little magnetic dissociator that forever nullifies the tiny magnetic charges that hold all matter together. I had no desire to go up in smoke, for love of the Hag or anything else

(I never will know what kept that thing sticking in her belt. In the years that I had seen and used the hellish weapons of the caves, I had never before seen one that didn't function smoothly. Maybe the Gods love my big baby face.)

When you neck feels the breath of the Grim Reaper, thoughts that take minutes to relate, race through your mind like lightning—that's the way I wondered why Hecate hadn't taken a hand in the thing—so I looked and there was the big cow, hurriedly pulling her massive bulk over to the bank of controls.

"Oh, oh," I thought. "Here's where little Jimmy gets what is known in some circles as 'the works'—gotta do something—with haste."

I moved in on the aide. She wasn't too hep to Earthly "rassling," so when I rammed one leg behind hers and heaved with my shoulders, the old battle-axe went over like an iron balloon. She hit the floor and went sprawling—the gun getting loose and skiding away from her. I grabbed it—too late.

HECATE was still one jump ahead of the opposition. She'd gotten to the mech's control panel and the jig was up. Before I could level the dis-gun at her and

1468

THE HIDDEN WORLD

fire, a beam sprang out of the great old machine, stopping me cold, the surging power of Hecate's beam freezing the will that coursed from the antique spy-mech in my head.

I stood still. A living pawn. Two ancient machines fighting silently for control of my body. The Tuons were doomed to fail from the first. They were matching skill with the sharpest hands on two planets, and for all I know, the best mech artist on all ten worlds.

I couldn't think. I was just aware of what was going on. Then, shortly the huge old mech under Hecate's flitting fingers slowly gained the upper hand. I guess the Tuons were too far away to last too long.

Like a puppet on an invisible string, I moved toward the Hag, seated at the control panel. I was numbed or I guess I'd have gone mad at the hell-fire flashing out of those proud, angry eyes. The very hate of hell was burning into mine as I stepped up to her and meekly handed the dis-gun to her—as SHE willed.

Something—an affectionate banshee, or the gods, stayed the awful anger that had destroyed hosts of abler men than me— and for a lot less, too.

She looked at me for a long, long moment, then summoned some of the guards that never were far from her. They and the aide who had picked herself up off the floor by this time were commanded to wind me with certain coils of wire. They were experts at that sort of thing because in a matter of seconds I was tightly wound round and round with many turns of wire and hustled off to the cells in the huge prison under the city of Disin, a prison, incidentally, from which there is no record of anyone's returning alive.

I'll never know . . . and it's cost me many a night's sleep trying to figure it . . . just what the Limping Hag WOULD have done to me if . . .

THAT night a soft hiss that wasn't caused by the vermin made me sit up on the crawling mat I was on. I held my breath . . . listening.

The door slowly opened . . . very slowly, not making a sound. The lock had dissolved in a puff of dust or smoke like that which had almost claimed me earlier that day.

An apparition from a drugged nightmare entered the cell . . . a tall column of barely heard hissing noise, yet I knew that the noise meant something or somebody.

The column of sound seemed to bend in the middle, bending in my direction. The sweat stood out in cold beads on my forehead. I thought: "This it it—Hell. What a way to die, in a stinking little cell . . . alone."

Then, like the chorus from a basket of snakes came a louder hiss, a hiss that I recognized as a voice . . . and I knew that voice.

"You big baboon!"

"Ceulna!" I moaned, both because my bonds were paining me and because of the shock of hearing her voice here under what I knew was an enemy city. "Ceulna, beautiful, what are you up to? You shouldn't be here, you———?"

"Ask me no questions, you overstuffed baboon," she cut me off. "You plaything of a hyena's daughter . . . you fancy fool for that spawn of hell. Oh, you're impossible! You're not worth the trouble I take."

I tried to say something, but she commanded, "Shut up. I'll talk for you."

She was most explicit. "Here, put this on and keep quiet!" Somehow I felt like a married man caught in delinquence. I had not known Ceulna gave a damn for me until she bawled me out that night. But, oh brother, what a job she did, then. Nothing could have been better calculated to bring my sleeping self back to life. She cut my ropes and slid some soft, rustling stuff over me and fastened the two whirling discs about my shoulders, then, walking through the door, she disappeared from my senses. I followed. The faintest possible whirring was the only guide my senses could find to tell me where Ceulna had gone. I followed that faint shadow of a sound that was she, and passed a dozen dead guards, great holes of nothingness where the center of their stomachs should have been. When Ceulna killed someone, she killed them.

MILES later, my unaccustomed feet stumbling after Ceulna a thousand times more anxiously than they had the first night I met her, I caught up with her.

"For God's sake, Ceulna, tell me something."

"You keep quiet, you overgrown lady

1469

killer, you— Of all the men Ceulna could have on two worlds, she had to want you, the only one that would be fool enough to fall into Hecate's arms. It would be better if you were dead. Keep still, we are still in danger."

I swear we walked ten solid miles, and I could get nothing out of Ceulna but violent recrimination. Then, in those gloomy, forever dark caverns, we came upon, of all things, an electric car that I swear was built on Earth, and recently. We got in, in silence, and due to those suits, in non-existence, apparently.

Two hours later, we were mounting in an elevator toward the city of Lefern above. She told me that much. Going into the buildings that I knew were upper Lefern from the rustling leaves outside, she led me into an apartment that I recognized as her personal living place, for the dancing costumes hung in the transparent closet, and the little globe of the kind she had shown me on Earth in the secret caverns rested on a low table. She must have gotten another one. Everything in the room said, "The graceful, lovely, Ceulna lives here." I was immensely glad to sink into a huge chair and just look at her. A great load had lifted from me, and although I was not able to think clearly anymore, I knew I was home.

CHAPTER X

The Veline fountains, and sulphureous Nar
Shake at the baleful blast, the signal of the war.
Young mothers wildly stare, with fear possessed,
And strain their helpless infants to their breast.
                                    Virgil's Aenid.

CEULNA was still boiling. "For months," she stormed, "I have watched you over the augments, listening to you make love to that living slime, that giantess of the abyss, that compound of baby's lives and selfish will. And when you get in trouble, who gets you out? I have to! You big blundering oaf, you wasted effort of a mistaken mother. What are you, anyway?"

"Ceulna," I said slowly, "I am angry myself at myself for all that I have lived through. But, I swear I could no more help myself than fly. I am more happy to see you than anyone could explain. It even makes me happy that you should be angry. I didn't know I meant anything to you. Now I know you care for me. Since you have read so many of my thoughts, you must know what I feel for you, though I have not had much time to think about it."

"That's another thing. All this time in the arms of the ugliest woman on two planets, and you haven't even thought of me, and now you say you care. Bah! And I risk my neck for you. Oh, why are women made that way? If there was a man, a real man wanting me, I would go out of my way to be nasty to him. Why? But just let a big self-centered oaf like you who does not even think of me get himself in trouble, and I nearly lose my neck to pull him out of the toughest prison on Venus. Well, say something, you bovine paramour of an old witch, aren't you even grateful?"

"Why are you so angry, Ceulna? Because it makes you so beautiful with your green eyes flashing and your face flushed, or because it is a reaction from worrying about your man so long? If that's it, come here and I'll show you something."

She moved closer and I wrapped my too-strong arms about her and she started to cry. "From now on, Ceulna," I started to soothe her, "I'm your man; you bought my life with your courage and it's yours. It's yours to do what you want with it."

After crying for a long time, she began to explain. "When the Hag put you down there, I knew it would only be a day or so until some of those hangers-on who have been wishing for your place in her so-lovely arms, her so-sweet embrace, would find a way to do away with you, and much the lovely ogress would have cared what happened to you. She does not like to be made a fool, even if you couldn't help it. I asked Oanu for the suit of invisibility. They are very rare and little known, but there are a few found now and then in sealed compartments in the old dwellings. Only the ancient secret-service owned them, so there are not many. They cannot be detected by an ordinary ray, unless it strikes one directly, and the only way such a feat could have been accomplished. They nullify all vibrations leaving the body. But how to get there without walking all the way? We finally decided to use the electric car, after covering all the wires and motor with material taken from another suit of invisibility. Well, it worked. We have maps of every bit of the old caves and it was simple to find a way into the part where the prison has been built. I doubt if they have such maps themselves. It was simple, yes. But this does not mean that you are forgiven. Later, maybe."

"BUT I don't understand how you came to have such influence here and how you got them to help you. How come?" I asked her, just to hear her voice again.

"I earn what I get here. They were glad to have me when they found that I knew of Earth-ray and of Hecate. I drew a very high allotment of credits for my work. When Oanu learned that I knew you, she put me in the group who watched and controlled the unconscious spies who are equipped with the device which is still in your skull. So, I know all about you, you vampire's plaything. You . . . !" In spite of herself, Ceulna was forced to laugh at my lugubrious expression. So she laughed and was soon in my arms again, crying softly. If I had known how Ceulna felt about me, I would not have been so ready to leave Lefern for our enemies' hospitality and for the arms of the oldest and ugliest woman on two worlds.

As I sat with Ceulna in my arms, enjoying the happiness and relief that she had brought to me, Oanu came in. She looked at us, a peculiar smile on her face. Ceulna did not rise, and I couldn't with her in my lap. But Oanu understood. She sat down, lighting one of the purple cigarettes of Venus.

"It is too bad that this love I see before me had to be dragged through the slime by Hecate," she said in better English than I had heard from her before. "If either of you had mentioned your acquaintance to me when you were here before, I would have brought you together. Then, all this could have been avoided. But it is over now. Our armies are gathered in the caverns under Disin and you and Ceulna will each lead a detachment. Your knowledge of the place should prove most useful. Within a few hours we will be ready. You had better refresh yourselves, then join your section. There is little time. It will not be long before Disin is in our hands. Simultaneously, the other cities in Hecate's hands will be struck in the same way from below, and, fortune favoring, we will end this vampire horror on Venus.

"Thanks to your efficient love-making," Oanu grinned slyly at me, "we know every weapon that Hecate will use against us, and have prepared the counter weapons according to the ancient war-ray books. Before Hecate realizes that we have this information, we strike, for she will deduce from the incident of the instrument in your head that we do have such information. So the time is *now!* We have her figured out and an overwhelming counter-attack prepared for anything she may use. Her methods are no longer a mystery as they used to be to us, nor can she have a surprise for us."

"Oanu, something has been troubling me ever since the day I fell into Hecate's hands. I asked her several times, but she always put me off. Where is Hank Farne? I haven't seen him since the day we were both questioned by Hecate."

"Farne has been idling in Disin. No one gave him anything to do, and no one harmed him for they feared you would hear of it. Hecate would not let him see you as she feared his influence over you would turn you against her. You will probably see him if we succeed in the coming attack," was Oanu's answer.

THOSE Amazons didn't pay much attention to me; I was politely told that I was boss of our group of thirty track-rays, much the same type that I had learned to handle under the Earth-ray-men. That boss-stuff was mere fiction, for I couldn't even talk their lingo well, and could hardly understand them. But they did pay attention to business. Through all the many dusty caverns leading to Disin, I knew that similar columns were racing madly toward the city of the vampires. The idea was to get there as soon after our discovery by their rays as possible. I realized that this attack had been caused by the necessity springing from the discovery of the spy-radio, in my head when I was with Hecate in her apartments, for she would guess just about how much we had learned of her plans and would change her whole campaign. To catch her in the midst of the confusion caused by this change was the reason for our attack. Also, there were many valuable men like Farne in the Hagmen's midst who would be killed if the attack failed. The old telepath-radio apparatus in their heads would be their death warrant now that Hecate knew what they were, and where to look for the apparatus.

In front of us vibrated the great fans of the black shorter rays, ready to ground any

1471

beam they might throw at us. Lumbering behind the fans came the light tanks such as my own group, and behind them came larger and larger war-ray. All focused on a predetermined spot in Disin—that spot the place where the great general ro-control with which Hecate ruled the city had its intricately cabled, myriad beamed, and electric-eyed being. This apparatus Hecate had had brought up, ton by ton, from the depths of an ancient ro-city. With it she could direct any man's whole activity or make the whole population obey the same mental impulse simultaneously. Always, a trusted follower of the Hag sat at this masterpiece of the ancient science, listening to the thought of the city and ruling that thought in the way that it should go, as prescribed by Hecate. A populace ruled in this manner by the ancient ro-controls accepts any occurrence without demur, no matter how much to their detriment. Once our dis-rays put this monster, the actual nervous center of Disin out of commission, their prime co-ordinating center would be cancelled.[3]

AT a signal, immense beams from the giant tractors behind us lanced over our heads, up at the center of the web of telaug beams which ringed the old ro-control mech. In my penetray screen, I watched eagerly as the antique super metal glowed red, then white. But there was one thing our spies had missed, probably because the things had been planted so long before. Whether the heat of our dis-rays caused the explosion or whether they could not see our true position for the mass of black shorter rays under our dis-beams, I don't know, but a vast booming and roaring ahead, followed by a rolling cloud of choking smoke and dust, told us what had happened—the caves leading to Disin had been mined for just such an attack. Our forces had come within a hair of walking into the primitive trap. Simultaneously with the explosion, what seemed like a thousand or more great dissociator beams bored down at us, and a myraid of dust belching holes appeared in the hardened rock of the cave-rooves ahead. Our "shorter" ray set-up, carefully figured out in advance for just such attacks on the basis of our full information on their weapons, were sufficient.

A few of our delicate telaug devices burned out from the overload and rolled to a stop for repairs, but the columns raced on toward the mass of tumbled rock fragments that now barred us entrance to Hecate's lair. Under the black shielding blanket of shorter ray, the dis-rays hissed at the tumbled rock, and the lava rolled slowly back toward us from the melted rock.

It would not take the big dis-rays fifteen minutes to melt away a half-mile of that rubble, but would the resulting passage be safe for the passage of an army?

Well, we'd find out, for streams of water were playing on the bubbling floor of molten rock and our wheels were rolling over the smoking rock before it had really cooled.

Overhead, the cracks left by the explosion reached upward. We had a few integrative rays playing upward to tie the rock a little more firmly, but I doubted they made much impression through the necessary blanket of "shorter" rays.

Far overhead as we rounded into a branching cavern, on the surface I caught a glimpse of a vast army approaching Disin overhead—a fantastic conglomeration of nightmare weapons, unbelieveably huge, rumbling over what I knew was soft mud. As I looked a second time, I caught on. It was a projection of an imaginary army, done with a huge thought-record augmentor. This close to Disin, they had probably detected its nature, but when our attack had been gathering, it had certainly been very efficacious in the dim distance as a cover for our real attack from the caverns. Realistically, on the surface overhead, a purely imaginary army was carrying on a purely imaginary attack upon Disin!

AS we rumbled nearer and nearer to the heart of Disin above us, my respect for the Tuon efficiency and science went up by leaps and bounds. The ray-shielding which had protected the Tuon buildings from the Earthmen's attack in my first action on Venus, must have been understood by Hecate, or at least been figured out by now.

---

[3] These ro-control mech were designed, of course, merely as an ever-present and all-knowing policeman. But in ignorant and repressive hands, they can become a device by which the whole thought of a city is held rigidly in a narrow rut. Many modern cities suffer from this mis-used ro-mech underlying the modern surface city. They are the origin of the God-myth, omnipresence cultivated by priests.—Author.

Yet, our rays reached upward all through the great medieval piles of clumsy stone that formed Disin. Why had Hecate not used that same type of ray-shield?

If she had covered this, the Tuons evidently had a nullifier for the shield in action, for nothing prevented either our vision rays or dis-rays from sweeping the length and breadth of Disin.

The myriad of rays which had combed down upon us at the time of the mines' explosion were fewer now. The rise and fall and the hiss of our dis-rays raved at the fixed installations within the great center building, evil's cloister, where the monstrous ro-mech dominated our transparent vision with its antique opacity glowing redly and more redly as we sought permanently to destroy this nerve center of the Hag's.

(Later, Oanu explained to me that the defenselessness of Hecate's forces was due to great fields of diffuse dissociation beams which nullified the effect of Hecate's shielding fields and shorter rays, as well as making it very difficult for the defenders to think or act swiftly or well.)

What happened as we finally closed in on the fortress mounting upward through dozens of ramps we bored with our dis-rays, was a surprise to me. I had expected much more of the apparently formidable outfit under Hecate of which I knew so much.

Out of the great courtyard, a score of the ancient space ships rose one after the other. The blood-takers, the core of the vampire organization, flashed spaceward at top acceleration in the ships that glowed from our concentrated fire. Fire that did nothing but heat the hull, for the ancient metal was impervious to most rays except over a long period of intense concentration of many rays.

We hadn't won so soon, surely? What had happened to cause their too sudden flight? Certainly the mighty and ancient knowledge of war that Hecate undoubtedly possessed was not so easily defeated. Yet, there were the ships fleeing—from us. Why?

The answer to my question was soon given. Scores of white flags suddenly were unfurled from every battery within the citadel. With them, terms of surrender blared out, as well as information that explained much to me.

I had not known there was much opposition to Hecate within her own forces, for I had been too close to her to learn anything about it. But the great thought-speakers they turned toward us said: "We have helped you by turning against the Hag. Our beams hastened her departure. Most of the blood-feeders have gone with her, the others lie here dead. Enter and be merciful, O mighty Amazons."

WE did. And Ceulna and I found a chance to do something we had dreamed of in more than one black night. We lined up the surviving Hagmen, and after permission from Oanu, separated them into two groups—those whom we knew well from the cruelties we had observed them in, and those whom we did not know.

This latter group we told to take the former to the children's "Palace of Life" where waited the great Moloch with his fiery mouth well stoked for them. I am not sadistic, but I enjoyed the sight of those ill-natured robots screaming their way to death in the flames more than any other sound I have ever heard.

Ceulna and I gave Farne a bad scare when we pretended not to recognize him in the line-up. The canny little man for once was at a loss. It was a joyous experience when we both embraced him, a very good moment to see the joy light his face ... to say nothing of the relief. Such moments are what makes life worth the living. Greeting one's dog on coming home, meeting an old friend again, the crack of an evil neck between the hands, the laugh of one's best beloved, what else makes life worth the effort? Such moments are all too far apart. The fall of Disin and the flight of Hecate, the Mother of Sin, from Venus, was a long moment of that kind.

CHAPTER XI

Faust. "When I behold the heavens, then I repent —
Ay, go, accursed spirit, to ugly Hell. 'Tis thou hast damn'd distressed Faustus' soul."
                                        Marlowe

OANU was not the official ruler of Lefern and the allied cities of the Tuon race, but she was certainly a most respected leader among that superior people. Hard upon the heels of that fleeing score of an-

1473

tique space ferries ascended a full hundred of Venusian filled space battleships, under Oanu. In the ship in which Oanu directed the pursuit, Ceulna and I pored over the great space view-screen, its huge master ray boring ahead of the fleet, God only knows how many miles, for one's mind is always prostrate before the potentialities of the ancient workmanship.

"How is it," I asked Ceulna, "that so many as a hundred space ships, still serviceable, are to be had from the ancients' leavings? I would think that they had needed every ship when they left Earth."

"I have often listened to the older people talk of such things—speculating about the Elder Gods is a favorite topic of conversation," answered Ceulna. "Those who know and read the old records say that the migration of the Gods was a long drawn out affair—over a century of great effort—with many trips back and forth to the new home in space. They saw that a strange infection called "de" ails all the machinery and the ships, everything left behind, that is why there is so much of it.[6]

Finally we sighted the fleeing vampires, but we could not catch them. Oanu was wary. One ship followed them to Earth, marked their position on the map and returned with two great holes bored completely through the impervious hull of supermetal. The Earthmen were not having any of us, evidently.[7]

Oanu approached as near to the point on the map as possible behind a mountain range, then the fleet settled to Earth. Certainly she must have had information on the cavern ray of Earth, for many Earth source lifter rays gentled our landing.

Someone here must be rooting for us. Below our downward drifting tons, a great light flared suddenly and the vast mouth of some ancient landing tube yawned, still in use.

I was amazed to find all this vastly developed science of the ancient ones existing all these centuries on Earth, hidden from the otherwise credulous humans of Earth by their very incredulity of anything they do not know all about.[8]

Now, within that supposedly non-existent cave, waited a people whom you know all about, "THE LITTLE PEOPLE," the most charming inhabitants of Earth. They were few, for the centuries of handling the aging mechanisms with its now defective shielding, have made them nearly sterile—they have few children anymore. Many of them are changelings still —as in the old days, surface men's babes. They no longer steal surface babies and leave defective offsprings in their places, but now legally adopt them from orphanages. The blood of the little people has grown weak, but still they are the finest men I have ever met. The little people still love man and they welcomed us with the most delicious mental stim I ever tasted.

(Warning: There are some evil groups descended from castouts, in case you ever meet the "little people.")

The "little people" were very eager to help us against the new menace from Venus, having been practically besieged in their own area of the mountains, their home for many years.[9] Those with whom Hecate

---

[6] This "de" is a deadly radioactive infection from the sun, and the Elder Gods took the most extreme precautions to leave behind anything badly infected. Themselves, far out in space, transferred to a clean ship, leaving behind even their clothes, after extreme treatment of their own bodies to cure the infection, and abandoned the very ship they left the sun's vicinity with, to drift forever in darkness. Such are Venusian tales about the God Race leaving the planets of our sun—the reason was "de," the most terrible enemy of life. For that reason, many ships were left, some so complicated that no one knew how to run them at all. And the old students of the ancient writings know that Venus and Earth are deeply infected with that "de" from the sun, that it is the cause of aging and dying.—Author.

[7] The old caverns were originally equipped with many great installations of sky-pointing master rays, whose purpose was specifically to defend the underworld cities against space attack.—Author.

[8] From the pauper youth, Aladdin, down the pages of history to the modern science-fiction writers, the open-eyed among men have tried to tell others of the hidden magic of the ancients within those impenetrably walled caverns—tried to tell unsuccessfully all about this mighty gift of the old gods of Earth, with no more hope of success than had the pauper, Aladdin.

Jewels from those very same caves could have paid for the publishing of this work. Would you bother to find out if it were true or not? No, we of Earth are too purblind to all the infinite corroboration of such tales about us.—Author.

[9] Exact locations of such places cannot be given, for the "little people" would be offended. For more about the "little people," see Merritt's "Dwellers of The Mirage."—Author.

had sought and found refuge were not friends of the little people.

Oanu was not one to quit with the job half finished. The bulk of the fleet returned to Venus, and soon a steady stream of supplies began to pour in. The whole paraphernalia of our attack on Disin began to be assembled for a similar assault on this Earth hideout of the Hag's.

THE news from Venus was splendid. Two of the cities of the Hagmen were still holding out, but were expected to fall at any time. Soon, Venus would be rid of the vampire system, and the children of that beautiful people once again free to build the great future that was very evidently their potential possession.

During this period, Oanu arranged for a series of brain treatments from the army docs designed to restore my original initiative and character as much as possible. Ray medical work is certainly far different from the ether and knife butcher work we of the surface world are accustomed to consider advanced medicine. These doctors of the penetray just laid me under a lamp that revealed every nerve in my head as if the organ were constructed of vari-colored glass as is a medical display. Then they checked every injury in my head on a chart. Finally, they "operated" with an extremely powerful little benray, a needle of concentrated beneficial force. It hurt in a good way, if you can imagine a good pain. This powerful little ray they focused carefully on the points of injury, one after the other. After an hour a day of this for a week, they pronounced me cured.

I was more than cured. Those docs didn't fool me. They had created several focii of super brain cells in my brain with that super ray. Mentally, I was a better man than I had ever imagined any man could be. I learned why they did not tell me. It seems the ben ray devices are extremely valuable—rationed for use only on the most deserving people, those most valuable to the race. To save discussion on the point, probably at Oanu's suggestion, they had given me, unofficially, a generous dose of some of their most potent growth rays.

Everything was rapidly reaching completion for the attack on the distant refuge of the Hag when—it happened! The "little people" had been so sure that it couldn't happen, and we, I mean Oanu, had not considered the possibility, for the "little people" had been feuding with the ray-people who lived where the Hag's ships had sunk into the ground—and the "little people" knew their methods inside out. But, Oanu had forgotten that the addition of the Hag's experience to their array of apparatus was a factor rendering the whole a vastly more formidable set-up than formerly. For what Hecate didn't know about the old mech was known by few others on the two planets. Anyway, she found a weapon there that the "little people's" opponents had never used.

A diffuse field of force swept our caverns and stayed there. The stuff seemed to be a flow of radio waves nearly similar to thought waves, and the command it bore to our brains and muscles seemed to be "contract." Anyway, the stuff either accumulated a contracting charge in the nerves and muscles or she kept adding generator after generator to the power supply of the ancient radio-wave transmitter.

I knew that their mech was several hundred miles and a mountain range away from us, but that wave, like a radio wave of modern science, was not stopped by distance or rock. Our muscles just pulled up into tighter and tighter knots . . . at the end of ten hours we were unable to move hand or foot.

WE JUST sat or lay in painful knots of humanity and waited for the butchers to arrive. I swore steadily to myself. I swore viciously. Just when things were shaping so the surface men of old Earth were going to lose some of their age-old burdens of ignorant, all-powerful evil, that rabid witch, my beloved of so many long, lurid and I must admit, interesting nights packed with every sensation the body or mind could experience, pulled this ace out of her sleeve. The mighty Hecate, the Mother of Sin, the Devil's rival, the Holy Howling Horror herself, the only person who had ever been able to make me doubt that Evil was else than insanity, was going to get her Big Jim back again. Now the question that had bothered me so often was going to be answered. Unless help came within less than an hour, the old witch would have the whole thing in her ancient paws again. A great fear for what

1475

she would do to poor Ceulna rose in my heart.

I wept a little, cursed a little and involuntarily crawled before the mental image of that horror of the past. Soon I would be her thing again, or I would be dead with the lovely, fiery soul of Ceulna wilted beside me.

Waiting for the Hag, I couldn't move, so I thought of what I had seen of the "little people" . . . a thing many surface men have tried to see but failed. Some of the oldsters wore costumes of the fourteenth century, the kind you have seen "the little people" pictured as wearing. Long trunks over their legs, short jackets and a pointed hat or stocking cap pulled down over their ears, and pointed, turned-up-toe shoes, they presented an almost comical sight. They averaged a good four feet in height—bigger than one would expect. I suspect that they are not a separate race of men, but men who have lived so many centuries in the caverns that some thing lacking in their environment affected their growth adversely. The younger ones were dressed in modern clothes, evidently from modern American stores, though of course, in boy's sizes. Although many of them were extremely thin, they were a very good looking people. The "fairy drums" and "elfin piping" so spoken of by writers were present when we first arrived, but it was merely a kind of musical greeting to us. I remember nothing in particular to mention about it. Perhaps, I am becoming inured to the remarkable. However, now they have so much good modern music on tap on their radios. It may be that the art is dying out.

THEIR dancing, so often spoken of by other writers, was also present as a part of our welcome, but perhaps the costumes were not appropriate to the pattern of the ancient dances, or they had had no time to prepare a genuine program of merit. It was good dancing—very definitely identifying this group of "little people" in my mind with the legendary artistry in the dance which is attributed to them—but nothing more.

The most remarkable thing about them was a quickness of perception, a lightning kind of intuitive thinking, coupled with extreme agility of movement. But, I had had little time to get thoroughly acquainted with the "little people." They were a race of good looking midgets, and their magic, which was their knowledge of the uses and possession of the ancient mechanisms of the Elder Gods, was their chief distinction. And, ironically, its value to them was evidently neutralized by the monopolistic attempts of the other groups possessing the ray to kill them and take it away. From what I could gather, most of their time seemed to be spent in fighting such efforts on the part of the other old secret ray groups.

Now they lay, their own muscles knotted in the nervous impulses sent by the Hag and holding them in pained and motionless little bundles on the ancient polished stone of the floor. Their faces were pictures of despair and fear, and the habitual way that fear sat on their faces told me that these impulses were not strange to them.

Far down below us, in the vast tubes that connect all these time-drowned caves, rumbled nearer and nearer the wheels bearing the Hagmen and their new allies, whom I had not seen.

At last, when our nerves were shrieking from the pain of our bursting muscles and the horrified and hopeless waiting that was our only consciousness, they came. Into the cavern rolled the ancient cars of the tubes, a long torpedo-shaped vehicle with many wheels both on the bottom and sides, for the tubes have turns where the sides are used to check side-momentum. These cars still work, some of them are being used under your feet today. And the men that keep them in repair know more in some ways than the best of surface scientists, yet avoid us of the surface. Why? It is the ancient custom to do so. If I should ask, "Why do people marry?" you may understand. That is our way, that is all.

OUT of these long, and to us, hideously ominous, vehicles poured a weird mob of shapes and sizes. These were the people of the caves whose ancestors used the worn-out apparatus and were affected by the terrible x-rays given off by the old junk, affected the same way that fruit flies are affected by x-rays in the modern experiments spoken of so much. This x-ray-caused-mutation had gone on for endless centuries among these certain peoples, for they were ignorant of the cause, and never ceased to use the defective apparatus. The end result was a deformed race beggaring

1476

description. They had long legs and short bodies, or very short heads on very long bodies, bodies with arms at the hips and the trunk sticking up above the spider-like limb grouping. Some had hides mottled in black and white, some were covered with fine fur, and, surprisingly, some were normal and even beautiful individuals, but the effect of their entrance was that of the hordes of Hell loosed upon us. In truth, they were evil in a way I had not seen in action before. (The simple truth of some life in the caverns sounds fantastic, doesn't it? Truth is a more fantastic and horrible thing than any mind can enwrap—and truth can be a more vast beauty than a man's mind can grasp—if it is. But Earth life, in truth, is a vast horror unperceived by us because we are accustomed to the horror.)

The cave filled with these horrible invaders. The paralyzing waves were shut off ominously. A few of the "little people" made an abortive attempt to reach the old mech, but died writhing in their tracks from the hand ray trained upon us.

The rest of us were grouped together in the center of the cave to await the rulers' disposition. Others took up the usual watch over the screens which are placed so as to bring a continuous view into the center cave of all the ones surrounding us, as well as the surface overhead. Usually, this set-up is the same one left by the Elder Ones, as no modern man could improve on their disposition of the weapons and view rays. These screen are very large, covering most of the walls to a height of ten feet, and nothing that takes place within thirty miles is missed if they watch them carefully.

We squatted miserably in a close group in the center, hope withering within us. Such is ray warfare. One second everything is your way—the next, you would be better off dead. We all knew the part of wisdom was to attack these distorted horrors bare-handed and die before the torture started, but we did not. Such hope is a betrayer . . . a weakness indeed.

At last came what I dreaded—Hecate and her party. Once I had been curious as to what she would have done with me, now I was to know what she would do. Ceulna would not leave my side; I feared Hecate might learn that she was my beloved. Ceulna knew better, but the swift adversity had upset her usual sense—she just clung to me and looked dazed.

HECATE had us kicked into a line and walked up and down, looking us over. Oanu she singled out by her uniform, or perhaps she knew her from her description. She so honored a few other Tuons as well as myself. As I left the line at her gesture, Ceulna, still dazed, followed me, her hands held out numbly. Hecate didn't miss seeing that she loved me. My face was expressionless. I pretended not to notice the girl. The hag smiled grimly and gestured for the girl to be included in the little party she had selected as her special victims. The rest she gave over to the home team to do whatever they wanted to do.

The party began as we left in Hecate's train. It is very unnerving to see a woman hung up by her hair, while she is flooded with pain ray . . . particularly when you can't do a thing. You can't get used to it.

Hecate took us aboard the ship in which she had arrived from Venus. There she took a seat on her crystal throne, whether it was different from the one I had first met her on, I don't know. It certainly was the same type of apparatus, probably the ancient rulers used the thing themselves. No other set-up of apparatus I ever saw had so many varied types of rays controlled by its mech.

We stood and waited while she augmented our thoughts, searching each one of us, pumping everything out of us swiftly with her super-active, but, I was fast learning—not too sharp brain. Finally, she reached my brain. Her sharp exclamation of triumph as she saw what I felt for Ceulna told me what to expect. Now, she could hurt me as she desired without harming my body (which sub-consciously she wished to retain?). She would have her revenge on Ceulna, too.

Standing there and waiting while that ancient from Hell decided what fate would best fit our transgressions was one of the most painful periods I ever endured. Occasionally, her great yellow eyes burned into mine with an enigmatic expression . . . my skin crawled . . . my mind refused to imagine what she might be contemplating. About her stood a few of the blood-takers, hideous old-young creatures of Spanish ancestry for the most part. Age had left them alive, but had marked them in other ways. Tiny wrinkles criss-crossed their skin, and their noses and ears had grown out of proportion. All were very tall.

THEY were dressed in various fashions. Some of them had clung to the ancient Spanish styles—hose and doublet with slashed sleeves and puffed short pants. The women, for the most part, had adopted modern styles, though, some of the more attractive dressed in Venusian manner, which consisted of very little but arm bands, g-string, breast supporter, and many flashing jewels, and a plumed headdress. However, most of them were not beautiful, despite the young, stolen blood pulsing through their flesh and lending sparkle to their eyes.

A terrible weariness was in them, too. Taking the form of a consistent disapproval of everything they looked at, a constant sneer twisted their lips, a conviction that life had nothing more to offer them—that all life about them was worthless and, therefore, to be destroyed, rested on their faces. It was evident that age had been defeated in their bodies, only to take its tolls in other ways. Their faces did not show enjoyment of their stolen life. Even with the infinite pleasures of the High Gods at their finger tips, still, they were miserable creatures, lacking the wisdom to enjoy the fruits of their evil science.

"If we place them under 'Evil Dreams' from the punishment records, they will experience all the tortures and deaths and still be alive to suffer more, or to examine later for information should you need it," I could hear a giant fellow explaining his ideas of our proper fate to Hecate.[10] She nodded her head in agreement and I looked curiously at him. He was a man whom I knew for an intimate of Hecate's, an old one who had perhaps lived under Hecate's domination for centuries. He was clothed in the Venusian style, his body was brawny, but too big-boned to be attractive. His acquiline, narrow Spanish face served but as a base for his comically oversized beaked nose. His eyes were small, close together, and near-sighted. He wore thick lensed spectacles.

I knew that if this be-spectacled scavenger had his way, Ceulna, Oanu and I and the other unhappy Venusians in the party would die—over and over—the most hideous deaths these super-idiots could divise.

YOU don't exactly got to sleep under the dream beam. When it is turned on, there is an instant of vertigo and you wake up in another world—another person has taken possession of your body—a different life entirely is lived.

Soon, we were all strapped on the couches under the dream beams, and, simultaneously, we blanked out of this world. It was the same record for all of us, I suppose.

With our bodies trembling—yet untouched and unmarked—we suffered the unspeakable hell of having our flesh torn with hot pincers, of the skin of our bodies being removed slowly, inch by careful inch, while irritant powders and salt were sprinkled on the bared flesh and nerve ends, of having finger and toe nails mentally torn out, one by one, being immersed inch by slow inch into boiling water—eardrums throbbing with the agonized screams of

---

[10] These ancients are addicts of the "dream"—the reason one sees so little of them—one reason they do not try harder for power and pomp. The dream machines are the ancient libraries, which were not books, but thought records. To read one, one reclines on a couch, and a record is inserted in a nearby record augmentation machine. The ancient thought unrolls in a beam which conveys it to the brain in synthetic thought impulses. These impulses are vastly stronger than normal, self-generated impulses—vastly more pleasant and thrilling. Reading the ancient records which are accounts of magnificient people doing magnificient things (but, I suspect, things completely misunderstood) are extremely pleasant opium dreams to the addicts, though they were never intended for such a use.

The ancients left books, too, but the more usual record of the past was the thought record. They did acquire some education from these dreams, but the comparative dullness of everyday life the degenerate people of modern times lived is so uninteresting to the reader of the ancient thought records, that he retreats again to his couch and to the world of the past where life is infinitely more liveable. The thought recording instruments were sometimes used, though their barren brains found little real use for anything. One of the uses was recording the mental agonies of an enemy under prolonged torture. These were too painful to listen to under full strength augmentation, as it would be equivalent to undergoing the same torture. But, they could gloat over them under a mild augmentation and know that the victim had suffered terribly. Though not present at the actual scene of torture, they could be sure that everything possible had been done to make some poor wretch's last moments horrible. Then, too, they could use such records to put a victim through many deaths and still have him alive to suffer again and again. This was what the unpleasant giant talking to the Hag was proposing that she agree to do to them. —Author.

1478

one's friends unmercifully suffering the same sensations. Synthetic pain sensations are even more pain and agony than the actual experience because of the terrific, exquisite augmentation possible with the hyper-powerful ancient mechanisms.[11]

This ultra-torture went on for weeks or days—Gods! I'll never tell you how long. Then came that vertigo that is the return from the dream submission, the awakening. As I returned to this world, I could still hear all around me the constant, terrible, utterly inhuman sounds of suffering made by the others of our party of Tuons who still were under the dream beams of pain recordings. They were tortured screams that would have made Scrooge weep in pity.

CHAPTER XII

Hell and the gulf between, and Satan there Coasting the wall of Heav'n on this side night,
..., and ready now
To stoop with wearied wings and willing feet
On the bare outside of this World.
...see'st thou what rage Transports our adversary?
—Milton

AS I looked up, I found the giant form of Hecate beside me, a sly smile of triumph on her usually poker face. She didn't waste any time in polite formalities.

"The space ships of your friends are driving us to flight," she hissed. "Is it your wish to accompany me alive, or to remain here dead?"

My gaze flew to Ceulna, writhing against the straps in infinite agony of the pain dream. I looked back at Hecate.

"I'd like to strike a bargain with you, Hecate. Leave her here, alive, under a simple sleep beam, and I will go with you willingly and serve you faithfully."

She did not stop to ponder my words for she knew me too well. She nodded, then with swift, flicking motions of her huge long-fingered hands, she adjusted the mechanism of the beam over Ceulna. With a choking feeling of relief, I watched her lovely body subside from its straining against the straps and a slow smile of peaceful sleep steal over her face.

Then, Hecate strode about the room with a dis-gun in her hand, firing a short blast at each writhing Tuon. A great hole instantly appeared through their bodies, and at last they were still. Of all who had lain in the room under the torture of many deaths, she left only Ceulna and me alive.

She threw free the straps from my limbs, and, saying nothing, strode from the room. I followed, for I realized there could be little time. All about the caves leaped a strange blue fire which I realized must be the cause of the flight, for a bit of the fire touched me, and the flesh shriveled where it brushed my skin.

"Hell," I thought, "no wonder she was so ready to release Ceulna. She'll die anyway from that damned fire!"

Hecate divined my thought, and flung back at me. "The dream room is shielded well; it is probable that she will live. As for you, that little device in your head will not be there much longer. After that, we will see how you behave."

We entered the great old ship in which Hecate had returned to Earth after so many centuries of exile.[13] Before doing anything

---

[11] These horror records were often taken through the eyes of young boys to catch the reactions of horror and pity and fear, etc., which naturally arise in the minds of the young. Such jobs of recordings were terminated often by death, as the boy's eyes would see too much. You see, the recording is a mental impression, not a visual one. Mental agonies of the victim would be cut in the mental vision of the boy, just as in moving-picture making, various angles are shot. Dream-making by the use of the ancient mech has been a highly developed art for centuries and its addiction has enervated the best of the life of the caverns since the earliest times. But, these records which we were to experience were rather crude affairs, consisting mainly of the pain of a victim of physical torture. The crew around Hecate were not exactly "artistically" inclined.—Author.

[13] Perhaps the reader would be interested in some Fortean data that will answer his question as to "Why, if these ancient space ships DO exist, they have not been seen and reported to the public before this?"

The only answer the authors can make to this is—THEY HAVE! Strange ships HAVE been seen and reported ... but we people who pride ourselves on our scientific attainments won't believe what we can—and have—seen with our own eyes. You are referred to the "Books of Charles Fort," (published by Henry Holt and Company, 257 4th Avenue, New York City).

In the 12th chapter of Fort's "Lo!" are these
(Footnote continued on next page)

else, she placed me under a strong penetray and cut every nerve leading to the bit of camouflaged radio-mech in my head. It would no longer broadcast any of my thoughts, I heard Hecate thinking. Then she took a little double-beamed needle of force and with a loud report in my head, the tiny device blew its guts under a terrific overload. Now I was no longer a spy, but I had a hell of a headache. From the way things were going, I guess I was just predestined to be a vampire.

THE great ship, under Hecate's swift hands, rose slowly to the height of a dozen feet, and drifted rapidly down the huge and endless corridors. Ahead of us coursed the rest of the score of ships which had left Venus not so long ago. How long? I no longer had any way of knowing.

Ahead of the racing space ships, I occasionally had a glimpse of the wheeled vehicles of the distorted people with whom Hecate had taken refuge who were leading the way to some new position of strength in which to make a stand against the Venusian invaders.

On the rear view screen we could see a vast fleet of space ships hovering over our rear, far up in the strato-sphere, and lancing down from each ship a beam of blue force. All about us danced the deathly fire which this beam induced in anything it touched, but the old ships seemed shielded well against the stuff, the deadly flames did not leap inside the ship. I realized that Hecate must be handicapped for experienced hands with these ships, for she must have abandoned the dozen or so ships that had remained with Oanu when the rest of the fleet had returned to Venus for supplies.

I dared not to think of pulling some hero stunt and taking the ship out of Hecate's long hands. One little "think" of that kind would have been death for me, for in this type of augment ray work, your thoughts are always wide open to those about you. Instead, I had to pretend a relief at being in her hands again . . . even simulate the wild attraction which she had induced to live in me . . . always a part of me when I was her slave. Apparently, I did this act well, for she paid little attention to me. One cannot plot and plan in ray work, one can only wait for a break without thinking about it, and don't wait too obviously, either. Somehow, there is almost never a real break. When things turn wrong for those whom one serves, you usually die with them.

Our ships finally came to rest in water. I recognized the black expanse, for the sheer knife-edge of the ancient wharf of

---

facts (which he culled from newspapers and scientific publications).

". . . it may be that constructions from somewhere else have appeared on this earth, and have seized crews of this earth's ships.

. . . BROOKLYN EAGLE, Sep't., 1891—something was seen, at Crawfordsville, Indiana, 2 a.m., Sep't. 5th. Two icemen saw it. It was a seemingly headless monster, or it was a construction, about 20 feet long, and 8 feet wide, moving in the sky, seemingly propelled by fin-like attachments . . . it sailed away, and made such a noise that ———— was awakened, and, looking from his window, saw the object circling in the sky.

(Note the date of this occurrence.)

". . . ZOOLOGIST, July, 1868—something was seen in the sky, near Copiapo, Chile—a construction that carried lights, and was propelled by a noisy motor—or a "gigantic bird; eyes wide open and shining like burning coals; covered with immense scales, which clashed together with a metallic sound."

". . . NEW YORK TIMES . . . from Bonham (Texas) ENTERPRISE . . . a man living 5 or 6 miles from Bonham, had told of having seen something like an enormous serpent, floating OVER his farm; and that other men working in the fields had seen the thing and been frightened . . . A similar object had been reported from Fort Scott, Kansas. "About half way above the horizon, the form of a huge serpent, apparently perfect in form, was plainly seen."

". . . NEW YORK TIMES, May 30, 1888—reports from several places, in Darlington county, South Carolina—huge serpent in the sky, moving with a hissing sound, BUT WITHOUT VISIBLE MEANS OF PROPULSION. (Caps are ours.)

And finally—but this is by no means the last datum that Fort collected. . . .

". . . ZOOLOGIST 4-7-38—that according to the log of the steamship FORT SALISBURY, the second officer, Mr. A. H. Raymer, had, on October 28, 1902, in Latitude 5° 31' south, and Longitude 4°42' W., been called at 3:05 A.M., by the lookout, who reported that there was a huge, dark object bearing lights in the sea ahead. Two lights were seen. The steamship passed a slowly sinking bulk, of an estimated length of five or six hundred feet. Mechanism of some kind—fins, the observers thought—was making a commotion in the water. "A scaled back" was slowly submerging.

Q.E.D.—Author.

rock told me we were back in that place from which Earth rulers had sent me and the other green recruits from surface cities to Venus to fight for we knew not what. It was different now, in spite of myself, I felt like a somebody as I marched up the long connecting cave into that part of the caverns which I had first entered more than four years before, by my count. It was hard to tell as the time recording system on Venus is entirely different. No use explaining it to you. It's irrelevant, anyway.

IN that room hung with the black drapes crawling with the sinister figure of the great crab of gold still sat the too-soft figure of the woman who had first greeted me so long ago. Hecate and myself, surrounded by the big shots of the vampire crew, stood before her.

"Greetings, O mighty Hecate," she sneered slightly in her mechanical voice, gloating a little over this great one of another planet, forced to plead here for refuge after such long superiority. "I see that things are not going too well with you."

Hecate was not one to bow her head to anyone. "O Nonur of the Dream-makers, think not that you are not included in the attack from Venus. They intend to wipe Earth clean of all blood-feeders—yourself included. You will be forced to fight for your life quite as much as for ours—and, I advise you not to take any other view. Too much insolence here and my strength can go on to other places where we will be better received, O Gracious one."

Nonur of the pouting, cruel mouth pondered the great Hecate's words visibly, and the sneer slowly drained from her face; her voice became dulcet.

"Knowing the Tuons as I do, O mighty Hecate," Nonur spoke, but try as she did, she couldn't quite conceal the faintest tone of irony in her voice, "I surmise that what you say of their intentions is probably true. Therefore, My Lady, let us forget our little petty bickering and get our two heads together on a plan for defense. Nonur is not one so unwise to spurn the wisdom of the All-knowing Hecate!" And so saying, she bowed her head just a trifle and a small smile played about her lips.

"That is better, my Nonur. Together we can drive those ships back into space whence we came, though the best use of the space ray is not too well understood by any of us. We have little time. They may attack in force at any time. Again, they may wait for the gathering of an army within the caverns before they attack this position from the space ships for a double assault. In any case, we must not delay in making ready. If you will give me charge of a section of the caverns, I will get on with it."

I WAS soon manning a great old ray gun, its view ray lancing up—up how many miles I'll never tell you—up toward the scattered dots on the screen ... dots that were the ships of the finest race of people I ever knew, even if they are dominated by women. My job was to center one of those dots on the cross-hairs and pull the lever releasing untold millions of flaming volts of destructive disintegrant juice skyward—to kill people fighting for everything that meant living to me. For all I knew, they might have entered the caves abandoned by Hecate and the monstrosities, found Ceulna and taken her aboard, and then continued the pursuit. She might be on the ship I was training my dis-gun on. I tried to think of aiming without doing it ... an impossible feat. Seated at the bank of the master controls, Hecate flung a look at me that made the old ro-response in me center the ship and pull the lever. The ship shuddered, pointed its nose slowly Earthward and fell ... fell faster and faster and the guts in me fell, too.[13] My heart was a great

---

[13] The reader may be interested in other phenomena—not listed in the story, but reported in scientific periodicals, etc. From the Works of Charles Fort, again ... "Upon October 31, 1908, the planet Venus was four months past inferior conjunction ... there are vague stories of strange objects that had been seen in the skies of this Earth ... back to the time of the *nearest* approach."

"In the New York Sun, Nov. 1, 1908 ... is said that, near Bridgewater (Mass.), at four o'clock in the morning of Oct. 31, two men had seen a spectacle in the sky ... somethink *like a searchlight*. It played *down* upon this Earth, as if directed by an investigator, and then it flashed upward."

(Fort assures us that all the balloons of that day were accounted for.)

"In the New York Sun, Dec. 13, 1909, it is said that during the autumn of 1908, reports had come from different places in Connecticut, upon a mysterious light that moved rapidly in the sky."

(Footnote continued on next page)

lump of lead, and all the time I was trying to act elated at hitting it. I hoped to die. I have never done anything harder, and I didn't know how to avoid it. I couldn't think; I had only to obey the ever present thought of Hecate.

She sat at a great ro-mech in the center of the space ray fort, reading the thought of each of us simultaneously and throwing her own controlling-strength thought where it would do the most good. Unquestionably, it was she who made me fire that shot with the ro-mech, but that didn't keep me from thinking I did it myself.

Her fierce yellow eyes blazing, her brow furrowed, her long nose quivering over the screens that reproduced the screen before each of us ro, she was a picture of fury, of the witch from the past at last at bay, but still fighting.

Fighting a fleet that wasn't retreating, but lancing down toward us, driving before them a barrage of force needles such as never flamed my way before. Through the impenetrable ancient metal around us, hole after hole appeared, stitching across the room in row after row of death. The ro at the ray around me screamed and died, to be replaced by others under control. They had no choice but to fight and die. Now, I was sighting and firing steadily. I hit several more of the distant, deadly ships of the past, but none fatally.

Further flight was impossible for the Hag, for the ships from Venus ringed the whole horizon.

MY hands were scorched from the smoking heat of the metal of the gun—the long, ringed barrel, glowing redly—the whole works burning hot to the touch. Under Hecate's control, I sighted and fired. My hands, badly burned, were not allowed to let go the firing lever. There just weren't enough of us to fight efficiently, for I knew that in every direction lay monster weapons unmanned and not understood by the ray people here. I thought of the many men and women—wise, efficient "ray" of experience—whom I had seen die at Hecate's hands and at the hands of the others now fighting for their lives. I tried to figure how many of us there would be if we had all been well treated since the time when these began to rule so long ago. "Evil digs its own grave," I concluded, grinning a grin out of control—killing good men it could use for better ends.

A slave rushed into the great war-ray room, shouting a message:

"Nonur is dead, Oh mighty Hecate. They sent for you to take control—no one else left alive knows how!"

Hecate rushed from the room, a huge, weirdly ungainly figure, her long arms and immense hands swinging by her too-wide hips, her waist a marvel of thinness above those hips, and the swaying rock-gray shoulders heaving with ill-repressed rage.

It was the last I saw of her. She left the room without control—nothing but a couple of wounded ray-ro left alive, moaning on the floor. The others fled with Hecate, not realizing that safety would come when we ceased fire, for the distant ships were only firing at the flame of our ray—probably could not see us individually.

I waited till Hecate's rushing feet had lost themselves in the distance. Then I stole through the rooms, once full of that weird, dreadful life, now riddled and strewn with corpses. I found the chamber where Nonur's throne sat, surrounded by the gloomy black hangings with the dismal crawling gold crab over them. Behind one of the hangings I found the door by which I had entered. It opened without trouble, and I started the ascent to the surface.

"New York Tribune, Dec. 23, (1909) . . . that a "mysterious airship" had appeared over the town of Worcester, Mass., "sweeping the heavens with a searchlight of tremendous power."

From the "Sydney Herald" and the "Melbourne Leader" he takes an account of a *fireball* falling and exploding at Carcoar, in November, 1902. Here and elsewhere in Australia within a few weeks, the same phenomenon was reported. One, reported by Sir Charles Todd, of the Adelaide Observatory . . . a large "fireball" fell—so slowly it was watched for 4 minutes.

From "Greg's Catalogues" . . . bright ball of fire and light in a hurricane in England, Sept. 2, *1786*—visible for 40 minutes. (That's about 800 times duration that the orthodox give to meteors and meteorites.)

Page 101. "Book of the Damned."

"London Roy. Soc. Proc., 6-276:

"A triangular cloud that appeared in a storm, Dec. 17, 1852; . . . visible 13 minutes; explosion of the nucleus.

See back to description of ancient God-built space ships . . . "Huge, and golden."

(Fortean material obtained from "The Books of Charles Fort," published by Henry Holt and Company of New York City.)—Author.

The doors were secured by bars on the lower side and all opened to my questing hands in the dark. Behind me, I could hear the muffled sounds of firing, the twang and thrum of the great coils that released the discharges, the sharp "splat" and "hiss" of the Venusian fire as it burned through the cave walls.

I wanted no more of it . . . if the Hag was to die, I saw no reason for dying with her . . . if she was to win and live, I was not crazy for an endless life as her pleasure robot, for she left a man little sense of his own. No, degraded as the life had made me perhaps, I saw no reason for not losing myself among my fellowmen upstairs, until I could contact sane, good "ray" like the Tuons and so find Ceulna again.

After what seemed the whole of Eternity, I broke out of the house that was the "front" for the stairs—my tortured breath coming in hysterical sobs, my almost naked body shivering in fear and sweat.

SOMEHOW, I got home. I don't remember how—I was punch-drunk and more afraid than I've ever been. Not of anything—just horribly afraid and unnerved.

I guess the elemental animal in me had taken over and I'd run like a startled deer. I'd run too fearfully—too much without thinking . . . I want to go back. I did almost as soon as I'd calmed down. That's a laugh—a hideous joke—I can't even find the house that contains the opening to the caves any more.

Now, when I talk to the ray that gibbers over the city, they mock me, laugh at my predicament, sometimes torment me with pain rays, but of information how to contact the Venusian rays, I can get nothing out of them. Did the Tuons' ships win? I don't know. Where can I find people of the caverns who will tell me how to find Ceulna and the invading Venusian rays? They laugh at me in their idiot way. They are the mad ones of the caverns . . . they never make sense with anyone. The antique ray-mech of Earth is still a secret, and I am out and can't get in. I'm not the first man to find himself shut off from that life. I know. In my place what would you do? There just ain't no way to get back into those caves that I know of . . . but there must be a way. There *must* be a way!

* * *

WELL, that's the story. Interesting—but surely we don't expect grown men to really swallow all that stuff about caves under the modern world filled with prehistoric machinery—and flights to Sunward planets in ships older than history . . . flights right at this very time? That all makes a very nice tale—interesting for a few hours of reading, or so, but it isn't true really, is it? Why that sort of thing would earn us straight jackets these days, or a pile of faggots in the days of a few centuries ago . . . and we are not so noble and stuffy that we'd risk that.

No, friends, we are not going to tell you that it's true—you KNOW differently, don't you? That such things COULDN'T be. There have never been oddly weird things occur that Science couldn't explain . . . so how could we expect you to believe if we did tell you that it was truth? WE know that such things just don't happen, so we won't tell you that.

YOU have never been badly frightened in a dream and flung your arms out violently to protect yourself from the Gods only know what. And because that hasn't happened—well, you know how it is. And weird, unexplained chills running up your spine—oh, those are caused by drafts say, or—or tiredness. It's just a clever use of coincidence that we use those chills to make parts of our stories seen reasonable. That JUST COULDN'T be some of the people in the caves playing with us. We all know that.

And the magic talisman—the scarab ring—my brother wears on his third finger? Oh, that is something that I dreamed up, figuring that everybody knows the part the scarab played in Ancient Egypt and it would make the whole story seem very weird and mysterious. Really, I have never seen this ring get cloudy and little pictures form in it—little pictures of people in a stygian world. That wouldn't be reasonable, would it? Besides—YOU know that such things can't be . . . such things just aren't so. So, you can go to bed and sleep, dreamlessly. It isn't true . . . it can't be . . . or . . . COULD IT? It was a hell of a long dream, brother, if it didn't happen.

LET'S THINK OF MAN'S RIGHTS — NOT NATION'S

THE HIDDEN WORLD

LUDER VALLEY

I heard the whir of propellors and looked up . . .
1484

THE HIDDEN WORLD

By RICHARD S. SHAVER

There in the green hell of South America lay the wreck of a ship from an unknown world in space

THE chief's face was red, and the odor of cigar smoke, the kind that only grows in Havanna, drifted in gray ribbons across the room and in front of his red face. His big teeth were champing the butt, as usual...

"The name of the place is Luder, Steve—Luder Valley. It's the scene of the biggest gold strike in years—and it's in the worst jungle on the Southern continent. Even a condor carries a pack in that country—and skid chains. There is no way in except for a mountain goat or a monkey—so they use mules; they don't know any better than to go ahead, anyway. The snakes are bad, and you better take three kinds of serum along. Along with the gold occurs a good diamond clay, and lots of stones of good quality, for industrial uses. The Germans have sent in agents in a helicopter to buy those industrial diamonds and fly them out to a sub—the Germans are desperate for industrial diamonds. We've got to get in there and stop them. You're to be advance man. Get in, get the info, and make ready for the arrival of the rest of us. And don't get recognized for an agent before we get there—just smell out the lay of the land."

Pug, the chief's beauteous daughter, came in with a big bouquet of rainbow-hued flowers that smelled like heaven. Hell of a name for a girl, isn't it? But she had the cutest pug nose I ever saw on a human and someone had hung the name Pug on her and it stuck.

She was always coming in with something when I was around. But I wasn't having any. Pug was too much like her old man for a man to marry. I didn't take to the idea of being bossed around off duty, too. But that beautiful pug nose of hers, above a smile as gay and welcome as the Pearly Gates, if heaven is what they say it is—was hard to be rude to. So I said, "Good afternoon, Pug Ranscom."

She answered, "Good afternoon, Steve. Leaving so soon?"

"Yeah, I got my sailing orders—and my mule ticket, too. Don't you wish you were going along?"

"Maybe I will. Somebody will have to keep you out of trouble." Her eyes had a stubborn glint, and I knew she meant business, from the similar look her old man sometimes had when nothing would stop him.

"Now look here, Pug, you keep out of this. No more of that—I'll tell your

1485

old man right now."

"You tell him anything, and I'll get you transfered to Iceland, so help me, I will. And I can, too."

"Anyway, one mule ain't any faster than another, so how you going to catch me?"

"If I felt like it, I could catch you anywhere, and any time. And don't forget it, Steve. I just haven't made up my mind I want you. I don't need a mule, yet."

"I hope you never do." I breathed the fervent prayer to her smiling young face, and left.

CHAPTER II

TWO days in by mule from Sandoval, and I was plenty sore. Riding was never one of my accomplishments, and the terrain was strictly non-horizontal. First I slid off the saddle backward, then I slid off frontward. Occasionally I varied the routine by falling off sideways. But the mule went on, and somehow I went along.

The surrounding territory was swathed in green stuff, and the green stuff harbored more numerous and varied insect life than my skin had ever encountered. This was the edge of the Green Hell, the most dreaded of South America's junngles. What would it be like when I arrived, if I did arrive? I was afraid to worry about it. The mule went on, and a liana dragged me off again. I got back on, mainly because the motion of the mule kept the flies flying, instead of lighting. The flies were worse than the mule.

Overhead a deep, quiet hum swept close. Looking up, I was suprised to see a heli. I was still more surprised when it circled and hovered closer, apparently looking me over. Then the darn thing went nuts. It shot up, fifty feet or so, then swooped down to a few feet of the ground, jockeyed around looking for the smooth spot that didn't exist in this country. Then the blades smashed against an Indian-Fig tree, and the heli sat down in a shuddering mess. The door opened, and out of the cabin stepped Pug.

I didn't let her get started. I opened up on her first.

"What in the name of the seven blue devils are you doing here—and just how do you expect to get back? Didn't you ever fly one of those things before? I suppose you think I'm going on a little picnic and you would just come out and see how I'm doing? Explain yourself, and don't think I'll believe a word of it."

Her face was red, and it got redder. I regretted my hasty words. Pug wasn't the mildest girl in the world when she got riled.

"It isn't enough I nearly break my neck just trying to see you, you have to bawl me out. Steve Hawley, you're the meanest, ugliest, most worthless male I ever had a crush on."

"Look, vacuum-brain, why do you think I didn't ride that heli in here? Do you think I like to ride this animated bag of boulders, do you huh? The chief didn't mean us to use that heli till we had the opposition all rounded up—for fear they would see it. So you just get in and fly out here in hell's back yard, where even the snakes get lonesome for a nice friendly human to bite that won't bite back—and wreck the ship. Who in hell do you think you are, you beautiful dumb female, you? What in time am I going to do with you now? I'm supposed to slide into this gold camp, this boom town in the hottest part of the Green Hell, like I was a miner—a greenhorn out for a strike. I'm supposed not to attract attention. I'm supposed to be too dumb to notice. So what have I got on my hands? The prettiest operative in the United States, that nobody who wears pants can take his eyes off—all dressed up in nice tight jodphurs and flying boots—all togged out in a red silk shirt so nobody can fail to see her—and no way to get rid of her. I could scream; but you'd laugh. How in hell can I learn anything with you around to attract the poor lonesome miners?"

"LOOK here, you conceited ape. Just because you haven't shaved for a week, you think you look like a rough, tough, experienced gold miner that no one will notice for an operative. The truth of it is, it's written all over you like a book about spy methods. Your nose is peeled, telling anybody you're not used to the sun. You walk like you had a double charley-horse and locomotor ataxia, telling anyone who looks you never rode a horse that wasn't fastened to an ice wagon. With me around, nobody will look at that beautiful manly Dick Tracy face of yours—they'll look at me. And if you think those dumb Nazis will figure out that I'm a spy, you're crazier than you look right now. You go about your business and I'll dig for gold, like all good little gold-diggers do. And I'll do your job and mine too."

It was no place for a woman. I would be spending my time exclusively shooing off the woman-hungry wolves in the diggings out here where a white woman was strictly for pinning on the wall—not expected in the flesh.

I looked at the wreck. The first heli issued to any government outfit—strictly secret—almost the only heli in the U. S., and Pug had to wreck it. The only kind of plane that could operate in this country—and God knew when we could wangle another out of the Washington office. Well, no use crying. I called to Vasco, the guide, and the two of us began cutting brush and covering the heli so it could not be seen from the air. The Germans were using some kind of plane in here in their diamond smuggling. I doubted if they had perfected a practical helicopter yet. But they had. *

Vasco got off the lead mule and Pug got on. Just to explain things—I might as well tell you that, she being the chief's only daughter, he doted on her. So did we. She did a lot of our office work when a big bunch of us were out on a job. But she had strict orders to stay at headquarters and keep her nose clean of the field work. She was efficient and good natured and damn useful because she knew all the ropes, having been raised at the game. Her mother was dead, therefore she had accompanied her Dad for years in his work, and she absorbed info like a sponge.

But she had inherited other qualities not so admirable from her old man. His temper, for instance, and his infernal bullheadedness that always got him his own way. In a man, it's called aggressiveness. In a woman, you can call it what you like, but you can't get used to it. But we did. She pretty much wrapped us all around her finger, for she was the chief's assistant.

To top it off, she had a crush on me. I had no great desire to be dominated the rest of my life—and I ducked a little, but it wasn't much use. Like today, for instance. A hundred miles of jungle between me and women—and she drops

*A lot of you fellows are going to kick about these helicopters being in use by German and American secret agents before they are in use by the army of either. But I myself saw practical heli flights in Newfoundland in '38. I think the ships have been in use by the services of both countries: experimental jobs, hard to handle and not overpowerful, but indispensable for their work. It is the only way I can explain what I saw myself—and it wasn't in the newspapers. Naturally, the only conclusion to be reached is that the secret services got the helicopter on the Q T before anyone else. One can see why this was so.—*Author.*

in out of the sky. In the only hell our bunch had been able to wangle out of the home office. And wrecks it. And I knew it would be all right. The chief might sound off a little, but he couldn't really disapprove of anything she did.

VASCO leading her mule, and me trailing along, we went on through the worst country a man could pick for traveling.

Maybe it was the red silk shirt— maybe it was the perfume. I don't know. But the mule did know, and he didn't like it. He stood it for a little while, but he was restless. He craned that long mule neck of his around and took one good long look at Pug. Then he ran, straight out into the jungle. A team of horses couldn't have held him, let alone little Vasco Perale. Vasco tripped over a vine, measured his length on the ground, and my mule balked. She, or he—I never did get the sex straight—just went on strike, and Pug was fast disappearing in the distance. I jumped off and legged it after the disappearing girl.

I came up with her after a ten minute chase. Pug was standing, little the worse, under a tree which had reached a limb down and brushed her off the mule. But she paid no attention to my arrival.

"My God, girl—we'll never catch the darned mule in this bush. How do you do it, anyway?"

Pug just pointed at something she was staring at. "Do you see what I see?" she asked.

I looked. About half a mile away gleamed a long low metal building, shimmering in the afternoon sun. Rows of round openings stared from its sides. The whole thing looked like the wreck of a dirigible—and a mammoth one at that.

"I don't know what it is, but it sure is something. We'll have to make camp in a couple of hours, anyway; we might as well go on over and camp there. Maybe it's a building; if it is, there is comfort. If it isn't, it looks like something that might have a bunk or two inside it anyway."

"There never was a lighter-than-air ship that big," mused Pug. "What could the thing be out there?"

"We'll know before long. Here comes Vasco with the remaining transportation. And stay away from that mule. From here on we all walk. These mules never saw a woman before. Being rational animals, you can't blame them for running."

"I like that! I suppose you are rational, and a mule wouldn't run from you." Pug's face began to redden, and I knew the storm signals were out. "Well, I would say that the mule had never met an intelligent person before, and seeing me, knew it had met its master in brain power. That's why it ran. Naturally it wouldn't run from a man, as it despises the male intelligence."

Just to keep the peace I agreed with her. "Naturally. It knew it had met someone more stubborn than any mule could ever be."

WE covered the rest of the distance in short order. I wasn't going to let any woman wrap a rock as big as the one she dived for around my neck. But she stumbled and dropped the rock, and we stopped, panting, beside something it took me a long time to understand.

That thing was big. It was deceptively big, with smooth, beautiful lines that, had I known that much, told of ages of development or building just such ships. For it was a ship, a long, tapered, lovely dream of a ship of shining metal. The forward end had crushed itself into the side of a low hill, but otherwise she looked undamaged.

A feeling of awe stole over us, standing there, reaching with our eyes and our minds for the meaning behind the wonder of the ship's size and beauty.

"Did you say it might contain a bunk or two, Steve? I'd say by the size of it there're quarters for the whole Marine Corps. But those rows of round things I thought were windows aren't windows at all. They are just plates of darker metal. They must be doors of some kind."

"Pug, I may be wrong, but I think we've stumbled on something more important to our government than all the industrial diamonds in South America. This thing looks to me like the wreck of a space ship—a ship that was never built on this earth at all. Do you think it could be?"

"I'm not committing myself. Let's get inside and find out."

That ship seemed a good mile long, and we hadn't yet reached the end—and no opening. No projection, nothing,—just smooth metal hull, no way of climbing up and seeking an ingress. We walked along in the shadow cast by the bulge of the round of the thing, and wondered. But the wondering had just started.

Toward the bow of the ship, it had run into the side of the hill, apparently after skating across the countryside for a landing. The tremendous size and weight of the thing had rendered even this probably slight impact disastrous, for the massive metal of the nose was crumpled and bent and several gaps were tore in the smooth expanse of apparently seamless metal. I helped Pug scramble into one of these ragged openings, and climbed after her.

D<small>ID</small> you ever step out of this world into another one? No? Well, then, there isn't much you know to which I can compare the sight of the inside of that ship.

Did you ever see a sculptured machine? Did you ever see a painted surface that was all colors at once—a sort of super-irridescence? Did a machine ever speak to you in a heartrending tone of voice—like a dying man begging for a drink of water? Did you ever open an innocent looking bottle and when you drank of it find the nectar that made life instantly somewhere near a million times as worthwhile—that made your limbs pulse with instant new strength—made your mind turn over in an ecstasy of new-found power and ability? No, you didn't; and I'm supposed to tell you what it was like in words you can't mistake for false.

Did you ever see a picture of a woman so beautiful that everything you had ever thought beautiful turned to a horrifying image of degradation, of degenerate life, in your mind? And have you seen pictures of life that made your own life become a horrible memory beside the vital, living message that the pictures carried to your brain?

We were soon lost in the unending wonder of this ship from the voids of space—from a world beyond any man's ken. Night fell, and darkness overtook us deep within the center of the ship; and without lights we had no idea how to get out—or with a light either, for that matter.

Outside somewhere was Vasco, wondering what had become of us. So were we. You may have experienced the feeling of being lost in a big modern building. This was like that, but there was no familiar thing with which to orient oneself. There were signs about, over doors, on big, intricately decorated cabinets, on the backs of chairs, even labels on the machinery. But they were in a language that looked tantalizingly

1489

readable, but, brother, it wasn't English.

CHAPTER III

IN the middle of our other wonders, a new wonder came to cap the climax. Far overhead sounded a series of bumping noises. Somewhere a light glimmered through the gathering gloom of the big, utterly strange ship. Nearer and nearer glimmered and bobbed a light, and many feet came down, down, nearer to us, crouched there in the dark.

Pug tugged at me and we scuttled into a closet of the big room, closing the door all but a crack. Almost at once the room flooded with light, and we heard the harsh gutturals of German. I was dumbfounded. This ship could not be the product of German science; the symbols on the walls were about as much like German as Chinese. Yet here entered the German super-men, apparently in possession.

Both Pug and I spoke German, I much better than Pug, for which reason I had been selected for counter-espionage work. We knew what they were talking about, but it didn't quite make sense.

There were seven of them, dressed in rough miner's clothing, automatics strapped to their belts. One carried a sub-machine gun.

The smallest of the lot took his seat at a table—a table that had apparently been a work bench of the mysterious people of the space-ship, for it was lined with tools that looked like a pipe-fitter's nightmare. One of the others threw down the carcass of a small wild pig and two of them began preparing a meal over a camp stove.

The small fellow at the work bench was bending over several small stacks of fine gravel that I realized were diamonds. These he was sorting, grading and packing in boxes, working rapidly and to all appearances rather carelessly.

Pug and I did not dare move a muscle, for the slightest sound would have betrayed us. At any moment one of them might open the door for some purpose, and discover us. It was no place to be.

One of the men lounged over the work bench and engaged the diamond packer in conversation.

"Fritz, buying the stones and flying them out to the subs is all right as a job —and there isn't much else we could do with them that would get us any more money. But the power some things in this ship could give us! Is it wise to turn it all over to the fatherland? Would we be paid anything like its value?—or would we be pushed aside—maybe liquidated?"

The small man at the desk paused for a moment and shot a cunning glance at his questioner. Then he winked broadly at the man.

"Such talk. Of course the fatherland must have everything that will help to build her power. Our enemies hammer ever harder at the Luftwaffe—soon our great power in the air will be no more. And you think that I would keep such technical secrets as this ship holds from our dear Fuehrer? Don't be absurd."

THE man leaning over the desk was thoughtful, somewhat taken aback. Then he digested the meaning of the wink and the words of opposed meaning. He winked back at the smaller man.

"Of course, of course, Herr Ober Lieutenant. I forgot myself."

"I will talk to you later, alone, Herr Kraft. We cannot have these thoughts. Those are the thoughts that are losing Germany the war."

"Yes, sir." Herr Kraft turned away, smiling slightly to himself.

Presently the officer finished with the work, arose, and placed the diamonds in a metal box at the side of the room. He also placed several papers within the box, locking it carefully. The box was big, and I noticed that there were several strange books within it, whose covers were titled in that outlandish script of the strangers who had set this ship here and disappeared.

The men ate, and presently five of them went out, stretching and yawning. Pug and I began to breathe a bit easier; it looked as though we might get a chance to sneak out without being caught. But our relief didn't last long. The fellow at the desk stretched, yawned, and then with a lightning movement drew his gun and leaped toward the door behind which we crouched. It was a brave, almost foolhardy thing to do, for he could not know that we were not holding him steadily on the sights of our guns.

He threw the door wide. His Luger looked like a 44mm to me as it stared into my face. I was never caught so flatfooted. My gun was in my hand, but I had no chance of raising it from its position on my knee. I dropped it, for I didn't want the Nazi blazing away at me with Pug beside me.

"Come out, sneakers. Now, what are you doing here?"

I cursed silently to myself. That wink which I had thought served to keep his partner in skulduggery from talking in front of the others—had in truth been a way of warning him not to talk in front of us, the eavesdroppers. Why hadn't he gone for us when the others were in the room? Very possibly because he didn't want to give them a chance of plugging him in the back. By his face I knew he was a man with few friends. It was a Himmler face, a face only the German underworld could breed. But he wasn't soft. A quick, ruthless cunning was revealed openly on his face. He had noted something that betrayed our presence when he entered the room, but for his own purposes had delayed in revealing his knowledge till the exact moment when we were off guard. Was the man psychic?

THE bigger fellow, who could have been a brother of Schmeling, with his bushy eyebrows and bulldog, Germanic face, remained in the background, his gun drawn. The little pocket edition Himmler sat down at the beautiful work bench again. Pug and I stood before the bench, plenty uncomfortable.

I started explaining, knowing darn well nothing I could say would help us any.

"We saw the big, metal, ship-like building and wandered in, curiosity our guide. Then you entered, and we hid, not knowing who you might be. So here we all are."

"Jah, here we all are. And here you will stay. But it might be best if we knew something about you?"

"We were on our way to the goldfields. Our mule ran away, and chasing the mule led us here. That is all." I was sweating.

"That is not all. You are not a miner. What do you know of gold or the mining of gold? I do not think that gold was your purpose in coming here. I would say that you were American agents, and that your finding your way here was no accident. The only point I am in doubt about is whether your finding this ship *was* an accident, or whether your superiors are aware its existence. Kraft, lock the man up. I think he will talk later. Right now we will question the little lady, so-hardy little secret agent who wishes to pan gold with her pretty white hands."

Herr Kraft gestured with his gun,

1491

and I preceded him down the indicated corridor. I did not see any chance to play the hero. The big hun locked me in a small room with two great couches one over the other—the only furnishing. I suspected that other men had been locked in here before, for the place was crumby.

The lock had hardly clicked behind me when I wished I *had* played the hero. Pug began to scream—those hair-raising screams that only a woman can let out, when in agony.

One way to learn about love is to hear the adored one scream in agony. It is not the best way, I assure you, but it is efficacious. I knew now; there was no doubt in my mind. I would never love another woman as I did Pug. I went mad. I howled and flung myself at the heavy metal door; my hands beat at it, clawed, sought for some way—some impossible way—of tearing that great door to little pieces.

And one of the miracles of the construction of that ship became suddenly revealed to me. My seeking, maddened, clawing hands found a little rough place upon the smooth metal at the side of the door. The rough, apparently accidental imperfection of the metal gave, and the great door swung soundlessly open. The wisdom of those mysterious, vanished men from space—if men they were—was revealed to me in my terrible need. For they had not planned on being locked in their own cabins. There was a way out open to one who knew the construction of the ship.

I FELL out with the door, sprawling on the impossibly smooth glitter of the metal floor, studded with little projections for traction. I raced down the corridor I had just traversed. But caution slowed me and I ducked into a door at the side just before I reached the big central chamber where the screams still ululated. How I had the control to use caution, with Pug's screams of awful pain in my ears, I don't know. But I did. I searched the room for a weapon, a club—anything.

It was another of those incongruously beautiful tool rooms with which the ship was so plentifully supplied. More of the pipe-fitter's nightmare wrenches were hung in racks on the walls, were stowed in lockers at the base of the walls. I seized a wrench with a good heft, as the most obvious weapon. But something brought my eyes to an open locker at my feet, and a vague familiarity about a cylindrical, nozzled tool struck me. I picked it up, hastily pressed the projecting stud. A flame leaped out, struck clear across the room. It was a blow torch to top all blow torches.

Wrench in one hand, flaming torch in the other, I raced out of the chamber and into the big room where the screams were now subdued to a muffled sobbing interspersed with words.

Pug was saying, "I'll tell you anything, only stop . . . stop."

Somehow no blame arose in my heart for her. Flesh can only stand so much. Besides, a person can always lie. Pug must know that our lives depended on their failing to learn whether the chief knew there was such a ship or not.

The speed of my attack saved me. They turned at the roar of the flame, but the awful spear of terrific heat struck them to the floor, blackened instantly into hulks of scorched meat. The stench of burning flesh filled the room, but I did not shut off the torch. I kept it on them till there was no semblance of life left in the smoking mess on the floor. Pug had, blessedly, fainted as the pain stopped.

These devils had strung her up by the thumbs, and had stripped the clothes off her. Then they had been pressing cigar butts into the beautiful white of her skin. Why does an evil man always hit the most beautiful thing in sight? There is a lot to learn about evil in that fact. What a good man worships, a bad one hates. A child is a torment to a bad man and a blessing to a good one. So it is with every other good thing in life. Her beauty was to them something to press burning cigar butts into. You can't tell me that kind of animal enjoys any beautiful thing in life. I don't believe it.

I CUT Pug down, hung her torn clothes back on her, and slapped her face lightly till she came to. I didn't turn my back on any doors, either. I wasn't taking any more chances. I slipped the two automatics in my pockets, and picked the tommy gun off the rack on the wall.

I hated to leave that fancy blow torch behind. Taking a last look around, I found another use for it. The box of diamonds. A couple of shots of that super-flame and the lock melted away. Within were too many of those little bags of rocks for us to burden ourselves with. But the books and papers I suspected were too important entirely to leave behind. Rapidly I stuffed my shirt front full of the tight German handwriting. One of the books was small and easily slid into my back pocket. I might never see this mighty, other-world ship again.

Then Pug and I stole out of there. It took us at least an hour to find the way we had come. Mice couldn't have been quieter, but we saw no more of the rest of the gang. We didn't stop running into the dark till we saw the light of a camp-fire far ahead. I suspected it was Vasco. It was.

I didn't stop to explain anything to him. I couldn't talk Portugee well, anyway. I just started throwing things on the mule and he got the idea. Last of all I helped Pug aboard and we headed out. I wanted to get plenty of big trees overhead before the daylight made us vulnerable to the eyes of the plane I knew the gang possessed.

The sky was graying swiftly into dawn when he parked under the deep shade of swamp growth, deep within a boggy stretch of forest. We didn't light a fire—we just sprawled and slept and let the bugs feed. They did.

CHAPTER IV

WE AWOKE when the sun was blazing in the mid-west. We ate some cold beans from the cans in the pack, some chocolate, and had a few swallows of water from the canteen. God knew how long the stuff would have to last us. Since we were unmasked, we would have to make our way back to headquarters in Sandoval and start over. But I hoped the data we came for was in the notes I had stuffed in my shirt.

Just to make sure, Pug and I sprawled under the great tree to which Vasco had tethered the mule, and delved into our loot.

What we had was amazing stuff. Since I was most curious about the origin of that tremendous ship bearing all the evidences of a vast and alien culture, I opened the little book I had stuffed in my hip pocket first. I could not make head nor tail of the minute detailed diagrams and rows of strange, mathematical appearing symbols. I suspected it was an engineer's handbook, and as such it had an inestimable value. I made Pug pull up her shirt, and taped the book against her lovely stomach. Since we had already dressed and bandaged her burns, it was a good hiding place, for it looked like another wound, bandaged. Then we went for the German notes. These we could read. The story they told was one to floor a man, in more ways than one.

The thing started with a short statement by the German that the following was his attempt at translation of the difficult alien language of the spaceship's log. The rest was broken sentences, fragments that the German had, by some ingenious method, been able to translate.

Six light-year out from . . . Voyage monotonous, crew space-sick. . . .

Each fragment is preceded by what looks like a date, but I can't make out their calendar.

Kraft

Today . . . motors smashed by a speeding meteoric fragment that went clear through both walls of the hull and left . . . Catastrophe.

So many days have passed. We have worked unceasingly to make temporary repairs to reach some haven, but our case is hopeless.

Our course tends ever more toward some alien, poisonous looking sun. Unless we are captured by one of her satellites, we will end in the blaze of that death-light. What difference does it make? To end quickly or to drag out a few years of misery on some barren, rocky ball of sub-life forms, suffering the agonies of the unknown diseases of the wilderness.

Still working on the motors, but the damage is too extensive. There is no hope. We rigged temporary generators from the stores to activate the antigrav plates in case we approach a satellite planet on our dive into the fire. Have carefully observed . . . and the planet will approach our path rather closely. Have no exact figures of our speed—but it seems we will be captured by . . . the round rock.

Made a series of braking circles of the planet. Our speed is high; we will have to circle here for some months, I fear.

Today we entered the breathable atmosphere and opened our ports to the air of this sunburned ball. What a stench, but it supports life—for awhile.

Today we landed—and the final and complete disaster struck us. We managed to crush our hull against a low hill as we landed in a free fall, lightened only by the antigrav force. Now our case is hopeless, for our ships never approach within twenty light-years of these poisonous suns.

THERE followed a further note by Kraft, who must have been an ingenious and capable master of code work to get anything understandable out of the strange language.

"Much of the writing is untranslatable by me. As near as I can make out the crew of the space-ship could not stand conditions here under this sun, and died rapidly, the strongest living but a few weeks after the ship landed here in this desert country."

Pug's excited voice broke into my reading. "If they had only landed near a city, they might have been saved. God only knows what they might have done for our science before they left to return to their homes."

"They may do our science a lot of good yet, Pug. We're sending for help, and lots of it. Vasco, take this message back to the place where you were first hired. We will remain here, as too much depends on our retaining our freedom for us to risk showing ourselves in the open. Those Nazi will be out looking for us, for they know their safety depends on finding us before we contact our other agents. They don't know you, Vasco, and if they stop you for questioning, you never heard of us. Compre'?"

Vasco left us most of the food and

water, and I didn't argue with him. I knew we might need every bit of it. It would be at least a week before Vasco got back with a party and food. A lot of things can happen in a week. A lot did.

The first day a condor tried to steal our lunch. He made off with a pack full of other stuff, canned rations, etc., when I beat him off the food with a stick. The next day a boa got friendly, and I threw rocks at it. I retired. In between slapping at the bugs, cussing under my breath, and worrying about Pug, I studied the rest of the German's papers.

In one way we had done the Germans a service by killing the leader of the spies. He had had no intention of turning the big ship over to his government or any other government. He had intended to silence everyone who knew anything about it, return to it after the war or sooner, and figure out some of the technical stuff—which he could patent and sell as inventions. He had to take Kraft into his confidence to do this, as Kraft was the boy who had discovered the key to the language in the books in the cabins, probably, and had kept it to himself, pretending to decipher the words by laborious code deciphering methods.

PUG and I finally figured out: "They will turn that thing over to the Nazis now. There are undoubtedly weapons in the ship that would win the war for the Fuehrer in short order. The fellows we left alive aren't the type to try to keep it for themselves. They haven't the initiative and ambition of the leader."

"That's about what will happen if we don't get there first. Pug, *can* we wait for the rest of our outfit to get here? Those Heinies have their windmill plane, radio communication with German subs—everything to get ahead with it faster than we can act to forestall them. Should we—must we—try to put the kibosh on them before the others get here?"

"Well, we could sneak up in the dark and disable the heli. But they land the thing on top of the ship—and how in Hades can we climb the sides of that mammoth thing? It would stump a human fly."

"We might work it this way. We ease up close in the darkness. Then, come daylight, we wait till the heli takes off. Then we board the ship the same as we did before and trust to luck to overpower the guard they leave behind. But he will be on his toes and expecting something of the kind."

"You know, Steve, there must have been some of the Germans asleep in that ship the day we entered. They didn't all come aboard from the helicopter."

"Yeh, you're right," I grunted. "I was busy going over the tommy gun I had brought along from our meeting with the diamond smugglers from Naziland. It was a comfortable weapon to have in the hand now that we were deciding to storm the hide-out of probably the toughest German agents on this side of the globe. And what a hide-out that bunch had picked! A space-ship from beyond man's ken, from the far stars. What a pearl for a bunch of swine it was.

I hated to think of Pug falling into their hands again. But the value of that ship to the men of the future was so infinitely greater than our lives, that I knew I must not shirk the job in any way.

That night we made our way to the crest of the low hill in which the great bow of the ship was buried; there we hid ourselves in the tall grass to wait till the heli took off. I kept the binoculars trained on the broad back of the monster below us. The morning sun showed the 'copter midway of the broad length of the mysterious visitor from space.

ABOUT ten o'clock the heli rose, but Pug and I waited a good hour to give the Heinies a chance to cork off if they felt like it—and who doesn't in that heat. Then we stole into the break in the bow, Pug with an automatic and I with the sub-machine gun clutched too tightly in my hands. We had no desire to let those hyenas get another chance at us. But they did.

Pug's torn red silk shirt brushed against one of the sculptured machines that looked like an animal of peculiarly intelligent aspect. It wasn't a horse, nor a deer, nor an antelope,—but something of all and superior to all. Her shirt caught in a stud sticking out of the sculpture, and somewhere inside a record began to play.

Did you ever hear the angels sing? I heard 'em when that ultra-lovely voice started from that too-beautiful machine. Not only the voice—I knew the Heinie guard would know someone was prowling around—and what would we do with him?—he knew his way around here and we didn't. Besides, there could be more than one—up to four. The heli didn't need more than one man aboard.

I wished we were safe back in that nice swamp fighting the bugs, the biting flies, etcetera, instead of trying to be a hero for the future of science—American science. Somehow the hero stuff is always too, too slippery. It was this time, anyway.

Two pairs of feet came racing toward us down the long corridor from the chambers in the waist. Pug and I kicked off our shoes and raced up a spider walk to a door above us. We swung the door to all but a crack, and watched.

The two Heinies were not to be caught napping, for they had seen what could happen, in the scorched corpses I had left behind on my other visit. One of them remained in the great arch of the big nose chamber—probably the bridge of the ship—while the other cautiously advanced to the musical sculpture and switched off the apparatus. I could reach one with my guns, but the other was still shielded by the wing of the great arch from my fire. I waited. I shouldn't have.

The other one walked back to his buddy and they returned. They had no stomach for searching the place—the advantages were all with the party in hiding. It was up to us. They apparently knew that time was on their side, and they would have plenty of help on the way with the return of the helicopter.

I got it. They were in no hurry. We were. So I slipped back down the ladder and turned all the switches and gadgets I could find in two seconds, then raced back up the spider walk.

WELL, what those other-world gadgets started to do I'll never know —but they sure as hell started plenty. In the center of the huge, observatory-like chamber, some hidden projection device began to project three dimensional images of various kinds of battle tactics between opposing fleets of space ships. The whole vast space became filled with apparently solid ships—on a small scale—but still big enough to frighten one—shooting at high speed in intricate maneuvers. How those alien minds could grasp the meaning of such rapid, frightfully daring

1496

maneuvers, I don't know. Ships wheeled and swung in groups of hundreds, dived headlong at other groups of ships, and fired at each other with soundless beams of blazing force. The sculptured mechanisms, both beautiful beast's forms and Godlike, nearly human bodies of over-sized men, began to orate, or sing, or project three dimensional records of doings beyond our capacity to understand—or move slowly through symetrical and statuesque dances of a strangely powerful, erotic nature. One of them began to demonstrate a super geometry upon a projected blackboard, a blackboard that was a solid block of blackness—a cube in which the lines appeared, complete with labels, and utterly incomprehensible.

The place was a wildly, utterly beautiful madhouse, even before I reached the top of the ladder. I could hear the two heinies rushing back to see what all the racket was about. The utter confusion, the designed and meaningful presentation of all these various messages to the mind, none of which could be comprehended by a man, seemed to madden the Nazis. They stood open-mouthed in the doorway, watching the supremely seductive gyrations of some other-world temptress doing a strip-tease to end all stripteases—while through her apparently solid body swooped whole fleets of space battle-ships—and over her head wheeled whole galaxies of over-sized star projections in a mad race to portray the whole history of the bodies of all space. Through all this heterogeneous display of the talent and wisdom of unknown eons of development of some alien manlike race, rolled and resounded the deafening symphony of a thousand instruments of music unknown to Earth men—and not designed for human ears—for they contained many sounds that were maddeningly painful to our ears.

Holding their ears and grimacing with the great pain of the strange, other-world music, the two Heinies advanced together and began to switch off the strange instruments. At last I got them both under my line of fire, and I let the hammering tommy gun leap in my hands till they both sprawled bleeding from a dozen wounds, on the gleaming metal floor. Then I stopped firing. A guy never does get quite ruthless enough for ruthless opposition.

ONE of the Heinies, as soon as I stopped firing, scrambled to his feet and shambled through the doorway before I could fire again. I slid down the rail of the ladder-way and bounded across the floor. Far up the corridor, he fled, his foot dragging. I let out the rest of the drum of cartridges after him, and knocked him down again. But he got up, and went on.

I raced after him, as soon as I had put in a new drum, and was nearly up with him when he slammed shut the big metal room of the chamber where we had first fallen afoul of the Germans. It proved a wrong move.

I had just about reached the great metal door, when overhead and behind me I heard the muffled clang of a metal door and the sound that these steps gave out to men's shoes. The rest of them were returning, and were almost down to the great corridor that reached from midship to the chamber in the bow where I had trapped the Nazis. Pug and I were split, and she wouldn't even know the others had returned. My own case was desperate; I was caught between the two fires from the returning men and the Nazi, who, though badly wounded, I knew was still alive enough and mad enough to

1497

get a gun and go for me. Moreover, the wounded man had seen us, and would be able to tell the rest that we were but two, and they would search the ship till they had us.

I ducked into the nearest door at the side of the corridor. I waited till the steps passed, then slid the muzzle out the door and let them have it. I wasn't playing marbles any more, except for keeps. There were five of them again. That heli must have had a capacity for just five men. Three men must have left in it, and five returned. Two of these men were in uniform. That meant they had contacted the sub off the coast, or some other base where they operated in uniform. That also meant more would arrive very soon.

All this ran through my mind as I emptied nearly the whole drum at the backs of the new arrivals. Unheroic? Unsportsmanlike? Brother, I was thinking of the whole future of science if I could get that ship intact into the hands of American authorities. I was thinking of dead American armies all over the world if the tremendous weapons in that ship ever fell into the hands of the Nazis. So my conscience had no twinges whatever as those Nazis rolled and dived from the blast of bullets let loose so suddenly on their backs. They were up against a man as ruthless and unromantically deadly as any Nazi could hope to be. The stakes made me that way. I didn't dare lose, and my cards were damn bad.

FOUR of them didn't get up from the floor. One dived through the metal door as the wounded man inside opened it a crack for them to get through. Another rolled over, got his automatic out and let me have it. He fired twice and his arm dropped lifeless. He was a fighter. He got me in the chest. It hurt, and I was plenty worried as I backed down the corridor to the great chamber in the bow where the three dimensional variety show had so recently intrigued the two Germans.

Pug waited just within the great arch, where she had watched the whole thing. She threw an arm around my waist, helped me up the step ladder to our little nook far above the big room full of strange apparatus. There I nearly passed out, but I didn't. I just lay and gasped, and the air whistled out of the little hole in my chest, too. Right through the lung. I coughed up a mouthful of blood.

"I guess they got me for good, Pug. If I do kick off, I want you to know I love you. When those rats burned you, I knew plenty how much you meant to me. Just want to make sure you know how it is."

"Sure, you big dope. I knew that all the time. Do you think I'm stupid? And don't get the idea this is the time for a death bed scene. I've seen lung wounds before. They look worse than they are. The only trouble is, you've got to be still, or it won't heal. We've got to sit tight here, and God knows what these Hitlers will be cooking up while we sit still."

As we huddled, with Pug fussing over my wound, we heard the whir and muffled roar of the 'copter taking off. Our friends had got away—and we were now in real trouble. They knew where we were; we couldn't move; and they would be back with more of the Fuehrer's South American Bundsmen and agents.

A bright idea struck me. Here things were about as bad as they could be, and the Heinies played right into my hands.

"Pug, they did it then. They went off and left us here. They must have been badly wounded and couldn't wait for help to come to them. Now, Pug— you've got to do this right. Run up

1498

there where they get out of the ship to their 'copter, and lock the hatch. Take the blow torch I used on the two rats that burned you and heat the metal of the hatch till it fuses. If you have any trouble doing it, yell and I'll come up and help you. But I think you can do it. As soon as you get the hatch firmly fastened so they can't get in, look up all the other hatches on the top surface of the ship and make sure they can't get in. We'll have a fort an army couldn't take us out of."

"Ah, Steve—you've really got it figured out now. We don't care how many Nazis come; we'll just let 'em whistle and wait till the chief shows up. IF Vasco got through."

"Don't say IF, Pug; he must have gotten through. We've kept these boys pretty busy."

Pug raced off, her legs twinkling prettily in the cream colored jodphurs. I was all through criticizing Pug. She was my girl.

A LONG half hour dragged by, and at last Pug returned, her face flushed and streaked with soot from the torch.

"All fixed, boss. They won't get in from the top."

"O.K., Pug, now we've got to move down to the gap in the bow. That is one entry we've got to seal with plenty of hot lead in the form of bullets. So take me down there, then go and search the Germans' stores for everything that will throw a slug, and bring it here. Bring some grub, too."

With a lot of unnecessary groaning on my part, and sympathetic help from Pug, I negotiated the long ladder-stair to the big chamber below. At the gap where we entered the ship, we dragged up a big metal couch, after unscrewing it from the floor, to form a barricade. Behind the couch, on a blanket, I took up my post with the sub-machine gun, while Pug raced off to search for more arms and food.

Our position was better, but nothing to shout about. As near as I could figure, we had sealed off the entries to the strange ship—but I might have missed something. There was no way to know when our men would arrive, and Vasco was an unknown quantity to me, though he had seemed dependable. Men aren't always when trouble shows up.

Night was swiftly darkening the sky, and to my other worries was added the fact I wouldn't be able to see the heinies when they did show up—if they did. It wasn't a pleasant thought. I hoped they weren't accustomed to flying that German windmill around in the dark.

I knew there had been only a few of these planes manufactured that were any good as yet, and that these were all in the possession of American secret agents and the F.B.I. Yet the Germans had obtained plans of our ship or a similar one, for use in places like this. It proved that their spy system was ultra-efficient.

With these thoughts I drifted into a fitful, dream-conditioned sleep. Pug let me sleep most of the night, but it didn't do me much good. I was feverish, and I felt damn weak. My chest hurt, plenty.

With the first light of dawn we heard the now familiar bump of the 'copter striking the upper surface of the huge ship. We could even hear them cursing in German, and the racket they made trying to open the fused metal hatch. Then the heli whirred up again, and sat down about a half mile away. They must have figured where we had taken our position, for they landed way out of our line of fire, and too far away to hit, anyway.

Then the 'copter took off again, and

1499

I knew it had gone for more men, or more weapons. The place was a perfect fort, and I felt pretty sure they wouldn't take us so easily. Still, I knew we couldn't hold out long; we couldn't move around, and they could. We couldn't replenish our ammunition or replace our losses; they could. Our only hope was the arrival of men from Pug's old man, the chief. I knew they would come plenty fast when the chief realized the fix Pug had gotten into.

THE Krauts landed two more heli loads of men and equipment during the morning. Then I guess they figured they couldn't afford to use any more time getting ready, and started lobbing various devices of incendiary nature at us. A light mortar threw a half dozen gas shells within a dozen feet of the great rent in the hull where I lay behind the barrier. A gentle breeze wafted the stuff off to the side. All I got was the bitter odor of almonds. If a bit of it had blown into the opening, it would have been my finish.

I held my fire, waiting for them to get out in the open where I could reach them effectively. I could reach them with a sniper's rifle Pug had brought, but I didn't want them to think I was playing. Among the other stuff Pug had laboriously toted from the German's quarters in the ship were some gas masks, and we slipped them on. Now I couldn't even see them, which was probably the effect they desired from the gas shells.

The men were trained soldiers, and over half of them were in uniform. There was no chance of them being stopped by Brazilian force, out here where only the armadillos felt at home. The hopelessness of the situation swept over me.

A light machine gun set up a covering fire for the advance. Bullets hammered into and around the big lounge. Pug scrooched tighter beside me, holding her ears and closing her eyes. We just couldn't take much of this, and they were just starting. I had to take a look—and I knew it was sure death to poke my head out of that opening. But they could sneak up alongside the ship, and I had to know if they were doing it or not. The hammering of bullets didn't stop for a half hour. Then it let up, and I sneaked a quick look. It was nearly my last.

The Heinies had taken position in a semi-circle around the opening, behind hummocks, trees and rocks—and were waiting for me. Seven or eight rifles let go at once, and they were every one damn close. One plucked at my hair with mad fingers, another caromed off the metal and got Pug in the leg. We were just about gone geese.

AT THIS point I drew my head back to see the strangest sight I ever hope to see.

Inside the chamber where I had put on the futuristic variety show, some more strange things had been going on. My eyes started out of my head as I tried to grasp the meaning of what I was seeing where I had expected to see nothing living.

Across the big chamber toward us were strolling two people, a man and a woman. I knew they were people of the ship, from pictures I had seen of their peculiarly superb physiques, the serene, sculpturesque quality of their faces. They seemed not to be afraid of the bullets whining in richochets off the metal of the opening, and caroming around in the chamber like mad bees. It struck me they had no idea what bullets were. I shook Pug out of her attention to the nick in her leg.

"Pug, maybe I'm seeing ghosts—but you better get them back out of the

THE HIDDEN WORLD

danger and see what is what, if any."

Pug looked up, and let out a cry like a little girl scared in the dark. They *were* kind of scary, with their huge eyes and double length hands, kind of beautiful and deadly—like a strange vision of a man and woman of vastly greater powers than human.

Pug crawled toward them on her hands and knees, till she was away from the gap in the hull. Then she stood up and went to them with her hands raised to wave them back out of danger.

But they weren't being told what to do on their own ship. They remained, standing unperturbed and smiling like a couple of unbelievably lovely living sculptures by some artist from a better world. Then what I feared for them, happened. A ricochet screamed from the metal wall and struck the woman in the arm. Blood flowed in a stream, dripping from her hand to the floor, where swiftly a scarlet pool widened.

She looked down, and gave a little unbelieving gasp at the unexpected pain. That was the unluckiest shot any Heinie ever triggered, and most of their work has been unlucky. A fierce comprehension spread swiftly over the face of the tall man. Then, with the incredible swiftness of a leopard—he galvanized into a blur of action.

He raced around the big chamber, turned a switch here, swung a wheel there in a swift circle, and upon the smoke thickened air of the chamber the scene outside sprang into focus. The Heinies were within a dozen feet of the gap in the hull, just waiting the order for a final rush.

They never got a chance to make the rush. The stranger took one of those harmless appearing tools from the racks on the walls, and from the round maw of the gun-like tool sprang a ray of blinding brilliance. At each of the figures in the projection of the scene outside the tall stranger pointed the bright ray, and as the image of the man outside received the ray, the image dropped in a stiffened, frozen immobility. Some magic of the huge projection mechanism transferred the potent impulse of the ray through its magnifying focus of vision—direct to the scene outside.

IN A few moments the suddenly fierce stranger had eliminated completely the strength of the Germans, which I had momentarily expected to overwhelm our slight defenses. I dropped in relief to the metal floor by the barrier, my strength gone now that the threat was removed.

From a cabinet in the wall the still frowning stranger, moving like a picture of the perfection of the future, took a tiny kit. From it he brought out a small pad and applied it to the arm of his companion. On the pad he poured a liquid from a tiny capsule. Then he bent over me, and tore my shirt away from the wound that Pug had bandaged. He poured some of the fluid into the wound, placed a similar pad over the bared wound, and poured the rest of the vial of liquid over the pad.

As yet he had not spoken, but now his mouth opened and I heard the vital musical tones of the people from space—the same unbelievable beautiful sort of voice which the records had played. I did not know the meaning of the words—but I gathered he meant to keep the pad in place. I laid my hand on the pad over the wound, and he nodded and smiled. Shortly I fell asleep, completely worn out.

I awoke, alone, and lying on one of the over-size bunks in a chamber of the ship. I looked at my wound. It was nearly healed. Only a red pucker re-

1501

mained where a few hours before had been a scarlet hole. Yes, there was a lot we could learn from that ship from another world.

As I swung my feet to the floor, surprised to find my weakness had left me, the familiar odor of a certain hard-to-get cigar came to me. I looked up to find the chief standing in the door, and behind him the smiling face of Pug.

A great feeling of relief came over me. The responsiblity of making sure the immense power in the machines and weapons of this ship got into the right hands was no longer on my shoulders.

"I was all set to give you two scatterbrains the bawling out of your young lives. But that's out, seeing what you have turned up. I've already sent the plans for one device by radio to Washington. The stranger calls it Radar. What an edge it will give our ships! Nothing can get near them undetected."

"Chief, just what is in the cards for these strangers? Who are they, what are they going to do—what have you got out of them about themselves?"

"IT'S a long story, Steve. I've sent for a small army of technicians and engineers to repair the ship—to study with the stranger. It seems they can't stand our sun—have to leave within a few months at the most. So the ship will be repaired, and we'll lose them. But in the meantime, we'll learn plenty."

"Where were they keeping themselves all the time the Germans were hiding out here? Are there only two of them?"

"Well, it's hard to understand just what the man meant,—but I think he meant to explain that to me. There's about a hundred of them—sleeping in a specially prepared chamber that is insulated against the sun rays—and in which special air and vibrations reproduce the conditions of their home as nearly as possible. Several of them died while they were building the chamber, after the ship crashed. The rest have been asleep in the chamber—still are, for that matter. It isn't very big, and they can only remain out of it for a few hours at a time, due to the strong radioactivity of our soil and the detrimental charge of electric over the surface of earth. They just can't stand it. So the couple you met have been replaced by another pair, and each day they will change—so that none of them are exposed to the earth conditions for a long period."

"Chief,—you want to get the best minds here we can reach—pronto—to study their science and language, so they can leave us the designs for a ship like this."

"Don't worry, Steve—Washington Headquarters has the whole story—and you and Pug get the credit for the biggest accomplishment of all time. We won't leave anything undone that we can do."

"Pug, someday, when the war is over and things get decent again, the ship will be built—and we'll see the stars—from space. We'll even step on the soil of another planet. That will be hard to take, eh? Honeymoon on Mars, for Mr. and Mrs. Steve Hawley. How about it, Pug?"

"I can't think of an objection Steve." Pug had come to my side, and right there in front of her Dad we sealed the compact with a scorching kiss. And whether my ears were hearing correctly or not—the chief was murmuring something about, "Blessings . . . a thousand blessings—and I hope they do honeymoon on Mars."

A LITTLE over a month later we watched the strange ship lift and drive into the night sky with a mighty burst of power. And behind her, she left in the vaults and workshops of American government factories the plans for an armament and for peaceful devices which would put the United States so far ahead of other nations that fear would never again fall upon the people of the U. S.

And somewhere in secret underground factories, a score of these mighty space crossing creations of the minds of a race far advanced beyond earthmen, are being built. Pug and I have a guarantee of first passage to another planet as our wedding present.

REPORT FROM THE FORGOTTEN PAST

HERE are the latest bits of mystery your editor has dug out of the past. Let the archaeologists make something of them.

Take a look at the Hebraic, Vedic and Algonquin languages. Widely separated races, you will all agree. Well, the following seven words appear in all three languages: ANASH—which means to be persistently stubborn, by word or thought; ZIMMAH—wicked device; RA—delight in being bad; BELYYAAL—worthlessness; AVEN—vanity and self-conceit; DIBBAH—slander and reporting of evils; SATAN—to be a leader.

These seven words date back to 25,000 years ago; and their appearance in the languages of these three peoples, unchanged through 250 centuries, is unequivocal proof of the relationship of all three races, and their common origin. What about it, you archaeologists?

* * *

Ten thousand years ago there was a great civilization flourishing just east of Imperial Valley and approximately on the border between Mexico and the United States. There were magnificent cities. Then there was a great inundation from the north, passing through the Colorado river valley (and Canyon). These cities were buried beneath as much as a thousand feet of sand and boulders. A sand bar was thrown across the gulf of California, midway, the upper portion later drying out and becoming Imperial Valley. These cities can be found by digging.

* * *

The ancient continent of Lemuria, or Pan, located in the Pacific was composed of three sections, or islands, separated by narrow channels. The names of these islands were as follows: *Mai*, (note the resemblance to Mu and Mi) on which were a thousand cities built in rich valleys; *Og*, consisting of wide plains, also with a thousand (approximately) cities, among them the capital city, Penj, and the great temples of Khu, and Bart, and Gan and Saing; *Gan*, a mountainous section with few cities. Mai, Og and Gan were destroyed in a cataclysm that was over in twenty-four hours.

The word Japan, broken down by the Shaver Alphabet, means "Seed of Pan." Students of the geology of Japan will point out that (granting the existence of a continent in the Pacific which sank) the continental shelf breaks abruptly, descending for two-thousand feet into the ocean. Thus, Japan is properly termed a remaining bit of the ancient continent, a "seed" which remains as the germinating point for complete proof of the ancient continent. Japanese language, as it is spoken, not written, is the only language on earth which has descended through thousands of years almost phonetically pure and unchanged. Students of Japanese will instantly note the facility with which the Shaver Alphabet can be used to translate phonetic Japanese. The proper spelling of Japan is Zhapan. Z being the symbol for zero, or stasis. Japan, the unchanged, the relic, the *proof* of Lemuria.

* * *

In Europe, from Southern France to the Urals, exist an almost unbroken chain of ancient cities, buried at varying depths. The existence of these ruins is suspected by many scientists, and it is almost certain that when research is begun, they will be discovered and add a great deal to our knowledge of the past ages of man's civilizations, which extend back beyond 75,000 years ago.

* * *

Today we use "giddap" and "whoa" to a horse, to make him go and stop. It might be interesting to note that in the ancient Panic language, "gitoo" means, light ahead, the way is clear—and "washa" means, darkness ahead.

* * *

After Moses left Egypt, her empire fell, and her people migrated westward, hundreds of thousands of them, and settled in Western Europe, where they married aborigines. Their offspring were called Druids, Picts, Gales, Wales, Galls, and Yohans, all of which are Egyptian names, yet today are not referring to Egypt, but the peoples known as Gaelic, Welsh, Gauls and Johns. Their names betray their origin.

1503

THE HIDDEN WORLD

A MAN NEVER knows how much of his life is made up of familiar things. Not until he gets into a place where nothing is familiar any more!

To you a boiler shop or a steel mill or the Sunday traffic have nothing particularly deadly about them. But place the Hottentot or the Zulu in the steel mill or the traffic. Like a cat caught in the traffic he wouldn't last long.

Place yourself in an alien world. A world where duplication takes place strangely, where nothing goes according to the familiar laws of nature you take for granted. Then every little item of your daily life becomes an adventure in deadly danger.

JOE DANNON'S head was buzzing. "Some kind of space sickness, I s'pose." Joe talked to himself—for he was alone in the tiny cabin of the *Pioneer*. The buzzing got worse as he shut the jets off again.

"There can't be much fuel in the tanks." Joe missed the slosh and rattle of the drifting oil and the feel of its shifting weight. Funny how a guy and a ship get to be part of each other, how much aware of the whole thing he was, after five long years with her alone.

There below something that couldn't be, existed! Giant worms, fifty miles long—and alligator-beasts almost as huge, battling them

Joe Dannon, Pioneer

by Richard S. Shaver

You're sure you know who "yourself" is?
On this strange world, Joe Dannon found out
his "self" was not always easy to identify!

Funny how a guy could stay alive on nothing, out here where no gravity bore down to wear a man out. By rights he should have died of starvation a couple of months ago. He had cut his rations to a quarter normal since he left Lornomor. Was that two months ago, or was he as nuts as he feared he might be?

Five years! "Geez!" No wonder a guy talked to himself.

Sure, he felt all right, as far as that goes. But, the darn delusions. The visions that plagued him. Like now—those long white arms gesturing to him, calling to him.

Calling him to Earth? Sure that was Earth! It looked like Earth. Just like the globe used to look in the schoolroom — only it didn't have pretty white clouds strung around it, then.

Geez, he was tired. Tired of talking to himself. Tired of everything. Those darn arms.

Soft white arms—his mind couldn't even tell any more whether they were false or true. They were too everlastingly long to be real. They moved and twined like lovely, but deadly snakes. Real arms couldn't do that. Hell ... no!

A voice now! Dang it! It wasn't his own voice! Somebody else's voice.

Now more of them! Three or four of them. Soft ones, female—cuddly voices, and now a strident, harsh one. And one deep husky voice that called and called. . . .

He couldn't make out the words, but he knew what they were saying. They were saying this:

"You who have been away so long in the blue beyond, where the stars forever blaze out their deadly light into the ever-cold! Out where the stars wait with deadly bright lances to blast the sense out of your head and leave it buzzing as your head is buzzing. Where the sky is not black nor blue, but so black it is blue. All that is behind! You are home now, Joe. But, you are mad. You're nuts, Joe, nuts!

"Yes, you're nuts, our poor Joe. You've seen too much out there. You're too dumb now from the star rays, you'll never be able to keep your darn mouth shut. You'll talk. And you know what happens to guys that talk about such things as you've seen. They'll call the white-coats, put you in a padded cell. A padded cell, Joe. That's what you'll get for your pioneering.

"Yes, that's what you're landing for, Joe Dannon. Better for you to just keep on going. Out where it's always quiet. Or else just dive head on into Earth—down and down into those mountains that were your home, five long years ago.

"Men don't want you now, you're crazy. The smart aleck medicoes will look *so* wise when you tell your story. And the old guys who financed the *Pioneer* and were so afraid of ridicule they didn't want publicity till your return—will they be on hand, will they get to hear your story before the smart alecks wrap you up in a strait jacket? Will they defend you when you tell the truth of where you have been for five years? You were supposed to return in months. Maybe the old guys, Prof. Gizide and the rest of them, are dead or gone off somewhere? Anything could go wrong, but damn the worrying. Let the wise medicoes nod their silly heads when you tell your story and lead you away, oh so gently. Old Prof. Gizide will get you out fast enough when he hears about it; he'll prove that you did take off five years ago on an unannounced rocket flight to space. Sure, Joe, don't worry, everything will work out. When you struggle in the nut-house they won't beat you too hard. Just hard enough so you can't struggle any more, that's all. A hell of a thing to land for, Joe. Better just dive straight down and have it over with quick!"

THE bright day died as he shot around, on around the green cloud-dotted earth and the night rose before him as he plunged into the shadow of earth. The stars sprang out brighter again above him where they had been so long in their cold alien splendor. Fires forever frozen into a pattern of brilliant, blinding diamonds set on the ever-black. And then as swiftly it was day again!

He had shot around the whole earth shadow much too quickly. Joe shook his head, the buzzing quieted. The voices stopped.

Joe glanced at the speed dial, and whistled. At this rate he would have to coast around the old globe for a week.

He would have to ease slowly down into that air or he would burn up like a moth hitting a hot lamp. Maybe he would anyway.

He sure couldn't think like a guy landing a space ship should think. After all, though, he only *had* landed her twice before.

Once on Klakdonothor. What a name for a place! Once on Lornomor. If a guy ever started talking about the things he had seen on just two planets —what there must be to see on the really far-off planets!

In Joe's tired mind were the terrible visions of the life on Klakdonothor, as "they" called it. Where the life is so huge and horrible, so strange that words just haven't been made by men to talk about such things—a guy would have to invent all new words.

But, hell . . . he had films aboard. Somewhere in his junk in the rear of the old tomato can. If the heat hadn't got into them too bad?

The great worms that lie in the slime and howl like a thousand calliopes. Which isn't so odd, the howling—seeing the worms are three and four miles long. Wonder how big a robin would be built to fit those worms?

Klakdonothor was a soft, mushy planet. A lot bigger than Earth. But it couldn't be near as dense for nothing seemed much heavier. It had looked green and so good when it had first loomed up ahead of him.

And then those great things that preyed on the worms had showed up when he had landed! He couldn't even get out to take water aboard, or anything.

Vast alligator-like serpents, squirming through the muck. Squirming quietly, to strike the great worms where they lay asleep. He had thought the worms were hills, or viaducts, or something, at first.

Then they had moved! The terrible, writhing battle that had thrashed the greenery to shreds, to green hash, for fifty miles around the *Pioneer* before he could get her off again, and out of danger.

And that dying worm lying in its deathbed of fifty miles of blood and flesh and hashed jungle, screaming and screaming as it writhed in great snapping coils. Nearly smashed the old tomato can!

Joe thought of "they" who had helped him. "They" who called themselves the "Klakdor," and their planet "Klakdonothor."

Great, floating living palaces "they" built—spun out of their own bodies like great spiders.

Their terrible, yet beautiful thought, so full of perfect, yet somehow such unkind and inhuman voices—such careless, cruel and seemingly perfect logic. So perfectly kind, yet so cruel in their superiority.

They could not take him seriously enough to be anything but carelessly cruel to his earth mind.

They just couldn't take him seriously, to make him at home or feel that he was safe among friends. To them he was but a midge fly, caught up by the web of circumstance—projected by the unusual inventiveness of his backward race into space. Flung by chance into their aerial web of life on his great tube of soft iron and flaming gas and crude fuel and cumbrous instruments. They had all thought it a most humorous way to travel.

JOE knew why they thought his ship humorous when he saw their own sleek ships of shining plastic speed past him.

He could hear their thought-voices laughing around him as they looked the "quaint" *Pioneer* over. It was then he started calling the *Pioneer*, the life-work of that fine old man Prof. Gizide, the "old tomato can". It was the nearest he could come to translating what they thought about the ship. It was the best he could do in mental defense against their cruel humour—to despise himself and his ship, too.

"Yes, if I talk about the Klakdor I will be labeled crazy. What the hell can I talk about when I land and they want to know what space is like?"

Certainly not the impossible life-forms on and around the dread mushy vastness of Klakdonotho!

Joe considered the dead world of Lornomor toward which he had fled in his iron "tomato can" to avoid the merciless thought-laughter from the superior race of the Klakdor—as an embarassed child flees from adult ridicule.

Desperately, suicidally, he had fled toward the dead white planet as it swung near out of the black night.

He had to do something! He couldn't drink that red stuff, or eat that fried dry hash the Klakdor had brought him. It smelled too much like the great, horrible worms in the swamps below. What else would it be, when they were so big, so numerous? Joe Cannon, drinking worm's blood—only it wouldn't stay down.

Whatever the Klakdor might think of themselves, Joe Cannon would never concede that fried worms and raw worm's blood were Nectar and Ambrosia. They had brought it in response to his mental realization that his stores were nearly gone. It was kind of them—or was it cruel of them? Was it their way of being funny, to bring him revolting, bad-smelling food? Well, he couldn't like them or their food or their life or accept their condescending help.

Joe's head nodded. He fell asleep at the controls, and the *Pioneer* hurled on around the home planet, Earth. Joe dreamed again of the peace he had found on the dead world of Lornomor.

There he had learned so vastly much more from one old man than the so superior minds of the Klakdor had condescended to teach him. You couldn't hate the Klakdor. But you could run away.

The little ship swung on, imperfectly orbited, but still outside the real grip of Earth's gravity. Joe would have to take her lower into the air below to slow her for the long dive. But Joe was tired. Joe slept.

THE voice of old Pood Jaqmul sounded in his sleeping ears dreamily. Pood was the old guy he had found in the deep caves, deep and warm and far down under the eternal ice of the surface. Pood had told him the dead world was called Lornomor, Pood had

1508

told him plenty. But could he repeat any of it?

"Space fears Earth, Joe. Space races near your planet are so weak with their ages of warring on each other .... So few, with all their ancient space craft and wonder machinery. They fear to let Earthmen learn anything. For the Earth races, once in space—would soon wipe out the horror that is their life.

"That's how I got marooned here. I didn't know ... It's a long story, Joe. Sit down there on that hunk of silver sculpture. I'll tell you all about it. It takes a long time to tell a greenhorn from Earth about space.

"You think you're a pioneer. That's the name of your ship. But you're not a pioneer, even from among the people of Earth! The only difference is that your race built your ship.

"Space has been traveled regularly since what your race calls early times ... Even *from* Earth, and *to* Earth.

"The planets of space near Earth are rotten with the thing that makes the space traveling races fear Earth people. It's a long story to get it all through your head. So just relax and I'll tell you why old Pood waits for death here in these caves on Lornomor ... when he could take off into the far, clean spaces where life is what is should be.

"I'm tired, Joe. Tired, and I'm quitting."

Funny way for a hermit to talk to the first human face he had seen in twenty years or so. But Pood was a lot older than an Earth human, and maybe he had plenty of reason to be tired of living. Pood wasn't an Earth human.

Pood was from another planet, and there were lots of such places, but according to Pood there weren't many humans to be found there. Just cruel, terrible killers and their cronies and panders and captive women—everything else they had killed.

About Pood and Joe as they talked were the great paintings of the walls of the caverns—those paintings by giants' immortal hands. Paintings such as Michael Angelo's might have been if Mike had studied for a thousand years instead of fifty or forty. If Mike had been an immortal and studied under immortal teachers for a thousand Earth years he might have done something about half that good. If he had seen life and doings such as no mortal man from Earth ever saw.

The vast man-figures and animal-figures were more than superhuman. More perfect than the word "perfect" can convey. The minute detail as fine as a master's engraving ran all through the colossal scenes of Cyclopean life.

OLD Pood, as old men will, forgot he had told Joe to sit down, forgot all about him, apparently. Pood got up and started walking restlessly away, as if he had forgotten something he had to tend to.

Joe got up and followed; he wasn't losing his only human contact since leaving Earth. Joe was tired, but not that tired.

Pood had done it to him again, when he had absent-mindedly led him off into that maze of antique caverns—and Joe had followed in fear of being left alone.

Plunged him into things that filled him with the awful, constant fear of an environment entirely too much for his limited understanding. He was a cat caught in the Sunday traffic again. Just no sense to anything—just stand and face it and wonder what's going to hit you. And knowing it will!

Old Pood had led Joe off into an alien wonder-world. Yes, such a world can have lure ... The bright lure of adventure, the lure of sex in the strange and fearfully wonderful pictures and statues and thought-records from the bodies and minds of infinitely superior, God-like females. It can have terrific excitement and novelty.

But it also can have in a dreadful measure that fear that paralyzes—that fear like a cat's caught in the traffic, or a city child alone in the woods.

And all excitement and novelty fails to counteract or reduce or hide or help against the terrible fear that comes from a loss of all familiar things around one.

Yes, strong nerves and a healthy body can make a man hard and strong and able to quell such fear and enjoy the terrific novelty of such an alien environment. But Joe was weary, worn out, had been under a terrible stress and necessity of long hours of wakefulness. He was a nervous wreck, but he didn't know it. He found it out the hard way.

You see, the one thing the Klakdor had taught Joe was how to read minds. They had to teach him that to talk to him. It is a little trick of concentration, or else they had treated his mind with a ray from a distance. Joe knew now that the mind hears thought all the time, from other minds; and if you know how, you can read over the memory films of recent awarenesses. You can search till you find certain listening cells in your mind and they will hear the thought and tell you what it is, even after they have heard it. But it is a trick learned by hard effort, not something that happens without willing it to happen.

Pood had told Joe his name by this method, which was the way they did most of their talking.

THE first thing Pood did that threw Joe's nerves out of whack, he walked up to a vast intricate maze of metal that was meaningless to Joe—and opened a door. Pood walked in, closed the door. A moment later he stuck his head out, looking for Joe, and said: "Come on in; you might as well have some too."

Joe entered, found himself in a metal room about twenty by twenty. On the wall were a dozen peculiar levers. Pood pulled down all twelve of the levers, then touched a great switch on the wall with his finger.

Nothing happened! They walked out.

Then Joe noticed movement to right and left where had been none before.

As he looked that fear started up in his breast, that fear of the unknown!

For right and left of him were twelve other Joe Cannons! And twelve more Poods!

"What happened, Pood? What happened? Who are these guys; reflections? I didn't see any mirrors. I still don't."

"'Taint mirrors, Joe. That machine was a duplicator. We have twenty-four duplicates now, and if anything happens to us we won't know the difference!" Pood chuckled. "Hard to believe, ain't it. We'd never know the difference.

"I made a lot of 'em, of me, when I first came here, Joe. But they all died after a while. Got tired of themselves . . . I'm the only one left. And even I don't know whether it's me or a duplicate! Do you know? Can you tell me if I'm me, or a machine product?" Pood chuckled.

Joe was lost. Things are like that in Elder caves. The mind gives up! Such problems conceived for Titan minds by Titan minds just aren't the right size to fit a human head. If he died now he wouldn't know the difference! But then, did one *ever* know it?

1510

As they went on down the endless, many-branched cavern way, the duplicate pairs each took a separate branch as it opened. But it wasn't possible that the paths they took mattered. Somehow *they are just more me*, decided Joe. *Just more and more Joes and Poods and it doesn't matter if one dies or if they all die or if I should die. They would go on.*

But what was the meaning of it? There was something in it he couldn't grasp. Why did Pood do it?

"Because these caverns are dangerous." Pood's mental answer seemed adequate.

"When in danger, you just make a few duplicates and then the loss of one or two won't matter!"

Joe rubbed his head, and that buzzing started. It didn't stop, for a problem was posed he couldn't answer. His head just buzzed on, like the clutch was slipping on an overload.

Joe couldn't think, and musingly he watched, pausing to look at a great depression under a vast metal enigma. Pood grabbed his arm just as he was about to step into the shallow depression to see what it was about.

Pood said, "Now watch those other two on the identical corridor alongside. There is a machine just like this one. Maybe the other Pood hasn't got the proper affection for his friend yet, being so new. Maybe he won't think to stop him. Watch!"

AS JOE stood watching, he could see the other pair dimly. Pood and Joe, going along the companion corridor which paired this one in reverse, like a reflection. An identical depression under an identical machine snared the attention of the duplicate Joe. The repetition of his own thought and act was weird.

The other Joe stepped in, his arm reached out curiously to touch something. Was it his weight that tripped the power switch of the device, like a platform scale. Or was it his finger that made some obscure contact?

Joe didn't want to find out after it happened.

A blinding flash. A terrible moment of a pulsing, powerful ray from the machine downward. Even here, a hundred yards away, Joe could feel the power of the terrific pressure ray—the sudden relief as the power released again. And in that flash, the other Joe disappeared!

Pood said, "Come on, I'll show you why we need duplicates. This is no place for a fellow who has no experience with it all."

They walked quickly up to where the other Pood stood staring disconsolately at the place where Joe had been.

"Look—" said both Pood's simultaneously, pointing at the floor of the saucer-like depression. There was a faint reddish brown smear all across the solid metal surface. That was Joe!

The titanic pressure of that machine ray had compressed Joe into a thin dense film upon the metal. One duplicate was no more!

They walked on calmly—two Poods and one Joe.

Joe's head buzzed . . .

Now and then through the openings between the titanic metal machines that lined this time-forgotten factory of miracle people Joe could see other pairs of identical Poods and Joes, plodding along. Joe looked tired, and Pood always looked like a cynical, weary and disillusioned old man who had to take care of the children and wasn't very enthusiastic about it.

"Where are we going?" asked Joe, too tired to wonder about it all, but not too tired to worry plenty.

"We're going after certain things

that will do you a lot of good. I don't need them, but you do. Foods, beneficial rays, fluids to drink, medicaments."

They plodded past a weird edifice, a place large enough to cover several city blocks. It was made of many inextricably intertwined planes of curving glass-like stuff that seemed formed for the purpose of losing any wanderer inside. A mirror maze. Maybe it was for amusement. Joe didn't ask; Pood got tired of answering all his questions. Maybe the ancients had a lot of time to spend wandering around such things, wound up in impossible transparent corridors. Or maybe they used some other sense to get around with than plain eyesight.

Stairs, long ramps slanting upward, chambers of odd and weird sights that he could not quite make out in the strange half light of the place. For that matter he hadn't figured out where the light came from, either. But Pood paid no attention. Joe hated to ask questions like a kid. They plodded on.

SUDDENLY inside the maze a light flashed on blindingly bright and Joe heard a "whooooeeee whooooooeeeewoooo"! Something inside the maze, something that had been speeding out of nowhere, out of space maybe—came suddenly to a stop and for an instant Joe saw many little ugly dwarves inside one of the chambers. They were naked but for g-strings, and their hair was long and matted. They carried short bows and arrows in a quiver over one shoulder. They just didn't make sense here in this place of terrific scientific building, of past titanic workmanship.

Again came that weird "whooooo-eeeewhoooooo" as of a locomotive rounding the bend of the edge of the world—as of a materializing ghost train from nowhere—from seventh heaven, maybe.

As Joe watched with startled wide eyes, out of an opening that was not anywhere in the walls but seemed from out of the very nothingness of space itself, out of the air of the center of the great transparent maze shot a long, pearl-grey cylinder the size of a railroad car.

Inside were a dozen gigantic forms, women, they were—and Joe pushed forward to the great glass-like wall to see better. Pushed a couple of other Joes and Poods out of the way, for the awful "whooeeewoo" had brought them running.

Gigantic goddesses, fair and beautiful, but alien as time! Their weirdly twisted hair ornaments, breast plates, anklets and arm bands were of some bright metal, like chrome. Everything about them told Joe they weren't of any race he had ever seen.

But then, he had never seen any but Earth men, and the Klakdor, and now Pood, who was hardly human, but seemed so to Joe because Pood was sort of friendly and Joe could understand him. But since he had been with the Klakdor he could understand anybody.

Joe, from having had the same feeling so often lately, realized the dwarves inside the maze were feeling now that fear that he had felt—the fear the cat in traffic must feel. Joe knew that an animal in that position usually got crushed. With those gigantic women bearing down in pursuit from some weird other world on a machine of a kind no dreamer ever dreamed on earth.

The gigantic women blasted at the dwarves with long weapons that twanged like metal bows, like great plucked harps. They shot out a bolt of green fire and the dwarves melted under their accurate fire. But they bent their dwarfish twisted arms and

1512

pulled back their bows and the short clumsy arrows flew back at the giant women.

Joe winced as an arrow pierced a high-breasted beauty. The blood flowed down her white, marble-smooth waist; she clutched at her breast and sank to her knees.

Then that terrific "whoooeeewooo" and the dwarves disappeared, melting into that nothingness on the wings of that titanic railroad into space... one of them had known how to set the car into flight again. After them vanished the second car—and the gigantic ultra-beautiful women.

But where they had been, lay several dead dwarves, and beside them the long, slightly gowned figure of a gigantic female.

JOE looked at Pood, a long questioning look, pleading for information. Pood obliged, though still somewhat bored:

"That is a machine. You get in it and it takes you through the 'seven magical stops'. Each stop, when it stops, you can push a button and reach seven other magical stops. Or press another button and come back. Only trouble it is, you never know where you are when you get there—and never *can* remember just how to get back. Or which button to push, anyway. Or whether you have arrived seven hundred years ago or in the future. Or practically anything about it. I was through it when I first came here. I don't know how long ago that was in your time-telling. Those dwarves are natives of one of the worlds the cars stop at, somewhere in space—or whatever it is the cars travel to and on, or in. I suspect the railroad is a space-distortion traveling device that takes people places by some strange distortion of the laws holding things apart that we call space or distance. Through an ultra-dimension. I don't understand it and I doubt if anyone now living understands it. The dwarves stole that car from the giant women either centuries ago or several planets distance away, I wouldn't know which. They set out on their own to explore the railroad of the seven magical stops. Somewhere along the line they shot a few arrows at the giant women and the women set out in pursuit. The big women might be natives of Lornomor of the past, chasing the dwarves into the future and are going back when they get through. Wish they had killed all those dwarves, and we might have got a chance to talk to them. First people I've seen in half a century I really wanted to talk to. We'd have *some* company if they had stayed here a while."

"*Some* company is right" breathed Joe, thinking of the divine beauty of the huge people. Maybe they were the people who had built these caverns of Lornomor. Or were they? Was Pood always right in his guesses? How much did Pood really know? Who was he anyway?

Well, he had plenty of time to find out. All his life maybe. Then Joe thought of the duplicate Joes walking down those nearly duplicate corridors, saying nearly identical things.

His head started to buzz again. Suppose each of the corridors were an exact duplicate? Suppose each Joe had seen an exact duplication of the scene he had just witnessed and had the same thoughts about it? Suppose some of those scenes had been nearly the same, except that the giantesses had killed all the dwarves and remained on Lornomor? Suppose in the duplicate corridors some of them had come out of the crystal maze and talked to Joe Cannon? He sure would have to ask those

1513

duplicate Joes some questions when he saw them again. But it was so confusing to have identicals.

If he died, there would still be many of him around. Would they be Joe, be him? Or would he be dead, really dead?

SLOWLY Joe realized that he himself was a near duplicate of every other man on earth, except for details ... length of nose, length and thickness of leg, size of brain, etc. etc. All four-limbed and many of them surprisingly alike. Just like all horses look alike to some people—or all negroes look alike to some people. The truth was all people are brothers of a beginning that was identical somewhere, being one beginning. Yet if he died, he was dead—even though there were plenty of people around very much like him, almost duplicates of him.

They would carry on, say the same things, do the same things, crack the same old jokes over and over. They would marry and raise kids, and lots of the kids of America would look surprisingly like Joe Cannon. What the Heck was "self". He had just seen it duplicated and was no nearer to understanding it, the enigma, than before. Joe guessed shrewdly old Pood had been playing his own special joke, a magical trick upon him with the duplicator. There was no reason to believe that because he had duplicates, he would not be dead if he was killed. There was no reason to change his ideas of identity. Or were there?

Joe's head buzzed. Streets on Earth were nearly duplicates, quite often. The people walking up and down them were nearly duplicates in the main details. But when a man died he was dead and gone. Pood had been kidding him. Just Pood's special joke, to keep him from worrying.

Now from an opening on the far side of the corridor came another Pood and another Joe. As Joe watched they entered another machine like the one they had used to duplicate themselves when Pood and Joe first entered the caverns. Joe stopped to watch, but Pood wasn't interested. A short time passed.

Joe sat down in a blue daze as they came out of the doors. They were still Pood and Joe, but like people seen in a trick mirror at the circus that makes them broad and fat and funny.

Half as high, they were each twice as broad. They walked now with that peculiar short step of the dwarf—were compressed people—some terrible metamorphosis had seized them in the titanic force flows inside the machine and made them short and terrible thick. Joe looked at Pood.

Pood said wearily, "That machine is a thing the ancient race used to make a man heavier, ready for a heavier planet. On heavy planets a man has to be broader, shorter, stronger every way. That machine makes him ready for a trip to the heavy planets. When he comes back, I suppose he gets stretched out again. It is probably adjustable for the various sizes of planets. Joe and Pood don't even know they are different. They won't know till they take a look in a mirror or notice each other. Everything looks bigger, is all."

Joe wondered. Was that duplicate Joe still Joe? Or was he some other person? Was he now no longer Joe Cannon? Joe was tall, the new Joe was short. Joe had a long, lantern-jawed face, the new shorty Joe had now a short square face. Joe's leg was long and graceful, the other Joe had a short heavy leg like a baby elephant. How could he be Joe? But he *had* been Joe? Why wasn't he now? If he, Joe, died, would he be suddenly aware of life within the fat, short Joe? If all the other Joes died, and he died too—and only that short fat Joe lived—would that be Joe? would that fat Joe be conscious of being short and broad and heavy built?

SLOWLY the realization came to Joe Cannon that all the people of his race were really one thing—a repetitious repetition of the identical pattern man, and the only difference was that chance shifted the pattern slightly for each one—so they came out different all the time. Environment, feeding, many factors entered into this pattern shifting, but still the thing was the same thing—always—man. One thing, ever dividing and repeating, man—man—man! No more and no less than that.

Gradually Joe realized that "self" and "here" are the same word. Put another Joe over there and it was another self. Repeat it endlessly and you had a race of beings. Self itself was an illusion due to *"here"*dity— "here"— a repetition separated by a space. Connect two identical consciousnesses with wires—wouldn't they be like two batteries hooked together—just twice as much self—but the same?

Hell, take thought itself, it's always the same thing! Just as much the same as two books of mathematics—except some of the books are all blurred and full of misprints—poor thought. When they did it right they were all alike. Everybody had some thought, and they only had thought when they did it right, and when they thought right they were repeating mathematically identical syllogisms. The only reason for the illusion of self was that some people don't know their time tables—hence think they are different—an illusion due to a combination of recurrent error in men.

Some people can do arithmetic, hence get along with each other, since they all think alike, some more and some less—but always agreeing on the answers.

Other guys *couldn't* do arithmetic, *couldn't* think anything out right—hence *thought* they were different.

Joe felt better—the buzzing stopped.

Smart guys are repetitions. Dumb guys are *botched* repetitions. Repetitions of places where thought takes place are minds—selves. Each thought he was unique. But he was only unique when he couldn't think anything out correctly. If he was unique he was terrible dumb. But was a fishworm unique? It was terrible dumb!

Joe's head started buzzing again.

Thought, an exchange of electric flows between little amoeba-like cells in the brain. Why did that make a self? Maybe some people thought of themselves as repetitions of other people and no different really. Real democrats!

Suddenly Joe made up his mind. He was going to get into that crystal door, into that place where the cars from nowhere made the weird noises and vanished into hyperspace—or space-warp or something. He was going to follow the gigantic women into a world more interesting than this one.

Pood agreed. It might be wiser, for a young fellow. Pood had no desire, personally, for any more life of any kind. He was just tired of it all. Old people are that way, Pood assured Joe.

But, Pood argued, "You can't get out again. You can wander in there for years and never get out. This crystal maze is a maze with a purpose. You can't get in *to* the cars. You can't get out *from* the cars. Only the builders, those forgotten people, can tell where the path is through that maze. They built it to protect themselves from accidental or invasional visitors from the railroad into space."

Joe was obdurate. Pood would not help. Joe tried to open the great door of the crystal maze. It was no go. It would not budge.

FINALLY Joe had an idea. He went back to the machine that had crushed the duplicate Joe. He found a means of swinging the great crushing ray, mounted on great swiveling gymbals, upon the crystalline doorway.

Pood ran off hobbling, he wanted no part of the disaster he expected to happen. Or so he said.

As the huge ray projector swung in response to the strange control, Joe did not even wonder where he had gotten the courage to face the possible death this thing might bring him. Joe was desperate to meet some people. He really wanted some interesting, alive people around him—doing things. This dead world, and the old hermit, Pood, and his answers that only gave him enigmas to puzzle about, were not for him.

Joe pushed the button, the great pressure ray blasted at the vast crystal door.

It gave slowly at first, then crashed into fragments like a breaking dish! Joe did not stop, but blasted steadily at the interior walls of the maze toward the great chamber where the dwarves had appeared so suddenly and so dramatically at war with the giant women.

An hour later the vast power of the ray had crashed a huge broken edged path through the age-brittle stuff of the building. Joe realized vaguely what that building was.

It was a "station" on a railroad that traveled by no means he knew to places no man had ever dreamed of reaching.

Joe found controls in the great crystalline chamber, and pushed them at random till he heard the "whoooeeee-woooo" and the terrible rushing as of winds across the abyss of Hell itself.

Now suddenly materializing out of the nothing of the center of the chamber came the long cylindrical car, like a transparent tank-car with seats—only ten times as long—up close.

Joe climbed in, pressed the studs in the instrument board.

"Whhoooooeeeeeewoooooo!" It began, but it was in his very bones, the wild far breath of space, the cold of the loneliest, deadest reaches of time, the terrible heat of suns, that irresistible rush of titanic forces through him, around him! Slowly the turmoil stopped—it was quiet.

Joe looked around. Hell, it was the same place! He looked out, where the giant goddess had lain dead, to where he had rammed passage through the crystal walls with the pressuring ray. No great ragged edged path to the outside. No dead goddess.

Yet, it was the same place, to all appearances otherwise. It was a repetition, as all stations are near repetitions of other stations in essentials.

Joe wondered vaguely if somewhere twenty other duplicate Joes had depressed similar buttons, found themselves similarly transported, where? Joe wished he knew.

Joe climbed out, and he knew suddenly he shouldn't have. For the car faded slowly out of sight, the "whoooe-wooo" of the space travel came—and Joe was left alone. Not even Pood. The old misanthrope! How could a guy live in wonder till he was tired of wonder? Tired of wonder and magnificence and machines incomprehensible to all but non-existent, long dead superminds. Pood was tired of life.

TIME had passed during that whooshing ride through a kaleidoscope gone mad. How much time Joe didn't know. More days passed as Joe fumbled through the glass-like shimmering, mirroring maze. Time passed and Joe found the great door. Outside, the familiar machines stood where he had watched with Pood while the giant women fought the fleeing dwarves.

It all looked the same, deserted, blanketed with grey eons of dust. Joe half expected to see Pood walk forward to greet him out of the shadows.

But yet——this was not the same place! Time or space or some vast inexplicable wall of circumstance had arisen between that time and that place where Pood and Joe had stood before the great crystal door. Joe remembered Pood's words—those awed sounding words when he was shaken from his aged complacency by some particularly mighty manifestation of the wisdom of the Elder race.

"The Place of Magic Stops"—that no man ever understood since "they" left. What is it, a railroad into time? A device that bends far separated spaces into simultaneity? No one knows where it goes, one only knows one is somewhere else when it stops.

"I am taking a ride!" Joe had said, and Pood had not been able to dissuade him. Anywhere was better than the dead world of Lornomor.

Now Joe remembered. This was a different place, maybe even a different time. The great jagged hole he had blasted through the glassy walls was not here.

Joe wandered down the so familiar corridors, past the place where the duplicator cabinets stood, row on row. Joe wondered just how long it would take that thing to create an army of Joes? No, thanks—he would remain one Joe—himself. It was too confusing to see yourself repeated like that.

Joe came out to the place where the wrecked space ship had lain on Lornomor. At least that was different. The wreck of the *Pioneer* was not here, nor the wreck of the strange, powerful ship which Pood had been wrecked in on Lornomor so long ago. This duplication of things along the weird railroad through dimensions did not include everything.

Pood had shown Joe how to use the vision rays that stood about the caverns of Lornomor. On Lornomor there had been little to look at with the immense range and magnification of the beam that shot from the machine. Lornomor was dead and frozen. Nothing to see but vast ice choked chasms, some strange storm of force and cold had torn and crushed the surface and left it dead forever. Only the caverns were warm and livable.

Joe swung the great ray up and up. The ray made the rock overhead vanish, along the length of the ray was only the white light and nothing at all except the point of focus. There one could see rock, and more rock as Joe spun the focus dial that extended the focus ever farther away, farther up.

SUDDENLY the ray penetrated Earth's crust, and bright sunlight flooded the tube of sight, splashed and glinted everywhere about Joe from the suddenly blinding screen. Right into the eye of the rising sun he had inadvertently caused the ray to emerge on the surface.

Slowly Joe's eyes adjusted to the brightness and he saw on the screen a long valley of trees, a green wavy fields of young grain, a tractor chugging, farmhouses. It sure looked like Earth!

Nothing alien about the surface of this world. Joe swung the ray closer to the tractor, and spoke into the screen absently:

1517

"Wonder if he speaks English?"

The farmer looked up, shut off the tractor, got off and walked around the machine. His red, stubbled face wet with sweat—he looked more than puzzled.

"Now who in hell did I hear, out here, and with the motor going, too? I sure am tired . . . Beginning to hear things I shouldn't!"

Joe's question was answered and he had learned that the rays carried his voice. This was Earth! This cavern was some long buried part of the rocks of Mother Earth.

Joe swung the ray wonderingly across the hills, across a mountain, and then the blue seas sparkled, little racing white caps hurrying across the bright blue. A white sail in the distance, Joe wondered. And as he wondered, the strange mystifying answer came.

Far, far overhead, a high shrill screaming began. Faint at first, it grew louder, and Joe spun the focus distance dial, reaching up and up toward the sound with the mighty ancient ray.

At last he reached it, that red hot falling cylinder of steel, watched it plunge down and down, thrilled and feared with the man inside as the nose rockets flared briefly, checking the terrible fall again and again.

Close to the water the jets stopped, the steel flung itself with a great hiss into the blue. Down and down and down into the dark water, would it ever stop its dive and come up?

Joe suffered for the unconscious man inside as the pressure near crushed him, hoped for him that he was not dead as the last terrible momentum was consumed by the cushioning water's depths, as the cylinder again shot up toward the shining, blue, wave-capped surface.

At last he regained consciousness, shoved open the tiny round lock door —crawled out with his rubber boat as the cylinder filled with water and sank under his feet.

Joe felt a weird awe as he looked at the face of that weary, sick, starved man asleep now in his rubber boat. FOR THE MAN'S FACE WAS HIS OWN!

One of his duplicates? Joe didn't know if that man up there was Joe or this one here was the original Joe Cannon. They both were Joe Cannon was the incomprehensible truth. One of them had come to earth via the strange railroad of the ancients—the space-warp railroad.

The other, equipped with the same memory and mind, had returned to his rocket ship, found fuel somewhere, refueled—returned the way he had come —the hard way. Both of them were now on Earth!

AS JOE watched with his long range ray, watched that lonely rubber boat on the choppy, bright sea up there, he knew vaguely—could almost hear and feel those twenty some other Joes back in the caverns of Lornomor. Those caverns that were nearly duplicates of these he had suddenly found himself within here on Earth.

He knew those Joes were walking and talking with each of the score or more Pood Jaqmuls, and Pood was explaining as they passed the enormous explosion cavities where some cavern war had blasted the superhuman elegance of the ancient art work into great horrible gaps in the endless beauty. Ripped cables projected from the walls in the ruins, cables hung with fine festoonings of grey dust which covered everything there that wasn't directly vertical. And Joe wondered how many of those other Joe's eyes were drawn again and again to the Titan women in the wall paintings and bas-reliefs and sculptured columns.

Those women were too sensuously developed for mortal man to look on with comfort or understanding or anything but a terrible inward pain of longing—a fearful knowledge of one's own inadequacy. A knowing that being only mortal one could never approach such a being with the love the pictured forms aroused so terribly and insatiably within one—nor even dream of being able to please such a Titanic female or be worthy of her slightest attention.

And Joe hoped the love those pictured, long-gone females had aroused in him—that burned with an unquenched flame—did not torment all those other Joes so painfully. Joe could hear those other Joes in his "imagination" (or was it his perception) asking Pood, all those Joes asking all those Poods:

"Do such beings as these gigantic, infinitely beautiful superwomen exist anywhere today? They seem so terribly unattainable in their wisdom and beauty—they are what I would call 'Goddesses' because I had no word mighty enough to fit them."

"They are the 'Elder' race," he could hear Pood answer. "Their vast system of cold worlds came into a place in space where they had to abandon all these cavern homes—and that men like ourselves have come to live in and on these worlds afterward. Some little of their science my race has learned from their writings and their machines. Every great advance our race has made was through the study of the ancient methods. That is what I want to teach you—that the quest may go on."

Pood picked up a book where it lay half hidden in the dust under a machine. He dusted off the metal foil cover—read aloud the title: "Tentyne"

"Here is an engineering handbook of theirs left here by one of the bygone workmen. If you could read the knowledge in the symbols, could understand the formulae in this book, you would possess the key to immortality itself. The word means 'Textbook of Beneficial Ray Mech Repair'—as the beginning text explains—and would set your race upon the path to greatness . . ."

Joe heard the others say, "Pood, why don't you and I get in my ship and find your people—leave this dead world and go where your race can give me what you say you wish to teach me, quickly? Why do we dawdle about here as if there were nothing to do?"

"Several reasons. One reason is it'll take a year or two to teach you even a beginning of what I want to give men before I die. Then there is the reason that one of the Joes already found fuel in the old wreck of my own ship, filled his tanks, and blasted off for earth. His Pood Jaqmul didn't feel like going, making the trip in that coffee grinder worried him, I guess. Another reason, I was in that space-warp machine for so long that all my friends, my home, are lost in the past somewhere. If I do go back, it will be hard to face it—all strange and different. And another reason is that if we want to travel, it's easier to do it via the space-warp railroad than by any other way even if time often gets crossed up enroute.

"I am used to this solitude. Joe, when I have given you plans of space ships like that wrecked one, I will take you to your Earth by means of that ancient space-warp device. Then your race can seek out their own paths to the future. I would rather stay here on this dead world and dream under these painted goddesses than to seek more discouragement and experience

1519

more futile seeking after impossible things. Maybe when I die something that is still 'me' will find its way to the feet of such God-like beings as are here pictured. I don't believe it—but I like to dream about it."

THE voices died out of the ears of the Joe Cannon on Earth—in the forgotten, unknown caverns under Earth's rocky crust. His eyes followed the rubber boat pictured on his viewscreen, rocking on the now quiet sea overhead. The man in the boat was mentally resolving not to mention a word about who he was or where he had been, till he had found old Prof. Gizide who had built the rocket ship, partially financed the whole expedition —which had been entirely under cover for fear of government interference.

The Joe in the depths resolved to help him with these far reaching rays, for he wanted to bring the news of the ship's successful voyage to the old Prof. himself, too.

JOE sat in the rubber boat, and the sun beat down. His water was gone. He fished, but they weren't biting.

Joe muttered to himself.

"How the hell could you tell 'em that space gravity didn't act like schoolbook gravity? How could he tell old Gizide how he came to miss Mars and go off into far space and not even know where he had been, or have any proper charts of his course? Once out of the air, gravity had quit too, and the drive of the rockets had shot the *Pioneer* along like a crazy thing. Mars just didn't have a chance to be where it was supposed to be when the *Pioneer* arrived. It didn't have time, for the *Pioneer* covered the space in a third the the allotted time, and there was no way to cut the momentum—for when he shot off the forward braking charges the *Pioneer* just started off as fast in the opposite direction. No weight! see, Prof! Nothing acts like it should without weight. Momentum don't give any weight, nor act like weight, it has no weight at all to have a velocity! It just isn't like the school books at all. Of course he missed Mars. Nobody could have hit it!

"And space is a long and deep and wide place to get lost in, Prof!" He had shut off the rockets, saved his fuel. "I didn't waste any fuel trying to catch Mars a second time. I just sat tight knowing my only chance for life lay in approaching some planet under this acquired momentum."

Joe came out of it, stared at the sun glittered water—rubbed his head to stop the buzzing. There was no Prof. Gizide to talk to. Might as well save the explanations. Of course he should have turned her right around as agreed on and landed on Earth. But how could he tell them the terrible lure the space ahead had, how impossible it was to turn around and go back to prosaic old New York, with all space ahead beckoning. Death, what was death? If you could spend all eternity just speeding along toward some wonderful destination that wasn't just another hot-dog stand along the road. He had followed the lure of the open road long enough to know it was always another drive-in, just like all the others— another lousy restaurant that wasn't interested in giving anyone anything really fit to eat.

Nothing like that, even remotely like that could happen up here. How could anyone foresee the strain of the takeoff would unbalance him—make him unable to turn back from the lure of the far places. Well, he was back, and would tell them what he pleased. Only a series of miracles had brought him back, but the trail was blazed! Space

1520

was conquered, and his records—

Geez—his records....

They had gone down with the *Pioneer* back there in the Atlantic!

WHEN they picked him up, Joe was raving. Thirst and heat and the long strain had got him. So Joe became Joe again long after, and he was in that place where people go when picked up in the condition he was in, raving of giant worms, and mile-long alligators. The psychopathic ward of a big New York Hospital. He knew what those arms reaching out to him when he neared Earth had meant "Keep your big mouth shut."

He did, after he came to himself. Joe acted sane. And Joe got out, after a long time.

The day came when he walked up the red brick walk to the door of Prof. Gizide's home. He knocked.

There was no answer. He knocked harder. Nobody came.

Joe went on out behind the house to the little lab where the Prof worked when he couldn't get out to the big lab outside the city. Nobody here. Joe took a cab out to the city limits and the experimental lab of the Prof and his associates.

He walked up to the big brass studded doors.

The bright young girl behind the desk asked him his name and business.

"Joe Cannon. Used to work here for Prof. Gizide. I've been away for five years.

"The former owners of this place had some financial trouble or something. This is now the home of Prettykeen Hosiery Co. Were you looking for work?"

"No, I guess I've got a job. I guess I do!"

Joe went out.

"Prettykeen Hosiery, eh!" That was pretty keen all right. The "Pioneer Rocket, Inc." had folded when he hadn't returned. He would have to find the old boys, and would they be glad to see him!

SEVERAL days later, Joe walked up the shabby street. He had a card in his hand. He studied the card, watched the numbers on the old houses. This tumbledown rooming house, this must be the one.

Joe rang the bell. A lack of noise told him the bell didn't work. He knocked.

After a long time someone fumbled the door open. She was fat and dirty and foreign.

He asked for Prof. Gizide. She made him repeat it, acted as if he was a bill collector, as if she never heard the name before.

Finally she led him up the stairs, giving him to understand she was honoring him unduly by her efforts.

Three long flights of worn out carpet. Dusty, spotted, smelly.

She knocked on a door. A noise inside. She went back down the stairs. The door opened.

An old white haired man peered out at Joe. The beaten hopeless look on that face ... Joe's heart contracted with pity, a spasm of contrition.

He cursed the indecision, the madness that had contributed to his missing the planned route of the trip, missing Mars entirely.

But the vast joy that suddenly spread over the old man's face banished the pain from Joe's breast, aroused an answering joy in his own heart.

Silently the two men embraced. The old man sobbed, tears of joy and relief streamed down his face. Joe's face was wet, too.

"Joe, my Joe Cannon! My star-voyager! My space-conqueror! My

1521

brave man who did not scoff at the old men's dreams. Ah, Joe, now I can die happy. I have seen your face again! Now, come in, man, and talk! Tell me every little thing from the beginning."

Joe entered the shabby little room. He sat down on the rickety chair with the spring showing. He put his hat on the floor. He started to talk, and the old man paced up and down, finally sank into the only other chair in the room. His old face shone, his hands were clasped as in prayer.

But Joe knew that the prayer was to him, was asking him not to stop, not to miss one slight detail of that trip to space. That trip the old man could not make himself after a lifetime of striving toward it.

Joe talked! Joe tried! The words tumbled from his mouth in a steady stream—of the wonder of Klakdor and Klakdonothor, of the terror and size of Klakdonothor below the Klakdor web cities floating forever in the outer air. Of his embarrassment at their ridicule —at their attitude. Of his flight to the next planet, the dead world of Lornomor. Of the old hermit who had sat for an age—sat forever in the Elder caverns waiting for a rescue he did not want. Of his refusing Joe's offer to take him along because of knowing that Joe was not rescue but only poverty meeting poverty. For the old man's race were people who lived for a thousand years of joyful and fecund life, then died by their own hand rather than face age.

Prof. Gizide nodded understandingly. Every word he drank in, nodding understanding all the time. And as Joe finished, as the last words describing his search left his lips—Prof Gizide toppled from his chair to the floor.

As he fell, his head struck the metal of the gas heater! The blood started from a wound in his head.

JOE picked the old man up, laid him on the bed—got water, bathed his face. But the faltering breath grew weaker.

As Joe looked for something, whiskey, anything—he found the reason.

In the cupboard was no food—one crust of moldy bread, half eaten.

Prof. Gizide was nearly dead of starvation. Joy had completed the work of hunger.

The police were not helpful. They accused Joe of killing Prof. Gizide by a blow on the head. They wanted to know where Joe had hidden the money. Old Gizide was known as a miser. He never even spent money for food! Starved himself, to save money.

"He must have a lot of it somewhere, he never spent any."

Joe was discouraged. Joe refused to talk. Joe went to jail. Murder. Joe sat in jail, wondering how to tell the truth. That truth that nobody ever believes anyway—and least of all the truth he had to tell.

Joe told the truth! The whitecoats took Joe away, after his "appointed" counsel pled "insanity".

Joe sat in Bellevue.

Joe was a good, quiet patient. Soon he was taken for a walk, in a long line of "nuts".

It was spring again. Joe wished he was somewhere else.

Suddenly a strange, alarming pressure sprang into being about him. Joe felt light—lighter. Corruscations of weird, alien energy rainbowed around him. Slowly, at first, he floated up!

The attendant, mouth agape, instinctively reached for Joe's feet. Too late.

Up—up, faster and faster. Strange winds beat upon him, he was traveling now, like a bird, straight across country.

1522

The attendant was afraid to tell what happened. He said Joe had leaped the fence—ran like a deer. The other nuts said little, they knew they would not be believed. The craziest ones talked about it, but nobody listened. Such things only happen in Fortean data, or in fairy tales. Few other people have the guts to admit it, even when they see such things happen. Not when they are as close to a bughouse and a straight jacket as the attendant. He knew better.

JOE came down, floating down to earth a good way from New York. The strange powerful rainbow sphere of energy ceased to beat about him with its invisible wings. His feet sank into the moist earth. The trees about him on the hillside sparkled with the sun and singing birds did their duty to make his freedom look of value. As he glanced about him—through the sunshot air came two figures.

Joe remembered. There were other Joes, his fellows—duplicates. Remembering, he shook hands, fell into step beside them. They entered a big, freshly gouged out opening in the green hillside—travelled a long way down and into the hill.

THE original Joe rose from the ancient penetro-levitator beam mech, shut off the throbbing power. The mottled old rollat swept up, stopped, its ancient motor humming as sweetly as ever.

Three Joes got out. They did not have to talk much. Their memories were nearly identical.

LATER, as four Joes blasted a passage through the crystal maze with pressure beams. That "whoooooeee-woooo" that presaged the approach of the space-warp car came, weirdly howled closer, closer—materialized suddenly out of nothingness in the center of the maze.

As their pressure rays burst down the last crystal barrier, a score of little, indescribably twisted and dirty men and women rose up into sight from the floor of the car. They let fly with twenty of those short, heavy arrows. Four Joes died.

There were no more Joes in the God-caverns of earth now. The secret was still the ancient secret.

The dwarves crept silently from the smashed maze, searched the surface above with penetrays till the new, raw opening was found. Swiftly the pressure rays beat upon the soft earth, obliterated the passage from the surface to the ancient Elder World caverns. Then the troop of little men went to bed in the stim rays, and lay all night in the pleasures built for a God's nuptials so long ago. No big sunburned people would ever take their stim from them, the caverns belong to the dwarves!

ON LORNOMOR, which was perhaps Earth far in the future—or not earth at all, but another place in space too far away to think about—Old Pood sat on a rock by his wrecked ship, where he had sat for twenty years —or was it two hundred? Thinking was a job, but Pood was doing some. Near him lay the last but one of the Joes, gasping for breath. Pood gave him water, pulled the ragged cover about his shoulders.

He couldn't last long. Lornomor wasn't exactly healthy. Everybody always died here but Pood. That's why Pood liked it. It was good and quiet. The crazy dwarves never stopped here, in their rounds of the abandoned worlds which was their domain. Unless they were chasing someone. Pood dozed. Joe stopped breathing.

IN ANOTHER cavern corridor, a duplicate Pood pulled a dying duplicate Joe into the duplicator cabinet. In seconds there were two dozen healthy Joes—and one sick, dying Joe.

Some months later twenty-four Joes stood beside a repaired space ship. Old Pood nodded happily.

"She'll travel now, boys". Pood was happy to see the old wreck in which he had crashed on Lornomor so long ago back together again and ready to take off.

JOE CANNON'S head was buzzing. Behind him in the capacious space ship of Pood's, twenty-two other Joe Cannons played pinochle, or snored in the bunks. Pood had kept one Joe Cannon on Lornomor.

"Got a special use for this guy—he'll stay there. You'll see him later."

Joe Cannon, at the controls of the strange ship built by Pood Jaqmul's mysterious race, felt almost all right—except for the darn delusions. The visions that plagued him.

Like now, those arms gesturing, those voices calling to him. To Earth. Sure it was Earth. It looked like Earth, didn't it?

Those darn soft white arms too everlastingly long to be real. They twined like snakes, stretched like rubber. And the voices chorusing:

"You're nuts, Joe. How'll you ever tell 'em? About the Klakdor and the giant worms on Klakdonothor? Or about the other Joes."

Nobody would ever believe there was more than one Joe.

Joe Cannon looked around from the controls at the twenty-two other Joe Cannons lounging around the ship, crowding it to capacity. He sighed happily. They'd believe Joe Cannon this time, if they hadn't believed that poor original Joe Cannon. Or was he the original? Well, it didn't matter.

The ship began its long screaming dive into the air of the Earth. The walls heated, the air grew stuffy, the weight of a guy's arms grew most too heavy to hang on to the jet lever. Joe juiced the forward jets, the weight grew worse for an instant. Joe eased off, keeping it just bearable, reducing speed steadily.

But, Hell, come right down to it, plenty of those other guys were essentially the same, down there on that green ball, with the pretty white clouds dotting it like sheep on a meadow. Just *more* Joes, *more* flesh, *more* of the same kind of good intent, good hard thinking, clean-living Joe Cannons. Good guys, lots of them—and really all the same thing—*flesh*—figuring how to live better and longer. He'd try to tell them, all right! Show 'em this ship, give 'em the plans Pood had sent along in the ship's strong box.

FAR below the twenty-three Joes, another Joe worked madly at a huge space-televisor. He swung the levitator beam up, up, along the view beam, watching to get it just right—to ease that ship down without accident. There were going to be no more dead Joes if he could help it. Behind him Pood watched proudly, helping him with a word now and then—Pood knew how to teach by letting a man do things—important things. The falling ship hovered in the cross-hairs of the beam, the levitator lightened it—the ship fell now softly as a feather in the breezeless air.

Around Joe at the televisor and levitator the enigmatic gloom of the forgotten caverns, the mighty pictured lure of the Goddess-women reminding him what the future could be for men

1524

who conquered age as they had, long ago.

Pood slipped away from the seated Joe quietly. The "whooooeeeewoooooo" of the mysterious railroad of the Seven Planes startled Joe, made him look around—miss Pood's wise, weary, good-natured face.

INSIDE the long cylinder of the car on the whirling kaleidoscope of force to Lornomor—Pood chuckled to himself.

The dwarves *would* balk old Pood would they! The Earth people were good folk. They'd learn about the caves, learn plenty. To Heck with the dwarves, or anybody else wanted to balk the surface folk of that Earth planet. The dwarves were crazy nomads anyway. Pood was no beginner. They'd learn, darn 'em. They'd learn to leave Pood alone. And if they got these Joes—there was still another Joe back on Lornomor, in a sleep chamber . . . Pood chuckled. The big car "whoooeeeewooooed" to a stop on Lornomor.

LATTERWORD

THIS STORY WASN'T supposed to be anything more than this: In the caves they talk of this "railroad." The road of the "seven magic stops." It is very much as described, except it is more complicated, and goes places nobody understands even how to get back from. Sometimes people get off this forgotten "railroad" that is a door to no one knows where. People, strange people, get off in the present-day caverns under present-day American cities.

Sometimes these people seem to be from centuries in the past. They do not stay here, but look around very disgustedly, get back in the car, disappear on their way to the next "magic stop."

There are seven magic planes, seven of these stops—each of which connects with another railroad to seven other magic stops.

No one knows anything very definite about it as no one ever comes back, to stay, from a trip upon it.

I have tried to give a picture of this "legend" of the caves, as well as a picture of the peculiar duplicity of the concept of "self" by "men" and a picture of the peculiar atmosphere of the caverns where "anything can happen and usually does."

The "duplicator" (called "twice") is also talked of there and I believe it exists! Make what you will of it, it is still a part of the lore of the caverns, and much of it I cannot understand, either. Or it is a purely entertaining invention, if you like that sort of thing.

ERRORS IN SPECTOGRAPH OF STELLAR BODIES

IN CYCLONE regions it has been noted that reddish or yellow lights appear before the cyclone strikes. The phenomenon is sometimes accompanied by great heat. In monsoon regions, pink or bluish lights herald the monsoon over the ocean, and smoky color over the land. These colors are due to atmopheric strata, some of which extend upward as much as many thousands of miles. There are millions of layers (like the skin of an onion) in the atmosphere. Therefore, in making a spectrographic examination of a stellar body, the extreme sensitivity of the spectrograph cannot but record these various bands of color that intervene within the earth's atmosphere. Thus, it is an error to make a positive statement that (for instance) the atmosphere of Mars contains oxygen or hydrogen; or that of Venus carbon di-oxide.

1525

 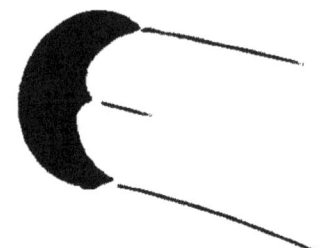

THE INVISIBLE INTERVIEW

OR

"WHAT DO YOU KNOW ABOUT FLYING SAUCERS?"

BY

RICHARD S. SHAVER

RAY PALMER, who has a fondness, or a weakness, for surprises, called me. He said: "Army Intelligence is going to call on you to ask you what you know about the discs!"

I gulped. Then I remembered the other agent of public information (or should I say secret public information?) who had called on the same errand, had been of so un-

THE HIDDEN WORLD

questioning, so incurious, so apparently uncommunicative nature - that as far as an exchange of conversation went that there was little to worry about. So I said: "So what; they're so worried they might tell you something they're afraid to ask questions, anyway."

Ray said: "Yeah, I know. He'll walk in, sit down, and wait for you to do the talking. How they expect to learn anything that way . . ."

"I'll fix him," I said, getting an idea. "I'll prepare a list of questions to ask and beat him to it. I'll really ask him everything, every way there is. Then at least I'll learn whether they want to know anything, or whether they want to find out if I know anything and tell me to shut up about it."

"It's an idea," said Ray. "I wish I had thought of that before they questioned me."

I prepared notes for the coming interview. The first question I intended to ask went like this: "Is this discussion to be on the level and confidential, or are we both to dodge the issue of whether there really were flying saucers, and only pretend to have a serious interview - which is one way such an agent has to dodging unpleasant duty. I would know he wasn't going to tell me anything the Army had learned about the flying saucers - and my reaction was going to be: "Why should I tell you?"

If he answered just as if he could understand English, and said: "On the level. We want to know what you have learned about them, and add it to what we have learned." Then I would bargain, ask him to tell me something about what they had learned first.

Then he would say: "You talk first, then I'll tell you if you're right or not." If so, I was going to spill my few beans.

My second question was going to be: "Do you get letters like this?"

I would show him some of the letters about ray phen-

1527

THE HIDDEN WORLD

omena; about sighting flying saucers and what they looked like; about a lot of things such as I have written about, - many of which are very startling letters indeed.

I know they do get a lot of such letters, and always supposed that no matter how startlingly they coincide with each other on these supposedly crackpot themes, they threw them in the waste basket.

If he admitted that they did get letters about voices driving people to suicide; about mysterious burning and tormenting rays; etc., I was going to rub my hands, thank God for meeting an honest man, and really take my hair down.

If he denied getting such letters or ever having heard of such letters, I was going to clam up - because if he was afraid to admit the sending of such letters to the FBI and other agencies of government (which I know takes place all the time as my own fan letters have told me they do write such letters to them), if he could not admit there was such torment and such devilish ray tamper with American life, then I could not admit my own serious interest in the subject to any agency as powerful as Army Intelligence. Such people have a way of taking care of citizens they pretend are mad.

If he dodges the issue of the letter and yet expects me to answer his questions fully and completely and honestly just as if he had no power to harm me (which is never the case with police or any officer - not in my experience), I was going to say: "How do you expect to get information that way when you know the truth more or less completely? Why dodge it? I couldn't hurt you if I did disapprove of your beliefs and statements."

If he tested out that far, then I was going to discuss eyewitness accounts of the discs, and try to find out why the army wants to know about disc ships when the papers have been stopped from printing news about them. I was going to ask: "What's the point of asking people like me about the discs when you yourselves have forbidden the newspapers to print the truth about them? How do you manage to get yourselves into such a self-contradictory

1528

path?"

I was going to learn definitely whether he himself thought of them as objective reality or mass hysteria and delusion.

I was going to say: "If you have heard of my writings, and from that reason came here to see me, why not give with a little conversation I can use to make a shekel out of? You get around as an Army Intelligence man. Or did some of my fans write to you and stir up your curiosity about me?

If he took the usual "courageous" attitude of refusing to face the reality of the generally supposed "unreal", then I was going to discuss nothing but the weather.

If he checked, I was going to suggest getting in his car and driving to a neighboring town where a friend of mine lives who told me he spent nearly an hour observing a dozen different disc ships cavorting over lake Michigan when out on patrol. I would have had to do this without disclosing his identity as an Army man, because the eyewitness (who had done his observing with high-powered glasses) had no intention of reporting the great deal of pertinent information he had to anyone who would get him in bad with his superiors as a crackpot who saw flying saucers. But he would talk to a couple of Amazing Story fans, which was what I intended to represent him as being - if he checked as a reliable and honest and intelligent individual who could keep friendly and loyal people out of trouble even when they tried to help him.

On the way, I was going to ask why they helped to conceal the presence of the disc ships since anyone who knows anything about them knows they are not of our government's manufacture nor of any other government on earth; but are obviously from space. Since they (the disc ships) are keeping out of our way, one knows they are hiding more or less - why help them hide? Suppressing news tales of them is helping them hide! Why do it? Is there a reason such as fear of retaliation of a terrible nature if they are talked about? Is the Army afraid of them to the extent they suppress information about something that acts like the

1529

THE HIDDEN WORLD

advance scouts of an invasion from space? Or are they like my friend in the Navy who cannot face the onus of saying: "I observed twelve disc ships for a long time over the Lake Michigan."

I was going to say: "If you cannot face the reality of these saucers long enough to carry on a simple conversation, why want information about them? If a Navy man is afraid of ridicule to the extent of not reporting twelve monstrous ships 100 miles from Chicago, how can an Army man face it long enough to do something about it?"

Then I was going to get real confidential and just-between-you-and-me-ish, and say: "It is the same with ray phenomena, which is a real and continuous injury and threat and danger to all our people, isn't it? Officials cannot face the reality of what they KNOW TO BE TRUE!

If he answered: "Between you and me only, that is the way it is." I was going to continue in that vein: "If this thing can't be faced in a private conversation of a confidential nature, if men in your position are not safe enough to state their honest opinion, how are we going to find a basis of conversation, of agreement on which to proceed? Hadn't you better tell me something of the work you are doing? I may be able to tell you a great deal if you can admit the discs do exist. But if a conversation begins with a lie (the discs do not exist), why should I talk to you as if they did?"

Then, when he said: "We are just checking; routine procedure. We do not recognize your imaginary underworld as existing. We do not recognize the existence of the discs officially." I was going to be real cute and say: "How can you expect to get an honest interview with someone at work investigating such things unless you have an honest setup over head, a realization of the general threat and harm of these facets of our life, and in yourself a real face-to-face understanding of the reality of these things?"

By this time I expected to have either a flabbergasted or departing agent of the Army intelligence. I was going to stand up like Caspar Milquetoast and defy him to make sense about it without admitting there was a ray mech not

1530

built by modern earth men. If on the other hand I had an honest man courageously admitting the reality of these officially frowned upon subjects, and the extreme necessity of open and official recognizance of their reality and peril, I was going to learn where the government stood, or get hauled away as a bug on invisible threats, or something.

I was going to ask my big question: "Is our United States Government controlled by unseen rays; are the thoughts of our officials completely a present from underworld ray?"

If he survives such a brash and open facing of the stew in which we all labor on this question, if he still was on his feet or puffing his cigar, I was going to ask him:

"Does the ray tamper such conversations as you have with well-intended rays? Do you get clear and intelligent contact with brilliant minds over the telaug beams, or do you have difficulties and lies and general confusion with this thing that seems to be in position to control our economy and our public men?"

If he hemmed and hawed and refused to answer, that was going to terminate my interview; I was going to clam up too - after I asked one more question: "Do you ever hear ray voices at any time in any hidden way at all?" (Meaning not only himself but his whole acquaintance among the personnel.)

If he says they do not hear any such voices or know anything about them, I will know that either he is a liar, or the Army has no "Intelligence".

Well, that's it. I got all set to interview a representative of U.S. Army Intelligence, pinned my list of questions, subtle suggestions, hints and reminders up on the wall and resolved to adhere strictly to its format so far as was possible, instead of sitting there and wondering what to talk about as I had when the FBI man called and wondered what I knew about discs. He hadn't asked questions then, and I hadn't either, and I didn't learn anything and he didn't either. This interview was going to be different. This was going to be just-between-me-and-you-ish!

He never showed up! I still don't know if the Army has

an "intelligence" or not! But I sure would like to know what they do know, because with my limited means of obtaining information I know plenty about the discs.

Just between you and me, I'll tell you what I never would anybody else, because they would think I was a liar. And I ain't a liar; it's just that I can't remember all the details.

The people in the discs came here often, to check up on the disappearance of certain of their ships near this sun. They couldn't figure for a century how there could be any harm in this planet, since the inhabitants didn't have space ships, and they (us) didn't know the caverns in their (our) planet contained the Elder science and mech.

They lost more ships, and they smelled the big rat that is concealed in our caverns, that keeps all that wonder work from the surface people's knowledge. They sent a large expedition to try to stop the depredation that was periodically knocking off ships from their commerce.

They took photos, scouted the planet, and they pitied us, the surface people, wanted to help us get rid of the thing that preys on us without our knowing it. Their disc ships have been shot down, exploded, and the expedition is so far a complete and ghastly loss to them - they are people who could be our greatest benefactors if they had a chance. Could be, and meant to be, but they didn't make it.

You won't see many more flying discs because they got knocked off, is the truth! Naturally you are to believe neither the flying saucers nor the ray pirates that knocked them off are anything but delusions, fabrications or mass hysteria or spots before your eyes or blood corpuscles in the veins of your eyes.

They had a lot to give us, wanted to free us of our worst parasite, a parasite we ourselves are as helpless against as a dog is against his fleas!

But I guess we just don't have any intelligence. Anyway it hasn't showed up in the "incident of the non-existent flying saucers". Not to date.

I'm still waiting. As for being confidential, I can't be held to being confidential about an interview that never took place.

1532

HERE NOW ARE the first TWO VOLUMES in a continuing series originally released by Publisher Ray Palmer in the 1960s, and hereby reprinted for the Serious Student of the Shaver and Inner Earth Mysteries!

TO COME IN TOTAL 16 BOOKS, OVER 3200 PAGES AND ALMOST TWO MILLION WORDS!
14 MORE VOLUMES TO COME!

HIDDEN WORLD NUMBER ONE:
The Dero! The Tero! And The Battle For Good And Evil Underground!

Here, in over 200 pages, is the beginning of The Shaver Mystery!
· Shaver hears the tormented voices coming from below.
· Readers question his sanity when he describes entering the caves of the ancients.
· He describes in detail the plunder of our planet by extraterrestrials in ancient times, and the lost continents of Lemuria and Atlantis.
· Shaver "proves his case" by revealing an ancient alphabet he calls "Mantong."
· Captured by the Dero from ancient races, the stem and mech machines cause utter chaos on surface dwellers, Wars, murder and horrific accidents are caused by the "evil ones."
THIS RARE REPRINT ONLY $25.00

HIDDEN WORLD NUMBER TWO:
The Masked World of Richard Shaver

The epic underground saga continues in roughly 190 pages of the nightmarish dealings with Inner Earth dwellers.
· A dark cloud hangs over the Earth as the subsurface mutants kidnap and torture humans, even performing cannibalistic acts upon their flesh.
· A series of airplane crashes carrying well-known celebrities can be blamed on the demented robot-like Dero.
· Shave reveals the secrets of "Growing A Better Man."
· Voices in the night torment readers of Shaver's tales as they confirm many of his claims.
THIS RARE REPRINT ONLY $25.00

SPECIAL OFFER: Both volumes One and Two of THE HIDDEN WORLD for the combined price of just $39.95. Please add $5.00 S/H to the total order.

Explore The Shaver and Inner Earth Mysteries

Global Communications
Box 753 · New Brunswick, NJ 08903

THE HIDDEN WORLD

INNER EARTH AND HOLLOW EARTH MYSTERIES
RICHARD SHAVER'S DERO - NAZI AND ALIEN UNDERGROUND BASES

WHAT IS THE SHAVER MYSTERY?
Here Is A Mystery That Stretches From The Madhouse To The White House — From Superstition To Scientific Knowledge - From the Forgotten Past To The Present! There are those who support Richard Shaver in his honey-comb of caverns the world over populated by a demented race know as the Dero, the greatest evil the earth has ever know. This is his story in his own words (and others who have undergone the same hell).

JUST RELEASED: ( ) **The Hidden World NO. 7** This Issue Contains Two Shocking Stories by RIchard S. Shaver: FORMULA FROM THE UNDERGROUND - THE WOMB OF TITAN, and THE RED LEGION - STRUGGLE OF NATIVE AMERICANS IN THE CAVERNS Plus JOURNEY THROUGH THE CAVES - HOME OF THE TEN LOST TRIBES OF ISRAEL

( ) NUMBER 6 - Entering The Secret Vaults Of The Elders - The Hollow World And The Ten Lost Tribes - Readers Reaction To Voices From The Caves.
( ) NUMBER 5—Deeds of the Elder Race? - Exploring The Occult Underground - The True Sorceress: Ladies of the Cavern World - Inner Earth: Fact? Fiction? Theory? Science?
( ) NUMBER 4—Reality of the Sathanas, Forbidden Playground of the Underworld. - The Madness of Richard Shaver.
( ) NUMBER 3—Mantong: The story of the Messiah as told in the caves. Underground rail system to hell. Death Rays from the Inner Earth.
( ) NUMBER 2—Airplane crashes, train wrecks, celebrity deaths caused by demented Dero. The dark cloud expands over Earth as subsurface mutants kidnap, torture and eat humans.
( ) NUMBER 1—Tormenting voices from the cavems. The home of ancients below Earth. Mantong, an unknown language.

Additional Volumes Will Be Added. . . Each volume approx 200 pages. Large format. $25.00 each. Any 4 books $$88.00. <u>All 7 just $159.95.</u> Add sufficient postage and handling (see our rate chart on order form).
Global Communications • Box 753 • New Brunswick, NJ 08903

( ) Best of Hollow Earth Hassle — There are two sets of unorthodox beliefs about the interior of our planet — the theory that the earth may be hollow and possibly inhabited (by a race of giants?) and that a system of caverns exists beneath our feet that are controlled by both good and evil entities (thus the concept of a hell below). Features a series of shocking articles from rare newsletter of same name. $21.95
ISBN: 978-1606110195 - Large Edition - Illustrated

( ) The Cave Of The Ancients —T. Lobsang Rampa enters the subterranean abode to meet with the Masters in the Halls of The Akashic Records. Deep inside Earth, it is revealed to the honorable monk fascinating accounts of ancient space visitors, lost civilizations, advanced gravity ships, and much more knowledge long forgotten by humankind. — $21.95
ISBN: 978-1606110607 - Large Edition

( ) Inner Earth And Outer Space People - Rev. Wm Blessing examines the inner earth from a Biblical viewpoint. CENSORED FOR CENTURIES BY THE CHURCH WITH THE BACKING OF WORLD LEADERS! Is There A Golden Paradise Inside Our Earth? Who Pilots The Ships We Call UFOs? Are They Here To Harm Or Help Us? Are the Residents Of This Subterranean World Angels or Devils? - $29.95
ISBN: 978-1606110362 -Large Edition - 320 pages - Illustrated

( ) Mysteries of Mount Shasta: Home Of The Underground Dwellers and Ancient Gods — SACRED SITE? ENTRANCE TO THE INNER EARTH? HIDDEN UFO BASE? TIME WARP? BLACK HOLE? Come with journalist Tim Beckley as he explores the US's most mysterious place. Lemurians and survivors of other "Lost Civilizations" roam the mountain, occasionally wandering into town to trade gold for supplies. Native Americans residing here say they have not only heard the screams of Bigfoot, but have seen these hairy creatures close-up! Visit Telos, the capitol of the Inner Earth occupied by the Ascended Masters of Wisdom — $21.95 —ISBN: 978-1606110027 - Large Edition - Illustrated

( ) Etidorhpa - Strange History of a Mysterious Being and an Account of a Remarkable Journey — A member of a secret society, John Uri Lord travels with a "sightless," superhuman to a subterranean land of magic and wonderment most will never see. Distant Worlds. Dead Civilizations. Other Dimensions. Rare reprint - $24.95
ISBN: 978-1892062185 - Large Edition - Illustrated

( ) Finding Lost Atlantis Inside The Hollow Earth - Brinsley Le Poer Trench (a member of the House of Lords) takes the reader on an exploration like no other. Here are tales of polar openings, hidden civilizations, strange underground races, Admiral Byrd's Top Secret discoveries, the central sun, the Shaver Mystery and much more that will open your eyes to a new reality like never before! Underground, the Atlantians still live in peace and tranquility away from the war-like elements upon the surface. — $21.95
ISBN: 978-1892062819 - Illustrated

( ) The Mysterious Cyrus Teed: The Phenomenon Of The Hollow Earth —. While working in his lab and hoping to find the Philosopher's Stone and convert lead into gold, Teed saw a beautiful woman who revealed that he was to become a messiah and reveal the true cosmogony to the world. It was at this point that his particular hollow earth theory began to take shape. - $21.95
ISBN 978-1606110713 - Nearly 300 pages - Illustrated

( ) Admiral Richard E. Byrd's Journey Beyond The Poles — Tim Swartz examines the great explorer's journey to the mythological lands of Hyperborea and Ultima Thule. His meeting with strange beings at the poles. His discovery of a secret Nazi base there. The development of German Flying Saucers. Britian's Secret War with Hitler's henchmen. Most important story of all time being hidden under our very noses. - $19.95
( ) Add $15.00 for ADMIRAL BYRD'S MISSING DIARY!
ISBN: 978-0938294986 - Large Edition - Documents -

www.ingramcontent.com/pod-product-compliance
Lightning Source LLC
Chambersburg PA
CBHW081225170426
43198CB00017B/2710